Co-operation

Conflict

and Consensus

B.C. Central and the Credit Union Movement to 1994

Ian MacPherson

Co-operation

Conflict

and Consensus

B.C. Central and the Credit Union Movement to 1994

Ian MacPherson

B.C. Central Credit Union
Vancouver, B.C. Canada
1995

B.C. Central Credit Union
1441 Creekside Drive,
Vancouver, B.C., Canada V6J 4S7

First published 1995
Copyright © 1995 by B.C. Central Credit Union

Project Management: Publications Department, B.C. Central Credit Union

Cover & Book Design: Baseline Type & Graphics Co-operative

Printed and bound in Canada.

Canadian Cataloguing in Publication Data

MacPherson, Ian, 1939-

Co-operation, Conflict and Consensus: B.C. Central and the credit union
movement to 1994

Includes bibliographical references and index.

ISBN 0-9699052-0-3 (bound)

ISBN 0-9699052-1-1 (pbk.)

1. Credit unions – British Columbia – History.

2. B.C. Central Credit Union – History. I. B.C. Central Credit Union. II. Title.

HG2039.C2M33 1995   334'.22'0971109   C95-900320-7

Co-operation, Conflict and Consensus
Contents

THE HISTORY OF ANY ORGANIZATION CAN BE NO MORE and is no less than the story of all those individuals who shaped its development. As a financial co-operative, a credit union is particularly indebted not only to its directors and its staff throughout the years, but also to its membership. Without their participation and support, none of B.C. Central's accomplishments could have been achieved.

This book is dedicated to those tens of thousands of volunteers and staff who, since the inception of the credit union system in British Columbia in 1936, have worked steadfastly to make financial services more readily available to the people of this province.

Finally, this book commemorates the fiftieth anniversary of B.C. Central Credit Union to recognize the men and women who have built the credit union movement in this province.

Michael J. Tarr
Chairperson
B.C. Central Credit Union

Co-operation, Conflict and Consensus
Acknowledgements

I AM INDEBTED TO THE BOARD OF DIRECTORS AND MANAGEment of B.C. Central Credit Union for the opportunity to write this book.

Preparing this study has been a pleasure; it has also been a practical exercise in co-operation. Many local credit unions have generously shared their records. Numerous individuals have donated time and effort to ensure that the record is as complete as time and space would permit. I am indebted to all of them.

The Corporate Information Centre at B.C. Central provided wonderful support for this project: I would like to express my gratitude for the efforts of its staff, particularly Georgia Fontaine, Diane Walker and Shirley Shipley. Their professionalism and courtesies were much appreciated.

Three students, Leslie Cooper, Kori Street, and Margie Ransford, assisted in some of the research at different times, as did Jonathan, Andrew and Elizabeth MacPherson; I appreciate their efforts and support very much.

I would particularly like to thank my advisory committee for our meetings and their commentaries. The committee consisted of Dr. Jean Barman of the University of British Columbia and four dedicated credit unionists with deep commitments to credit unions in this province: Wes Darling, Ross Montgomery, Phil Moore, and Ben Voth. George Viereck attended some of the early meetings before his untimely death; the book is the poorer for not having benefited more from his clear and compelling voice.

I would also like to thank the following employees of Central: Richard Thomas, for his careful readings and continuous support; Gayle Stevenson, for her many helpful suggestions; and Ian Smith, for his patience, care and commentaries.

For the errors of fact and interpretation that remain, I am, of course, entirely responsible.

Ian MacPherson
Victoria
September, 1995

Sources
1848-1935

> *They were cutting wood in return for groceries and growing vegetables in return for clothing and that is how they really managed, a lot of them during the dirty thirties.*

Gordon Holtby[1]

HELFER DER MENSCHHEIT · Raiffeisen

7 +3

DEUTSCHE BUNDESPOST

THE GREAT DEPRESSION. EVEN 60 YEARS AND TWO generations later, the images survive, the hardships are remembered. Shifting sands swallowing what were once grain fields on the Prairies. Desperate men and women hopping freight cars in search of work. Despondent casual workers following demoralizing daily routines from flop houses to soup kitchens in Vancouver's East Side. Charismatic evangelists – religious and political – preaching their panaceas and shouting their denunciations at church meetings and political gatherings. Relief camps located near isolated communities, housing the dispossessed, the young, the angry, the revolutionary. Armed confrontations between the unemployed and the police: the On-to-Ottawa trek in 1936; the sit-ins at the Hotel Georgia, the Art Gallery and the Post Office in Vancouver in the spring of 1938. Impoverished housewives in Burnaby, struggling to make a little food go farther and to keep demoralized husbands optimistic. Women choosing to have illegal and dangerous abortions because their families could not afford more children. It is a series of blurs in the communal memory now, but those images lie fixed in time, their familiar shapes and passionate tones suggestive of a fundamental change in our society that took place when grandma was young.

To a considerable extent, the Depression was a catalyst for the emergence of credit unions in British Columbia. During the 1930s, many British Columbians were in desperate need of places to save and, especially, to borrow funds. As the needs became greater, a small band, then a widening circle, of enthusiasts turned to the study and promotion of credit unions.

At that time, banks showed little interest in those who made small deposits or took out small loans. The main banks, in fact, closed branches in many small communities and withdrew services from even the middle class groups they had started to serve in the 1920s. Operators of small, independent businesses suffered, and those who hoped to start businesses had nowhere to turn for credit. As for those who sold their labour or operated marginal farms, the banks had never served them; their only sources of funds had been families, friends, local stores, pawn shops and usurious money lenders. In the midst of the Depression, even these sources were drying up or becoming more expensive.

And so the credit union movement found fertile ground in British Columbia some 60 years ago. Its ancestral roots, however, lay back in another, more sporadic but nevertheless severe, depression almost a century earlier. In the 1840s – the Hungry Forties as they were called

1. Interview with Gordon Holtby by Jac Schroeder and Miriam McTiernan, September 20, 1977, B.C. Central Credit Union Archives.

The surviving Rochdale Pioneers as they appeared in an 1865 photograph. Their efforts were popularized — and the rules they developed for their stores were stressed — by the leaders of the international co-operative movement.

in some parts of the Continent — Europe was at one of the crossroads of its modern history.

In that decade the consequences of industrialization and urbanization, those twin agents of social change in the modern era, became abundantly clear to many. In the Black Country of England, the belching smoke-stacks and teeming tenements were creating new, conflicting class divisions and quests for ways to better harness the promise of the new industrialism. In the town of Rochdale, a group of working people, many of them weavers, created in 1844 what would become a legendary consumer co-operative. It was, on one level, their effort to minimize their expenses in the marketplace; on another, it was a hopeful start towards the creation of a new world order.

The Rochdale experiment was replicated and built upon throughout industrial Britain for the remainder of the nineteenth century. By the early 1900s, the resultant movement was feeding one-quarter of the population of Great Britain; it was operating over 20 factories; it owned tea plantations in India and a 10,000-acre farm in Saskatchewan; and it had become a significant political force. It also had its own publicists and propagandists, from Beatrice and Sidney Webb to George Holyoake, who made the British move-ment the pre-eminent international co-operative experiment until at least the 1950s; it became the movement against which others —

The "Toad Lane" store established by the Rochdale Pioneers in 1844. It was carefully restored by the British consumer co-operative movement in the 1980s.

including for a long time the British Columbian movement – were measured.

Many of the British immigrants who came to British Columbia before and after World War One had been raised within the British movement; some had even paid for their voyages to Canada by using the "divy" or dividend that had been accumulated in their local co-ops. The British movement, therefore, would help shape the ideological underpinnings of the British Columbian movement, in both its credit union and broadly co-operative forms. From its principles and heroic story, many British Columbians would draw inspiration and sustenance as the twentieth century unfolded.

In a more direct sense, the B.C. credit union movement had its roots in the European co-operative banking movement. That movement took on life as the 1840s drew to a close, and its main centre was across the North Sea in the towns and small cities, in the villages and countryside, of the German people. To a considerable extent, its roots were the reverse of the crowded cities from which consumer co-operation emanated: they lay in the quandaries of peasants freed from their landlords but lacking the funds to buy the land and equipment to create a stable agriculture; they lay too with artisans unable to accumulate the money to start small manufacturing concerns or survive in the rapidly changing retail trades.

The harsh reality was that the new industrialism was draining the resources of the hinterland: capital flew to the big industries; people moved to the factories near the coal fields; traditional craftspeople and small family businesses could not compete. At the same time, the expanding cities created immense opportunities for farmers if they could specialize their production more than in the past and produce crops of reliable quality. They also provided some opportunities for artisans and small manufacturing or retail firms if they could find sufficient capital to compete effectively. The result was that there was a chronic shortage of capital, a shortage that sparked two co-operative banking movements.

The first was started by Hermann Schulze, a lawyer in the town of Delitsch in southern Germany. Elected as a Liberal to the National Assembly in 1847, he started a series of co-operative ventures among craftspeople in the late 1840s. In 1850, Schulze, who had adopted the name Schulze-Delitsch to differentiate himself from all the other Schulzes in the legislature, started his first credit co-operative.

That experiment failed within a year, but from it and the examples of other nearby co-operative banking schemes, Schulze-Delitsch fashioned his own theories of co-operative banking. His was a conservative approach, requiring relatively high membership fees, emphasizing careful lending policies based on strong securities, and serving artisans and small business people in the towns and cities. Thus, although it was a very successful movement in parts of Germany, the scheme had limited appeal outside of the towns and cities and among the less affluent classes – in Germany and elsewhere. In particular, its traditions, while constantly referred to in the literature of the B.C. movement, had only a limited direct impact.

A much more important direct source was the Raiffeisen movement. It was started in the early 1850s by Friedrich Raiffeisen, mayor of the borough of Heddesdorf in Neuwid, an industrializing city across the Rhine from Coblenz. Raiffeisen was primarily concerned about the plight of farm people, particularly after the severe winter of 1846-47. He diagnosed their chief problem as a lack of credit. Following involvement in a series of co-operative marketing and purchasing efforts among farmers between 1847 and 1852, Raiffeisen started a financial organization to help farm families in 1852.

The Raiffeisen approach was partly charitable in orientation and, in its first 50 years, relied upon the assistance of some wealthy friends. Within two years, however, Raiffeisen had determined that self-help was better than charity, and he organized a co-operative bank drawn partly on the precedent of the Schulze-Delitsch banks.

Between 1854 and 1864, Raiffeisen perfected his approach to co-operative banking. It featured an emphasis on ethical practices, a devotion to self-help principles, and a deep commitment to community. Above all, it based its lending policies on the character of the member, not on his or her financial securities: a radical idea (then as now) in banking circles. The Raiffeisen system was immediately successful, and it quickly spread in Germany, in time eclipsing the Schulze-Delitsch co-operatives.

The co-operative banking idea soon spread to Italy and France. In 1864, an Italian, Luigi Luzzatti, visited Germany and studied in particular the Schulze-Delitsch system. Returning to Italy, he started a co-operative banking network, but one which offered inexpensive membership, limited liability, and credit based on character. In the 1880s, another co-operative enthusiast, Leone Wollemborg, started rural co-operative banks based more directly on the Raiffeisen model. He, too, achieved success very quickly, and by the end of the nineteenth century Italy had a flourishing co-operative banking movement, one that provided the chief, direct inspiration for the movement in North America.[2]

In 1897, Alphonse Desjardins, a Hansard reporter in Ottawa, listened in dismay to a debate on usury and the heavy burden it imposed on the poor. It rang a bell. Desjardins had come from a large

Friedrich Raiffeisen (1818-1888) founded banking co-operatives among rural people in the middle of the nineteenth century. His work was widely popularized in North America during the early twentieth century because it was concerned about poorer people and because it was believed to be aimed at the improvement of communities.

2. The foregoing description of the European origins of the co-operative movement is based on J. Carroll Moody and Gilbert C. Fite, *The Credit Union Movement: Origins and Development, 1850-1970* (Lincoln: University of Nebraska, 1971), pp. 5-17.

family in Lévis, across the St. Lawrence River from Quebec City. His parents had been forced to leave their farm because of bankruptcy; his mother had become the family's sole bread-winner following the early death of his father; and he, along with his brothers and sisters, had known poverty at first hand – poverty that he came to understand was partly explained by the lack of credit.

Desjardins was also a deeply religious man, influenced by the liberal Catholicism of his day. He was immediately drawn to the structures and successes of the Italian experiments and to the moral urgency he found within them, within the Raiffeisen movement in Germany, and within the peoples' banks in France. In 1900, along with a few of his neighbours, he opened a co-operative bank, which they called the caisse populaire, in Lévis; it was the first continuing, successful co-operative bank in North America.

In 1908, Alphonse Desjardins travelled to Massachusetts where he explained his understanding of the co-operative banking movement to Edward A. Filene, a philanthropic Boston merchant who had first encountered co-operative banks in India during a visit in the preceding year. A progressive reformer concerned about the growing inequalities of American life, Filene was impressed and spent much of his remaining years (and a considerable part of his fortune) in promoting the co-operative banking movement within the United States. It was Filene who decided that the term "credit union" was better than people's bank or co-operative bank. He believed that the main problem confronting the poor was the absence of credit for worthwhile, prudent expenditures; consequently, he saw the extension of credit – not saving – as the most important activity. He also liked the word "union" because it reflected the kind of cohesive behaviour he believed should characterize co-operative banking.

Filene must have been at least partly correct. The movement he helped to start grew slowly at first but ultimately found receptive audiences. Its greatest successes were to be found on-the-job, in the places where people worked. In other words, Filene's movement early developed a deep commitment to what became known as closed-bond credit unions; associations of workers in specific companies or parishioners in a specific religious community. The great advantage of these closed bonds of association was that members could know each other well. Their knowledge of each

Above, Alphonse Desjardins (1854-1920), with the help of his wife Dorimene, started the first caisses populaires in Quebec at Lévis in 1900. He also contributed time and effort to assisting English-speaking people to start "credit unions" in the United States and, indirectly, in English Canada as well.

Right, Edward A. Filene (1860-1937) was a very successful merchant in Boston who first saw co-operative banks in India. After seeking advice from Alphonse Desjardins, he spent considerable time and much of his fortune developing credit unions in the United States.

15

other – and, if necessary, the social pressures they could bring upon each other – would ensure the operation of successful co-operative credit organizations.

Most American credit unions in the early decades, therefore, were organized on a company basis, almost like a fringe benefit in companies with an enlightened interest in their workers. They were almost invariably successful, reinforcing a belief in small credit unions, built on personal knowledge, and focused on simple saving and lending activities. It was a tradition that would long remain dominant within the American credit union movement – one that would be challenged in many key respects by the British Columbian movement.

The successes of the American credit unions were quickly noted in English Canada, particularly in Nova Scotia. During the 1920s, a powerful social movement had emerged at St. Francis Xavier University in Antigonish. Led initially by two priests, Moses Coady and Jimmy Tompkins, the movement was devoted to community renewal and development through the use of adult education and co-operative organizations.

By the early thirties the Antigonish movement, as it became widely known, had become a significant force, spreading to all the Maritime provinces and reaching out to Catholics and non-Catholics alike; it employed several talented men and women as community organizers using innovative study club techniques. The credit union was perfect for their purposes: it could be organized effectively even among the poor; it could be adapted to meet community needs; and it was an ideal way to bring people together for a variety of purposes.

The first credit union organized by the Antigonish movement was in Broad Cove, Nova Scotia, in 1932. By 1936, the field people from Antigonish had organized 106 credit unions in Nova Scotia alone and were organizing others in Prince Edward Island and New Brunswick as well. News of these successes soon spread to other parts of English Canada, including Ontario, the Prairies and the west coast. In none of those regions would the Antigonish impact be greater than in British Columbia.

British Columbians were experiencing a lot of frustration during the 1930s in large part because the 1920s had been so promising and profitable. In that decade Vancouver had finally achieved metropolitan status, a process that had started with the opening of the Panama Canal in 1914 but had gained momentum with the increased use of the port of Vancouver during World War One. Nevertheless, it was the rapid expansion following the recession of 1919-1923 that had made Vancouver a major city. Real wages for Vancouver residents increased 12% between 1922 and 1928, twice the national average.[3] The city experienced a building boom, symbolized in the downtown core by the

Moses Coady (1882-1959) was the foremost proponent of co-operative activism on behalf of human and community development. With the help of Father "Jimmy" Tompkins, A.B. MacDonald and numerous other organizers, he created the Antigonish Movement between 1929 and 1959.

3. Jean Barman, *The West Beyond the West: A History of British Columbia* (Toronto: University of Toronto Press, 1991), p. 239.

construction of the Devonshire and Georgia hotels, the Stock Exchange and the Marine Building. The growing population spread out to new subdivisions in the adjacent municipalities of South Vancouver and Point Grey, both of which amalgamated with Vancouver in 1929.[4] Indeed, by the end of the twenties, about 50% of Vancouver's homes were owner-occupied.[5]

Many families had even managed to build or buy cottages. The areas around the city, along the shore, in the shadow of the mountains, abounded in beautiful places for cottages: Boundary Bay, Horseshoe Bay, Deep Cove – the possibilities must have seemed endless to the newly-wealthy among the 200,000 who lived in the city in the later twenties. On the city streets, automobiles became commonplace, and the street railway made movement easy and cheap, not only within the city but also out to the "bedroom" communities in Burnaby, Richmond, and New Westminster. And, out along the harbour, the large grain elevators were built, attesting to the increasing influence the city had on its Prairie hinterland.

The importance of that hinterland became even more obvious when the Depression intensified its stranglehold on the city in the early thirties. The export of grain slowed to a dribble as markets collapsed, grain merchants could not pay their suppliers, and political turmoil decimated the Asian market. The promising trade with the Prairies in manufactured products – from prefabricated houses to canned salmon – fell off abruptly. The flourishing trade in apples and other fruits declined sharply, contributing to the crisis in marketing that depressed the orchards of the Okanagan Valley in the 1930s.

At the same time, the Prairies sent their young, their dispossessed, and their desperate. They hopped freights, drove such vehicles as they had, walked if they needed to. Many brought with them frustration from having seen old dreams die; equally, they brought with them a determination to start again. They also carried with them traditions of community building honed by the settlement period in the rural Prairies. Credit unions, when they emerged, would carry much of that Prairie inheritance.

The most important hinterland for Vancouver, however, did not lie across the Rockies; it was in the mines, forests, and farming areas of B.C. And, in that hinterland, geography was supreme. It created barriers even as it provided the resources on which the province largely depended. Good roads were rare, the railways reached only limited parts of the province, and many coastal communities were in direct contact with the outside only by steamer, usually once a week.

In a very literal and meaningful way, B.C. was a community of communities, which, while new for their non-Native settlers, quickly developed strong bonds. Those communal bonds were most readily

4. Patricia E. Roy, *Vancouver: An Illustrated History* (Toronto: James E. Lorimer & Co., 1980), p. 103.

5. Roy, *Vancouver,* p. 103. Even in 1939, and despite the Depression, Vancouver remained a well-housed city. Over 60% of families lived in homes they owned. Barman, *The West Beyond the West.*

developed around the workplace: the fishing fleet and cannery; the forests and the mill town; the orchards and the shipping point; the mine shaft and the mine town; the grain fields and the elevator. Men and women were thrown together in these communities, and, for those who stayed, the bonds of place and associations could become central to their existence; they would also be vitally important for many of the early credit unions that emerged.

British Columbia was divided in ways other than geography. In 1936, 70% of the population shared a British heritage, either directly from Great Britain or indirectly, following a sojourn somewhere else in North America. That group, though, was far from homogeneous. It included the offspring of aristocracy, educated people from the middle classes, skilled tradespeople, and those who had only strong backs. It included the full range of Christian religions, from austere forms of Anglicanism to the social gospel. It included all shades of political opinion, from the Clydeside radical to the conservative country squire. Very few of the debates that swept British society in the twentieth century were ignored in British Columbia; these debates would be reflected in the issues that beset credit unions, especially in their early days.

Similarly, the 20% of the population whose homelands lay in Continental Europe brought with them a rich diversity of languages, ideologies, cultures and traditions. Many of them were relatively old residents of the province, having come during the great immigration boom prior to World War One. Others had arrived during the optimism of the twenties or the despair of the thirties. Many of them had worked hard and long years in the primary resource industries, accumulating assets through the hardest of labour.

Many brought with them prior knowledge of co-operatives and cultural traditions that made it easy to support co-ops. Mennonite people who came into the Fraser Valley in the 1920s, for example, brought traditions of mutual self-help. Other Germanic peoples, who fled from Hitler during the 1930s, had belonged to consumer and banking co-operatives in their home country. Ukrainians and other Eastern Europeans came from regions where co-operatives had been well established since the nineteenth century. Though not always obvious, these traditions helped to make the idea of credit unionism less strange than it otherwise might have been.

The third major group in the non-Native population was made up of Asians, Chinese and Japanese people for the most part engaged in the primary industries – mining, fishing and agriculture. They too brought traditions of community that flowed easily into co-operative endeavours. They adapted co-operative techniques – more often informal than formal – into their fishing and agricultural activities, but they would not move easily or quickly into credit unions. Instead,

The Common Good Co-operative, from which credit unions in British Columbia grew, tried to organize its activities around the principle of rewarding people for the work they did. Pictured above is a certificate for 2 LU (Labour Units). A person could earn this scrip by working in one of the co-operative's activities and then exchange it for goods in the co-op store.

they tended to rely on their own financial resources even though there would be periodic efforts for decades to attract Asian Canadians to local credit unions. Those efforts would not be successful until the 1970s when they began to join community credit unions in significant numbers.

It was in the hinterlands, though, that the strongest co-operative traditions could be found when the 1930s began. As early as the 1890s, the provincial government had started to encourage co-operatives in order to facilitate the marketing of agricultural produce, to upgrade its quality and to encourage the bulk purchase of farm supplies. From early in the century, B.C. farmers had made careful studies of the development of co-operative marketing in various parts of the world; in fact, by the 1930s, they were as well informed on that topic as any farmers in the world.

Consequently, by the 1930s, co-operative marketing organizations were well established in the fruit industry of the Okanagan Valley and in the dairy industry in the Fraser Valley. Marketing co-operatives were also of growing importance in the fishing industry. They had started only in the 1920s, but they were increasingly powerful and determined organizations in the 1930s, linking most of the fishing communities on the coast and in the Fraser River estuary. These co-operatives would provide significant support for the credit union movement in its early stages of development.

The consumer co-operative movement would also provide important networks. That movement stretched back to the late nineteenth century, although none of the older co-operatives had survived. Nevertheless, in the mining towns of the Kootenays and Vancouver Island, there were consumer co-operatives that would contribute significantly to the development of credit unions. Others had recently been organized in Vancouver and Victoria, and more were being organized in the Okanagan and the North.

These consumer co-operatives were attempts to find ways to reduce the cost of consumer goods and to resist the growing power of chain stores. In 1938, some 20 consumer co-operatives organized a wholesale for the province, and would provide useful forums for the spread of the credit union idea in the 1940s and 1950s. In fact, many of the early credit unions were extensions of the stores, created as a way to deal with the bothersome problem of credit for members.

The consumer co-operative idea had particular cogency in the wake of the 1930s, arguably the period of the most intense ideological debates in Canadian history. Central to those debates was the idea of "production for use", a concept that production should be developed so as to provide maximum benefits for everyone and not primarily for speculative investors. The co-operative tradition as it had developed in Europe shared that vision and sought to reward people fairly for their labour and their investments. That tradition was well known among many British Columbians of a variety of political persuasions, and many B.C. co-operators spoke out on its behalf throughout the decade.

But if society was to be organized by the people to provide efficiently for their needs, capital could not be ignored. That is why the credit union was so important to the general co-operative movement: it was to be the financial heart for the entire movement. Such issues were widely discussed throughout the province in the thirties. The rapid growth of adult education, the increasing use of radio, and the popularity of pamphleteering made it possible for such issues to be addressed as never before by groups, families, workers and neighbours. The credit union (and co-operative) answers to contemporary problems, therefore, fell on fertile soil in B.C. Indeed, perhaps the soil was too fertile in that credit unionism and co-operativism in their most distinct meanings would always have a problem being accurately identified in a province where there was a wide, rich and competitive mixture of ideologies.

This problem of distinctiveness was not unique to British Columbia. It was a problem that had plagued co-operative movements in several parts of the world since the later nineteenth century. In its purest form, co-operativism was (and is) a unique ideology, with its own philosophical base and operating principles. It takes an optimistic view of human nature and believes that steadily larger groups of people are able to take control of their own economic affairs. It believes that democratic systems can be used effectively in the marketplace – in fact, they even offer advantages. It believes that economic organizations should have social goals that have to be kept in mind even as they compete in the marketplace. It believes that co-operatives, largely through integrated federated structures, can reshape the entire economy, and it believes that the profits of any enterprise should be distributed on the basis of participation, not investment. For many in British Columbia, Canada and the United States, credit unionism was just the financial variant of this vision.

That ideology, though, had fought a losing battle in the epic struggles between liberalism, conservatism, social democracy, Marxism – even anarchism – that convulsed much of the world from the 1860s onwards. Indeed, its distinctiveness had been submerged because advocates of all the competing systems could, and frequently did, embrace co-operative methods and encourage co-operative institutions. Liberals could like co-operatives because of their self-help emphasis; conservatives could appreciate their emphasis on community and social service; social democrats were attracted by their collectivist tendencies; Marxists saw co-operatives as useful, albeit temporary, instruments in their educational and fund-raising efforts; and anarchists (not an insignificant force in British Columbia) liked them because they demonstrated an alternative way to organize society, an alternative to big business and big government.

The need to define the essence of credit unionism, therefore, was evident in B.C. from the beginning. It would not be facilitated by the fact that credit unions would attract members from nearly all the ideological camps in an ideologically-rich province. That would be one of its greatest strengths; on occasion, it would become one of its greatest weaknesses.

In a very real sense, however, the ideological issues tended to be largely ignored in the early years of B.C. credit unionism.

The more obvious issues were usually much more mundane and practical. In that sense, the point is that the credit union idea from its inception in B.C. was successful: it met some very real and pressing needs, most particularly by providing places where people could save and borrow – people who were either not being served well or, in most instances, not being served at all by the existing banking system.

Thus, the earliest supporters of credit unions were from among those who generally never had credit: the underemployed, the relatively poorly paid. These were people who worked for low wages in factories or forests, who operated marginal farms, who made precarious incomes from fishing. For them, the most common problem was a periodic shortage of cash. It could be a long time between pay-days, there were financial emergencies, especially with health problems in those days before medicare. There could be the soul-destroying decline caused by the loss of steady employment, the type of decline that might be reversed by a stake to start a new kind of work.

Moreover, credit unions in the early stages were based primarily on character, not on wealth. Groups of people banded together to save money, but they loaned it, particularly in the early period of the movement, on the basis of reputation. In other words, collateral was important, but the more important factor was how peers thought of you. The mere fact that reputation could be important, that character could count, was in itself a powerful idea – especially in a time of economic collapse and in a society that increasingly tended to make the counting of shekels the measure of all things.

Beginnings
1936-1940

To be loyal to the
highest interests of the
citizens of Canada

To make honesty
and justice the
basis for
our dealings with
our fellow man

To think, act, and
speak constructively

Pledge of the
Army of the
Common Good

CREDIT UNIT #1.

T. W. PHILLIPS

ELSOM AVE

Of course, that not only are we taking a chance on you, but on the whole financial structure of our national economy . . .

1. Interview with Arthur Wirick, February 5, 1993.

*I*N THE 1930S, "BURNABY" WAS REALLY TWO RURAL COMMUNITIES – one stretching along Hastings Street, near Burrard Inlet; the other along the Kingsway on the route to New Westminster. Between them lay higher land still dominated by stands of fir trees, although even in the thirties the woods were giving way to clusters of houses and groupings of small farms or "ranches." Burnaby residents could readily reach the mills and offices of Vancouver and New Westminster on the interurban railway, but the communities were consciously different from Vancouver; they even believed they were significantly different from each other. Residents would maintain that belief for a decade. Thus, when they came to form credit unions, they would create two distinct groupings that would reflect, for a while, two different senses of community. In both communities, though, the homes were modest but generally attractive. They were the homes of working people, many of whom had small plots of land and found a variety of ways to support families: that is, until the Depression hit.

The Burnabys were among the B.C. communities most affected by the Dirty Thirties. In the fall of 1931 the workers at the Barnet mill in North Burnaby went on strike; it proved to be a disastrous mistake for them, since the mill, old and uncompetitive, never opened again.[1] Similarly, the Burnaby residents who worked in Vancouver tended to be among those who suffered earliest and longest: they were typically among the lowest paid – that was partly why they had sought the less expensive housing of the Burnabys – and they generally held the least secure jobs. Those who worked in New Westminster were also immediately affected by the cut-backs that started to occur in the mills in 1930.

The two communities, moreover, had few industries of their own and, therefore, little resilience as the times grew more difficult. The tax base for Burnaby was weak, meaning that it could not meet the relief expenditures as unemployment grew. By 1932, Burnaby had a larger proportion of its population unemployed than any other community in the province. The cost of relief soon soared beyond the financial capacity of the municipality, which, in effect, went bankrupt; Burnaby was the first region in B.C. to be placed under an appointed administrator.

Nevertheless, the people in the Burnabys were self-reliant and flexible. Most houses had small gardens; people worked at a wide variety of tasks to make ends meet; and it was commonplace for wives and children, as well as husbands, to work, even in the good times. It was an ideal environment for the emergence of the Army of the Common Good.

In a way, the Army had a long history of antecedents. It can be seen as a contemporary manifestation of a tradition of utopian community-building that stretched back a long time in North American history: at least to the experiments in Owenite utopianism of the early nineteenth century, if not to the efforts of the Pilgrims to create their Commonwealth in the early seventeenth century.

From those traditions had emerged a significant and widespread series of utopian movements in the United States and, to a lesser extent, in Canada throughout the nineteenth and early twentieth centuries. On an intellectual level, the immediate inspiration was more recent: it came from that classic study of alternative societies, Edward Bellamy's *Looking Backward*, and from the writings of Upton Sinclair, particularly his book *Co-op*. Practically, the inspiration came from the successes of a similarly-named organization in Pennsylvania, the activities of the Llano Colony in Louisiana, and the National Development Association in Salt Lake City.

All of these experiments were efforts to group people together in community (if not communal) activities in an effort to improve their lot in an ethically-acceptable way. The Army followed in that tradition and, for a while, played a significant role among the unemployed and marginally-employed in Vancouver. It also provided the spark that brought credit unions to British Columbia.

The principal leader of the Army of the Common Good was D.G. MacDonald. He was a visionary who dreamed, much in the tradition of co-operative utopians of the late nineteenth century, of creating an integrated co-operative society. It would be a society that would participate in the conventional marketplace as little as possible. Its members would swear "to make honesty and justice the basis of all [their] dealings with [their] fellow man."[2] There would be no salaries or wages — or, at least, as few as possible; members of the Army would work for scrip, which they would exchange among each other for goods or services. Only occasionally would the Army sell produce for money in the market, and then only to raise cash needed for the purchase of equipment or supplies it could not manufacture.

The Army was organized in 1931. A defiant statement of hope and self-help in a besieged community, it immediately attracted considerable interest. Its first stronghold was in South Burnaby, but it quickly attracted recruits in North Burnaby, New Westminster, North Vancouver, and Vancouver's East Side. Its first objective was to find work for its members, work that would produce goods and services the members could also use. It carefully recorded the backgrounds and skills of each member, then designed work for them. Since wood was a necessity, particularly in the winter, and since it was plentiful, as long as axes and saws were available, the Army concentrated on the

2. Common Good Co-operative Association Papers, BCCCU Archives.

harvesting of wood from nearby wood-lots. Then it turned to the working of a farm near Ladner, a variety of canning activities, the raising of rabbits, and the marketing of fruit. Special units were organized for workers who wanted to make furniture, for barbers, for shoemaking; women were organized into units for canning, knitting, operating a delicatessen, and dressmaking.

By 1932, the Army had 1,500 members enrolled on its books. In February of that year, when relief payments were cut back, the Army incorporated a consumer co-operative, the Common Good Co-operative, in South Burnaby. It leaders hoped that the store would enable members to secure good quality food at the lowest possible price. For the rest of the decade, the dream worked, and, for a while, attracted the support of city officials, the provincial government, the Board of Trade, and even the Stock Exchange.[3] In fact, some leaders of the Stock Exchange were particularly sympathetic and donated space in the Exchange's downtown building for the Army's Vancouver activities. The city police, too, were sympathetic and regularly ignored the Army's frequent abuse of the city by-law governing the licensing of its vehicle.[4]

The fundamental problem for the co-operative, as for so many people in the Depression, was a shortage of cash. The records of the organization throughout the 1930s demonstrate that there were never sufficient funds to carry out the envisioned projects;[5] the co-operative never had the capital to become large enough to meet the many needs of its numerous members. And that is why the idea of a credit union seemed to be so attractive.

In 1936, three individuals with some knowledge of credit unions urged enthusiasts within the Army to consider forming them. The first was Toyohiko Kagawa, the Japanese Christian co-operative leader who made a triumphant six-month tour of the United States and Canada during the first half of the year. Kagawa had played a prominent role in the establishment of agricultural, marketing and financial co-operatives in Japan, following theological training at Princeton during World War One. An eloquent speaker, a deeply committed co-operator who would be hounded and imprisoned by the Japanese government during World War Two, Kagawa had an immense impact.[6] He saw the co-operative movement as the economic embodiment of Christian thought. In Vancouver in April of 1936, he gained the admiration of large crowds of Christians. Many within those crowds, Protestant and Catholic, ministers and lay people, would become converts to credit unionism in the years ahead.

The second individual was George Keen from Brantford, Ontario, the general secretary of the Co-operative Union of Canada. At a meeting of co-operative leaders in Vancouver in July, a meeting called

3. See correspondence between D.G. MacDonald and George Keen, National Archives of Canada, Ottawa, Co-operative Union of Canada Papers, Vol. 164, "C.G. Co-op Assn (New Westminster) – 1935" File.

4. "Economic Adversity: Seed Bed for Credit Unions," *Enterprise*, February, 1967, pp. 10-11.

5. The records of the Army of the Common Good are in the Vancouver City Archives; a photocopy of those records is also available in the BCCCU Archives.

6. For a recent biography of Kagawa, see R. Schilgren, *Toyohiko Kagawa: Apostle of Love and Social Justice* (Berkeley: Centenary Books, 1988).

to consider the formation of a city-wide co-operative organization, he described the successes that had been achieved in developing credit unions in Nova Scotia. At the same meeting, the third individual, Mildred Osterhout, a member of the South Burnaby Army unit, reported on her recent visit to Nova Scotia when she had met with some credit union leaders. A month later, the Army, through the Common Good Co-operative membership, organized a financial co-operative.

It was not called a credit union; instead, it was called a "credit unit." The name may have been selected because of uncertainties over using the term "credit union" since there was no provincial legislation under which such a name could be used. The Army may also have preferred the word "unit" because all of its work activities, except for the store, were organized into "units." In any event, once formed, the credit unit carried on meeting some of the financial needs of a small but loyal membership of 20-30. More importantly, the credit unit helped to spark interest in the idea of financial co-operatives and of credit unions in particular.

In 1938, at least two other groups started to form credit unions. One of these was the B.C. Motor Transportation Ltd., whose drivers with Pacific Stage Lines learned about credit unions on their Seattle run. The other was made up of postal employees in Vancouver who met at lunch-time to discuss how they could improve their financial situations. They had, in fact, been engaged in an informal self-help banking system since 1933: the "Bootleg Lending Society," a pool of money to which each donated some funds and from which each borrowed small amounts when hard pressed for cash.[7] In time, this mutual aid activity would be formalized into Amalgamated Civil Servants Credit Union (Vancouver).

The main organization that carried forward the idea of credit unions, however, was the Vancouver and District Co-operative Council, which had been created as a result of the visit of Keen and Kagawa in 1936. The Council undertook a series of educational initiatives throughout the late 1930s, when co-operative enthusiasm was evident in many parts of the Vancouver area. It printed pamphlets, organized public meetings on co-operatives, and promoted existing co-operatives in the city.

Its most prominent activity was the sponsorship of large public celebrations of Co-operative Day, held each July in Stanley Park: in the late 1930s and early 1940s, those celebrations attracted hundreds of people. Its most important activity, however, was the sponsorship of study clubs out of which many credit unions would be formed, directly and indirectly, in the mid-1940s.

In early 1938, the council, on the urging of representatives from the fishing co-operatives,[8] formed a Credit Union Committee

7. *Federal Notes*, Quarterly Publication of the Vancouver Federal Employees Credit Union, December 1960, p. 1. There is some doubt that the Bootleg Lending Society started operations in 1933; it may have been as late as 1938.

8. *The Canadian Co-operator*, February, 1938, p. 9.

specifically to promote the development of credit unions. The committee was originally drawn from the council, but, as the intent was to create a provincial rather than city-based credit union movement, it was soon expanded and separated from the council. Ultimately, the committee included individuals from the fishermen's co-operatives, the Common Good Co-operative Credit Unit, the B.C. Co-operative Wholesale Society, and the University of British Columbia's Department of Extension. The key leaders on the committee were J. Deane of the Fishermen's Co-operative Association, A.S. Trotter from the Vancouver Council, George Cockburn from the Street Railwaymen's Union, and D.G. MacDonald of the Common Good.

The committee sponsored public meetings at which others who had visited Nova Scotian credit unions described their experiences.[9] On other occasions, it provided speakers or information for speakers on credit union topics at fishing co-operative and labour conferences. Throughout its existence, too, it distributed pamphlets, particularly to the various study clubs scattered around the city that were interested in credit unions.

The committee's main activity, though, was to lobby the provincial government for appropriate credit union legislation. The importance of good legislation could hardly have been overemphasized. Since few leaders for the credit unions that were being envisioned would have experience in operating businesses, the legislation would have to provide sufficient direction – with adequate policing – to ensure that adequate records were kept, that good loan policies were followed, that sufficient reserves were made to offset losses, and that sound procedures were used by the various committees. At the same time, the legislation would have to provide for an appropriate role for government, a difficult issue for any kind of co-operative, but particularly for financial co-operatives because of the fiduciary responsibilities of their leaders. It was a complicated area of negotiation between governments and credit unions, one that would remain continually significant for the B.C. movement to the present day; it was also an issue that would become fundamentally significant for B.C. Central Credit Union.

The efforts to gain legislation began in 1936 when Dorothy Steeves, the MLA for Vancouver North, introduced a private member's bill that would have regulated co-operative banking organizations. Steeves had been born in Holland and had married a Canadian prisoner-of-war at the end of World War One. She moved with her husband to Vancouver and soon became involved in pacifist and left-wing causes.

Her interest in credit unions and co-operatives grew during the 1930s, and she was a frequent speaker on the two topics at political and

9. Ibid., pp. 12-13.

public events from at least 1935 onward. She knew Mildred Osterhout well,[10] and no doubt learned about credit unions from her. She was also familiar with the European co-operative movement, perhaps as a result of her service as legal advisor to the Dutch Government's Wartime Prices and Trade Board. Her 1936 Bill, Number 13, suffered the fate of most private member's bills and was defeated by the government majority. A second Bill, introduced the following year, met the same fate. Nevertheless, Steeves's efforts publicized the need for legislation and raised the issue significantly at the legislative level.

In early 1938, negotiations for legislation became serious among those directly involved in credit unions. Members of the committee joined with representatives of the Vancouver Co-operative Council to meet with officials from the Attorney-General's Office to consider the preparation of co-operative legislation. The group prepared a brief on the value of credit unions and the nature of preferred legislation. Following precedent in other jurisdictions, it advocated separate legislation for co-operatives and credit unions, but, unlike the American tradition, it wanted co-operatives to have the right to be members of credit unions. The group based its specific recommendations on credit union legislation on a review of the Quebec, Saskatchewan, and Nova Scotia legislation; for that reason, the group was particularly well informed about the emerging trends in credit union law at the time.

The Liberal government received the brief and then melded its provisions together with parts of the B.C. Societies Act, the recently-passed B.C. Co-operative Association Act, and the B.C. Company's Act to create its own legislation: the Credit Union Act. The resulting legislation, while lengthy, made incorporation difficult and it ignored requests to make it possible to enrol junior members (those aged under 16). It also demonstrated its diverse origins and suffered from confusing wording.[11]

Following precedent in other jurisdictions, the government decided that credit unions would be incorporated under a different act from co-operatives, a decision that angered many co-operative enthusiasts. To make matters worse for the enthusiasts, the government appeared, at least to some, to have a hidden agenda. Throughout the province, merchants were having difficulty in collecting on overdue accounts. The government hoped that credit unions could be developed to help resolve this problem.

The government also wanted Chambers of Commerce to be involved in establishing credit unions, perhaps so that the merchants in the Chambers could then refer their debtors to credit unions to secure loans to pay their bills. The government sent the Legislative Counsel, Pitcairn Hogg, on a tour, with the help of

10. See Susan Walsh, "The Peacock and the Guinea Hen: Political Profiles of Dorothy Gretchen Steeves and Grace MacInnis," in *Not Just Pin Money: Selected Essays On The History of Women's Work in British Columbia*, ed. by Barbara K. Katham and Roberta J. Pazdo (Victoria: Camosun College, 1984), p. 368.

11. Holtby interview.

The patronage of Archbishop William Mark Duke helped in the formation of several credit unions among Roman Catholics in British Columbia. As in many parts of the world, the Roman Catholic Church supported credit unions in British Columbia as a way for working people to help themselves.

12. See interview with J.F. Grant by Schroeder and McTiernan, March 8, 1977, and Holtby interview, BCCCU Archives.

13. See A.V. Hill, *Tides of Change: A Story of Fishermen's Co-operatives in British Columbia* (Vancouver: Prince Rupert Fishermen's Co-operative Association, 1967).

14. *A History of Greater Vancouver Community Credit Union* (Vancouver: GVC News, 1990), p. 2.

Chambers of Commerce, to explain the legislation and promote credit unions. Hogg, however, was badly-informed about credit unions and he could not explain the Bill effectively. His first meetings with interested parties clearly demonstrated his lack of knowledge, and his tour was cancelled. It was not an auspicious beginning.[12]

Bad as it was, the legislation nevertheless contributed to the widespread interest in credit unions that had already appeared. By 1938 a substantial number of people had started to study and promote the formation of credit unions. Essentially, there were six networks of people promoting credit unions, with some of the networks having people in common.

The first and most prominent network was the nexus established around the Vancouver Co-operative Council and similar, though unorganized, groups in several communities. Their most common commitment was to the co-operative store and they were greatly influenced by the philosophy and perspective associated with British co-operatives and the International Co-operative Alliance. From that group would come several of the key leaders for the credit union movement during the 1940s.

The second was found within the fishing co-operatives that had emerged during the later 1920s. They were well established along the coast, Vancouver Island, and the Fraser Valley estuary.[13] Despite the Depression, they were successful, resourceful enterprises, built on the class interests of the fishing people, in many instances a shared Scandinavian heritage, and generally a left-wing political orientation. They were consistently promoting credit unions as early as 1937 and ultimately they would make a vitally-important contribution in the 1940s. Indeed, a significant amount of the success of B.C. Central Credit Union in its early years would depend upon the support of those organizations.

The third network was provided by several religious groupings, but particularly the Catholic Church. The example provided by the Catholic Church in the credit union movement in Nova Scotia was one reason for that interest. So, too, was the fact that the Archbishop of Vancouver, William Mark Duke, was a close personal friend of Moses Coady. Under Duke's leadership, the Catholic Church in B.C. created the Pacific Co-operative Institute in 1936 to foster study clubs for the organization of co-ops and credit unions.[14]

More fundamentally, though, the Catholic Church, from the 1890s through to the Great Depression, had been engaged in a deep debate over its role in the face of dislocations caused by virtually unregulated capitalism. Significant groups within the Canadian church participated in that debate and came to advocate support for self-help and

The first cash drawer

by Clarence Morin

The first "offices" of credit unions usually consisted of not much more than a single container for a few ledger cards, the corporate seal, and some stationery. Stry Credit Union used a small suitcase; a cardboard box under the treasurer's bed held OFI Credit Union's records; V.P. Credit Union's first office was Don MacKay's locker at the police station. Seldom did they begin with furniture or fixtures.

C.G. Credit Union probably owned the first real "cash drawer." Fabricated and donated by a carpenter (who had only one arm), the wooden insert converted a desk drawer into a cash drawer.

It didn't see much use in early years because deposits were so minimal — the problem of liability for funds was a very real deterrent to building deposits. Incorporation removed this barrier and the cash drawer became a most useful device.

Five curved bottom compartments for coins allowed easy removal; five rectangular compartments held paper currency. The insert served the credit union for many years, and after 50 years, it was still in excellent condition — a bit worn here and there but a solid testament to its craftsman.

It is truly unfortunate that no one can remember the name of the man who made such an interesting and useful contribution to the development of credit unions in British Columbia.

community organization as a way to improve living conditions and to forestall the growth of socialism. Catholicism in British Columbia had its share of such advocates, specifically a number of priests and lay people who encouraged the formation of credit unions in communities scattered across the province.

Similarly, within Protestant churches, there was a growing interest in social activism triggered by ethnic associations or the Social Gospel. Leaders from the Lutheran and, eventually, the Mennonite churches became strong supporters and several credit unions had their beginnings in church congregations. Many of the early leaders, such as Breen Melvin and A.S. Trotter, were also influenced by the Social Gospel, a reformist movement within Protestant Churches that argued for the creation of the New Jerusalem here on earth. It led several ministers and prominent lay people to encourage co-operatives of all kinds, but especially credit unions.

The fourth network was to be found within a political party, the Co-operative Commonwealth Federation. During the 1930s, the CCF had organized study clubs as key components of its activities in both provincial and federal riding associations. Many of these clubs devoted sessions to the careful study of co-operatives, including credit unions. Generally, it was the more moderate, even conservative, people within the CCF who favoured co-operatives.

Those within the CCF who were more influenced by Marxism tended to be less enthusiastic, even negative, since hard-line Marxists regarded co-operatives as diversions from the real struggles for working-class dominance. The point was that co-operatives represented self-help as opposed to government-led economic and social development, a difference that had produced considerable tension in European socialist/co-operative circles and would lead to problems later in B.C. In the 1930s and 1940s, though, the CCF networks that supported co-operatives would be important vehicles for their development.

The fifth network consisted of various employee groups. Some of these were trade unions and associations, such as the Amalgamated Civil Servants of Canada, the B.C. Motor Transit Workers, the Street Railwaymen and the Provincial Government Employees. A particularly important group was made up of federal, provincial, and municipal public servants. While they were fortunate enough to be employed during the 1930s, they received low salaries and required financial institutions where they could save and borrow funds. They were also well educated and easily contacted, especially by government officials who would be charged with developing the credit union movement. In fact, many of the important leaders for the movement and for Central in the early years would come from this network.

The sixth and last important network was provided by the University of British Columbia. During the 1930s, UBC, like many other Canadian universities, became increasingly interested in adult education. This was in striking contrast to the traditional "ivory tower" approach typical of Canadian universities before 1929. As the thirties unfolded, though, adult education gained many adherents. It aimed at the "emancipation" of working people from the effects of economic hardship and social dislocation;[15] it was a body of thought with natural and historic ties to the co-operative movement in both Europe and North America. St. Francis Xavier University, Laval University, the University of Toronto, and the University of Saskatchewan were leaders in this field in Canada, and UBC, under the leadership of the entrepreneurial Gordon Shrum, sought to join them.

In December of 1937, delegates from the three largest fishing co-ops in B.C. met with Shrum and asked him to start extension work on behalf of co-operatives. Soon after, he contacted St. Francis Xavier University to learn about its program, and specifically about how to secure funds from the federal Department of Fisheries for the promotion of co-operatives through adult education.[16] In 1938 he secured a promotional grant from the federal government, and in early 1939 he hired J.D. Nelson Macdonald, a Presbyterian minister who had worked for the Extension Department at St. Francis, to teach a short course on co-operatives.[17] It was the beginning of what would become a significant involvement in credit union/co-operative development by the University.

All of these networks became involved as various groups sought more appropriate legislation in late 1938 and early 1939. On the political level, Dorothy Steeves continued to press for legislative changes, but the most important lobbying was undertaken by a growing band of credit union activists. On May 10, 1939, representatives of all the major groups with a clear interest in credit unions met in Vancouver. They included some 81 representatives drawn from the Vancouver Co-operative Council, the Co-operative Wholesale, the fisheries co-operatives, the University of British Columbia, several trade unions, and the Common Good Credit Unit. The British Columbia Credit Union Association was formed to "promote and sustain the growth of the Credit Union Movement in the Province in an orderly and systematic manner during the period preceding the establishment of a Provincial League of Credit Unions." It would do so "by the employment of effective organisational, educational and protective policies which shall be calculated to secure and maintain for and within the Movement complete democratic control and strict neutrality in regard to race, class, politics and religion."[18]

A feature of the gathering was the presence of many public servants. Some, like A.L. Nicholas and J.W. "Jack" Burns, would play

15. For fuller discussions of the history of adult education in Canadian universities – and the tie to co-operatives – see Ron Faris, *The Passionate Educators: Voluntary Associations and the Struggle for Control of Adult Educational Broadcasting in Canada, 1941-1952* (Toronto: Peter Martin Associates, 1975) and Ian MacPherson, "Co-operatives, Adult Education and Community Development," in Frank Cassidy and Ron Faris, *Choosing our Future: Adult Education and Public Policy in Canada* (Toronto: The Ontario Institute for Studies in Education, 1987), pp. 50-61.

16. G. Shrum to M. Coady, November 16, 1938, University of British Columbia Archives, Extension Department Records, St. Francis Xavier Scrapbook.

17. See Gordon M. Shrum, "Among Canada's West Coast Fishermen," *Journal of Adult Education*, October, 1940, pp. 2-3.

18. *The Canadian Co-operator*, June, 1939, p. 11.

important roles in the development of B.C. Central in the 1940s. These public servants would be particularly important over the next few years as the Association struggled to gain the kind of legislation that was needed: in particular, legislation affecting how credit unions were organized, how they were inspected, how they could spend their deposits, how they could build and spend reserves, and how people under 16 could become junior members. Securing such changes would require several amendments throughout the early 1940s and some of them would not be gained until much later.[19] In time, lobbying for appropriate legislation, a never-ending and vitally important task, would become one of the key responsibilities of B.C. Central.

From the beginning, however, the provincial legislation reflected what was becoming Canadian practice. In keeping with the norms of English-Canadian credit union legislation in the 1930s, the B.C. Credit Union Act of 1939 allowed for the organization of both community-based and closed-bond credit unions. It also gave considerable regulatory power to the provincial government. It established an Inspector's Office to regulate the credit unions, and the Inspector was charged with an annual inspection of all credit unions.

The regulations accompanying the Act, along with the Act itself, gave the Inspector extensive powers, and under some conditions complete control over credit unions. The Inspector, for example, had the right to suspend those credit unions that did not provide him with required information or were operating in a frivolous manner. Credit unions in difficulty were required to submit extensive reports and had to have all major decisions approved by the Inspector's Office. In such cases, the Inspector could stop further deposits, restrict loans, or limit interest payments. In short, the legislation made the Inspector the policeman and the deposit protector for the province's credit union system. It was not an easy relationship to define satisfactorily, and the 1939 Act was just the first of a long series of attempts to do so.

It became particularly important, therefore, who would become Inspector. The position was offered first to A.S. Trotter, who had played a significant role in promoting credit unions since 1936. For some reason (perhaps politics, since Trotter, although very moderate, was associated with the CCF) the offer was withdrawn.[20] Instead, the position was given to E.K. DeBeck, who also served as Superintendent of Brokers. It turned out to be an excellent choice. DeBeck had been meeting with representatives of the co-operatives since 1936, and he had been closely involved with the passage of the Co-operatives Act in 1938.

Moreover, on a personal level, DeBeck, although somewhat paternalistic, was approachable and sympathetic. As Gordon Holtby, a credit union activist who became involved in the late thirties, later

19. The Act was amended in 1939, 1943, 1944, 1946 and 1948.

20. *The Canadian Co-operator*, March, 1939, p. 5.

recalled: "[The inspection of credit unions] was sort of a baby tossed into all his other work. But he took it seriously and we were very appreciative of the help he gave us."[21]

With the legislation passed and a bureaucrat in place, the various credit union groups around the province could now apply to be legally registered. Three groups rushed to be the first to be incorporated. The first to send in its application was the credit unit group in Burnaby, whose leaders were anxious to have the first charter. Unfortunately for them, their application had not been filled in correctly and so was returned. The first to apply and to be accepted – slightly before those wanting to form a credit union among federal public servants – was a group in Powell River on the Sunshine Coast.

During the late 1930s, there were actually two inter-related groups in Powell River seriously studying the co-operative movement. One formed a consumer co-operative in the summer of 1938 and it generally made good progress in its early years.[22] The other, stimulated by the Catholic priest, Father Leo Hobson, had started studying credit unions in 1938. In the autumn of that year, J.D. Nelson MacDonald visited the group as part of a familiarization tour he took shortly after arriving in the province to work for the University of British Columbia. He particularly impressed Father Hobson, who encouraged his brother, Tommy Hobson, a mill worker, and Walter Cavanaugh, a leader of the recently-formed union, to sign up their fellow workers for a proposed credit union. They were successful and the company made available to them "a little cubby hole of an office right opposite the mill gates…next to the watchman's office and…a big lunchroom…where the employees who formed what was called in those days the spare gang used to congregate."[23] They were ready for operation by the spring of 1939 and sent in their application in June. On the ninth day of that month, they were granted the province's first credit union charter.

During the winter of 1939-1940, there was considerable activity as groups around the province continued to study credit unions – what they were, how they were organized, what they could do. The Extension Department at the University of British Columbia spearheaded these activities. It had received a grant from the federal Department of Fisheries to start co-operatives in the same way as had been so successfully pioneered by St. Francis Xavier University in Antigonish, Nova Scotia.

The Antigonish approach, as the St. Francis program became known, was very simple. It was a kind of economic populism squarely within the traditions of the most distinctive version of co-operative thought. It believed – a deceptively radical idea – that the economy, no less than the political order, could be operated on democratic principles. It further believed (also a deeply radical idea) that broad segments of the population could be educated to take an interest in, and could operate,

21. Holtby interview.

22. *The Canadian Co-operator*, March, 1939, p. 10.

23. Ibid.

Romance in the Credit Union Movement

by Clarence Morin

Romance is, and always has been, widespread in the credit union movement. Many managers married directors, directors married directors, staff members married each other, and all sorts of other liaisons developed from encounters at conventions, workshops, study clubs, and training sessions.

The highest profile romance of all-time began in 1946 when the president of the B.C. Credit Union League, A.L. Nicholas, met Margaret Priestly, treasurer of Nepro Credit Union. They crossed paths again on the ferry taking them to a convention at Powell River and shared a table for lunch. At the convention, some delegates wondered why Nick, as he was called, seemed to be appointing Margaret only to the committees he chaired. They soon figured it out — Nick and Margaret had fallen in love; they married later that year. Margaret and A.L. Nicholas were one of the best known "credit union couples" during the forties and fifties.

Over the years, many credit unions had president-manager romances, but one had its own unique twist. When the manager did not appear for work one day, a call went out to the president. But he, too, was nowhere to be found. A hurried inspection and audit showed the credit union's affairs were in perfect order, every cent was where it was supposed to be, but the two officers were gone. Further investigation eventually revealed the couple had "eloped" for northern points. They never returned.

economic organizations, even those of some complexity. In that sense, it debunked the idea that only a narrow elite could run the economy. Even more, it attacked the capitalist form of enterprise for its tendencies to be exploitative and dictatorial. Finally, the Antigonish approach saw co-operatives as an effective way to bring about technological change with minimum dislocation of workers and communities.

Following from these basic principles, the Antigonish approach developed its own methods. It relied heavily on local leaders, often but not always priests; it required people in the local communities to meet together and systematically review the community's problems; it provided literature and training in group dynamics so that the people could learn about how to organize co-operatives to resolve, at least in part, some of their problems. It was an approach that was brought in its entirety to British Columbia and would have a powerful impact for a generation. It would also serve to instill attitudes within the B.C. movement that would help to establish its distinguishing characteristics.

The early missionaries for the Antigonish approach arrived in the autumn of 1939. One of them was Alex S. McIntyre. He was a coal miner from Cape Breton, a one-time Marxist who had rejected that philosophy in favour of co-operativism's "middle way" between capitalism and statism. The other was Norman MacKenzie, a United Church minister. The two of them brought the literature and the organizing methods of Antigonish. During the autumn of 1939, they visited fishing villages on Vancouver Island, the northern coast and the Queen Charlotte Islands. They organized 24 study clubs, a dozen credit unions, and a number of co-op stores.[24] In the winter term of 1940, they ran short courses in Vancouver and visited several groups in the Lower Mainland and the Okanagan.

By the spring of 1940, therefore, the credit union movement was poised to make significant gains. It had several networks through which information could flow and groups could be identified. It had a legislative framework that, while not completely satisfactory, could nevertheless be used. It had a sympathetic public servant. Above all, it had a cadre of devoted enthusiasts willing to pay the price inevitably involved in starting any movement.

The potential for the future, too, was not just a matter of dreams and musings. In February, the directors of the Common Good Credit

24. Shrum, "Among Canada's West Coast Fishermen," pp. 2-3.

Union received an invitation to attend the meeting of the Oregon State Credit Union League in Portland. Two of their number, Bill Campbell and George Cockburn, both at the time unemployed, volunteered to go, using their own money. Campbell had the money – $7.50 – and Cockburn had the car, a 1926 Ford, "which could do all of 40 when pressed."

The perils of the journey aside, the two men were impressed with what they saw in Portland. The convention was an inspiration. The speeches and enthusiasm shown at the banquet were "eye-openers" to Campbell and Cockburn. On the last day of the Convention, too, they

E.K. DeBeck was the first Superintendent of Credit Unions appointed by the provincial government.

met with Tom Doig, vice-president of the Credit Union National Association in the United States. For a few hours they tried to convince him that British Columbia – with only five credit unions registered – should have a league affiliated with CUNA. Doig was skeptical but their enthusiasm must have touched his building instincts and he promised to come to B.C. and help create a league as soon as he could.

On the way home the two men rejoiced over what had been a good trip and they even found a good omen. With only enough money to pay for the gas apparently left between them, Campbell made a last search through his pockets and found 15 cents – enough in those days to purchase two doughnuts and two cups of coffee in Bellingham – "as satisfactory as a weary desert traveller's stop at an oasis"[25] and an early dividend on what would become the B.C. Credit Union League.

25. Bill Campbell, "Birth of the B.C. Credit Union League," *B.C. Credit Unionist*, February, 1950, p. 15.

Dieppe Raid Mapped by Canadian Officers

Clay Model of Town Used in Attack Plans

CHUMS ARRIVE OVERSEAS

Dieppe Casualties
Canada's Roll of Honor
Two Injured

DAILY WARTIME PRICE REDUCTIONS
Watch for Daily Specials—Tomorrow's Specials 2–4 p.m.
KITCHEN UNITS   LEMON REAMERS

YOUR $100.00 BOND WILL FEED THIS NUMBER OF CANADA'S FIGHTING MEN FOR 15 DAYS

TIMES
SICKNESS
FINANCIAL DISTRESS

CREDIT UNION

HOW TO F
And Start Grou

What is a Credit

How Do C

Who S

E. K.

MALE AND FEMALE
EMPLOYMENT OFFICERS WANTED
By Civil Service Commission of Canada

10 Canadians Buried
In Britain Identified

B.C.
CREDIT
UNIONIST

November 1941   VOL. 1, NO.

B.C. CREDIT UNION LEAGUE

*Are we,
as Credit Unionists,
aware of the awful power
that lies within our grasp?*

Editorial
B.C. Credit Unionist

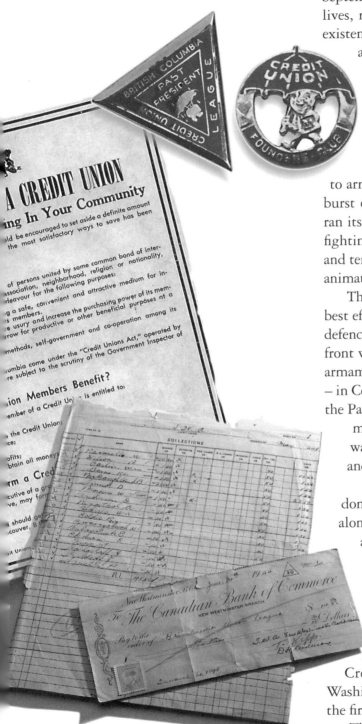

1. *B.C. Credit Unionist*, November, 1941, p. 2.

W HEN 1939 BEGAN, EUROPE MUST HAVE SEEMED FAR AWAY FOR most British Columbians; it would not be so when the dogs of war were unleashed. And, even for several months after war was declared in September, most British Columbians still went stolidly about their lives, many with the quiet desperation that had characterized their existence for a decade. Until late 1940, unemployment continued at about the same rate as it had for the previous 10 years; there were still lines of people at the soup kitchens; there were still the untidy exits from the flop houses and the beaches in the morning; there was still the anger and the ideological commitments the Depression had fostered.

The outbreak of war, then, did not immediately mean total involvement for most British Columbians. The initial rush to arms that occurred in the summer of 1939 soon dwindled as the burst of militantly pro-British and/or strong anti-fascist sentiment ran its course. Moreover, the so-called "phony war" – a time of little fighting for the British and their allies – lasted until well into 1940 and tended to dull people's apprehensions. It was a time of suspended animation; a brief interlude before the terror and the pain would begin.

The key to local change, however, was the economy and, despite the best efforts of the Vancouver Board of Trade to lobby government for defence contracts, nothing much changed immediately. The European front was too far away, and it was much more reasonable to place the armament orders – and to locate most of the new armament industries – in Central and Eastern Canada. Not even the ominous war clouds in the Pacific aroused too much concern in 1939 in British Columbia or, more particularly, back in Ottawa. A decade of nearly continuous war in Asia had confused what was in any event a rather dilatory and superficial Canadian understanding of Southeast Asia.

It would not be until 1941 that the war really became a vital, dominating factor in the life of the province, and at that point it, along with the economic changes it helped accelerate, would lead to a fundamental restructuring of the province. Ultimately, the credit union movement would be a part of that restructuring, shaped by it and contributing to it.

During the early years of the war, the credit union movement made steady progress. Perhaps the most important single event occurred in June, 1940, when Tom Doig arrived, as promised, to help launch the British Columbia Credit Union League. He came with representatives of the Washington State League and Oregon Mutual Credit Union to attend the first annual meeting of the Credit Union Association. The meetings were held in the Vancouver office of the Amalgamated Civil Servants of Canada trade union, then a strong supporter of the credit union movement. They joined 18 representatives from credit unions in Skidegate, Vancouver and Powell River, and study clubs sponsored by the Catholic Church and trade union locals.[2] On the afternoon of June 29, the delegates voted to disband the Association and form the Credit Union League of British Columbia (changed at the 1941 annual meeting to British Columbia Credit Union League).

The new League was patterned along the model developed by credit unions in the United States, but it was the first formed outside of that country. It was also an important step for the fledgling movement in B.C.: it demonstrated the commitment of the delegates and it gave the provincial movement access to the experience and support system of the growing American credit union movement.

During the 1930s, the American movement had experienced remarkable growth. In 1935, the leaders of the Credit Union Extension Bureau, the original organization established by Filene to foster credit unions in the United States, realized they had too many activities under one roof. They separated the Bureau into four new organizations with interlocking directorships. One of these, the Credit Union National Association (CUNA), was formed as the promotional, lobbying and educational wing of the movement. Another, CUNA Supply Co-operative, marketed a wide range of supplies – bookkeeping stationery, calendars, passbooks, children's piggybanks – for local credit unions. A third, CUNA Insurance Research, provided bonding insurance, while a fourth, CUNA Mutual Insurance, provided loan and life insurance for credit union members. The B.C. credit unions, therefore, were gaining access to a wide range of services and a rich source of information when they became part of the CUNA system.

The basis of that system, however, was the state or – in the case of Canada – provincial league. Leagues voluntarily brought together credit unions in their jurisdiction to deal with common problems and the purchase of services and supplies; the latter, it was hoped, from the CUNA organizations. Leagues were also primarily responsible for lobbying governments and undertaking vital educational activities. Education was particularly important because so many board members had limited experience – if any – in the operation of business organizations. Nowhere was that need more obvious than in British Columbia.

When Doig arrived, some 20 credit unions had been registered; by the end of the year there would be 43. Seventeen of the credit unions active at the end of the year would be organized on a community basis, seven of them on Vancouver Island, two on the Queen Charlotte Islands, two in the Okanagan, and the remainder in Vancouver. Fifteen would be occupational – seven of them among municipal, provincial, or federal public servants; two among telephone employees; and two among fishing people. Another three would be started by Catholic

2. Minutes, First Annual Meeting, B.C. Credit Union Association, June 29, 1940, BCCCU Archives.

parishioners, and one would be organized by Danish immigrants in Vancouver.[3]

The growth would continue over the following three years. In 1941, 16 were organized; in 1942, 32; and in 1943, 24.[4] By the latter year, there were 108 credit unions, 70 of them organized with community bonds, 35 with occupational bonds and three with religious or ethnic affiliations.[5] Among the new credit unions, nine were in the Okanagan, the northern interior, and the Kootenays. They were organized through the efforts of either League officers, government officials, or trade union enthusiasts. Nearly all of the new occupational credit unions were located in the greater Vancouver and Victoria areas. Again, government employees were the most prominent groups, but there were also such trade unions as the electrical trades and graphic arts. There were also some employee groups, such as workers at Buckerfields, Dairyland and Sullivan Concentrator.

This success in organizing employees partly reflects the industrialization – and the strength of worker consciousness – in British Columbia during the war. It also made the B.C. movement somewhat different from its counterparts in most of the other Canadian provinces. In Quebec the basis of organization tended to be the parish. Only in Ontario were workplace bonds as significant; in all other provinces, following the Antigonish precedent, the community-based credit union was supreme.

The difference was important. In those days, the community-based credit union typically embraced wider community concerns, was more supportive of the general co-operative movement, and was more likely to be involved in political issues. In contrast, employee-based credit unions tended to be focused, in keeping with the "bread-and-butter unionism" of the day, on gaining specific, tangible benefits for the membership. Some of the closed-bond credit unions, too, were organized among groups that inherently were both more conservative and more experienced in managing enterprises. These were important distinctions that would give rise to many of the arguments – and creative tensions – in succeeding decades.

To some extent, the tensions appeared as the League was being formed. The Credit Union Association had been influenced largely by community-oriented leaders drawn from the Common Good and the Vancouver Co-operative Council. Gradually, a more conservative group of leaders had become more influential, many of them coming from the closed-bond credit unions.

One of the new and more conservative leaders was Al Nicholas of Amalgamated Civil Servants of Canada (Vancouver) Credit Union, the second credit union incorporated in the province. Nicholas had succeeded A.S. Trotter as chair of the Credit Union Association in

3. Based on statistics in *B.C. Credit Unionist*, June, 1942, pp. 8-9, and the list of credit unions in ibid., June, 1950, p. 22.

4. *B.C. Credit Unionist*, October, 1944, p. 12.

5. Ibid., June, 1950, pp. 21-22.

October, 1939, and he played a major role at the League's founding meeting. Another was H.G. Pocock, from the same credit union, who would become secretary-treasurer of the League in September, 1940. He too would add a more cautious and circumspect voice to the provincial leadership.

It was Nicholas, though, who was the dominant figure. A deeply committed and capable credit unionist even as early as 1940, he would remain so until he died in 1960. Somewhat austere, possessed of a sharp temper, remarkably articulate, and meticulous in his attention to detail, Nicholas would play a powerful role in the movement for the succeeding 20 years. He was elected the first president of the League, and would serve for two years.

As the decade began, all of the credit unions were small: in total they had only 1,320 members and $18,790 in assets at the end of 1940.[6] They were almost entirely dependent upon volunteer labour, and all the volunteers had much to learn. Each credit union had between five and twelve directors, elected by the members at annual meetings. They in turn would elect one of their number president, another vice-president, and a third secretary-treasurer. These three were the officers of the credit union, and they formed the executive committee.

The executive committee was responsible for ensuring that the credit union operated properly on a day-to-day basis, in keeping with the Act and the policies set down by the board and the membership. Like all those who served the credit unions in the early days, they usually did so without pay, although a few secretary-treasurers received modest honoraria of $10-$15 per year.

There were two other committees in all credit unions, both required by legislation. The first of these was the credit (sometimes called loans) committee, which received, evaluated and decided upon loan applications. This was often the committee with the most difficult and usually the most sensitive work within the credit union. It could be argued that it was the most prestigious. Members of the committee had important responsibilities and played significant roles among their peers. In making decisions about loans, they also had a lot of power.

In the early days, the credit or loans committee made lending decisions almost entirely on the basis of character: Was the applicant judged to be reliable by his or her peers? Was the reason for the loan satisfactory? Was it for "providential or productive" purposes? How much could the credit union afford to lend to a single member? The latter problem quickly became crucial: even as early as 1942, members

The Government of British Columbia assisted credit unions in their early development by printing pamphlets informing people about how they could organize and operate a credit union.

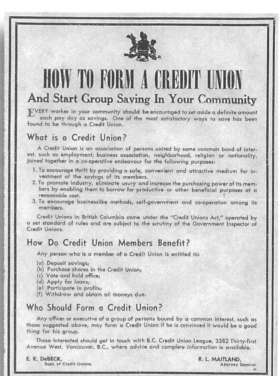

6. Ibid., June, 1942, p. 9.

42

The League was operated in its early years largely through the enthusiastic efforts of volunteers. Above is one of the first membership lists of the League, along with a cheque drawn on the Canadian Bank of Commerce: it would be many years before the credit union system would be independent from banks in managing its financial affairs.

7. Based on an article in the *B.C. Credit Unionist,* January, 1943, p. 5.

8. *B.C. Credit Unionist,* June, 1945, pp. 14-15.

were applying for loans to purchase houses, in some instances requesting as much as $2,000. When a credit union had only $4,000 or $5,000 in assets, should it make such a loan? Moreover, should it rely only on the applicant's character in making its decision? These were questions that could not be resolved easily.

The third committee was the supervisory committee. It acted as a watch-dog on the credit union's activities. At least every three months, it was to review the secretary-treasurer's books, the loans that had been made, and the efficiency of the organization. Based on these reviews, the committee could recommend how policies should be changed to improve the operations of the credit union. In exceptional circumstances, the committee could take action – calling a special meeting or appealing to the Inspector – if it deemed that the officers were abusing their powers or not meeting their obligations.[7]

The supervisory committee also had a mandate – shared with the executive committee – to encourage the involvement of members. This mandate was perhaps the most widely discussed (if usually the most frustrating) responsibility of any committee. The early enthusiasts were generally very committed to democratic procedures and keen on member involvement. In many credit unions they held monthly meetings open to the membership, rotated social evenings in members' homes, sponsored picnics, and supported bowling teams. Women played particularly important roles on supervisory committees in both watch-dog and social activities. It was often frustrating work because, although their efforts were often successful, these volunteers seemed almost inevitably to fall short of their ambitions.

As they developed in the early 1940s, credit unions were remarkable examples of volunteer activism. Although memberships generally ranged between 30 and 100 (50 and 1,350 at the end of 1944[8]), the number of people directly involved seems to have varied between 12 and 20 for each credit union, a remarkably high rate – and one which ensured that the credit union's business was widely known. The credit union also provided important opportunities for public service. In that sense, they could be a poorer person's "service club," a way to contribute to one's community and to achieve status. This was particularly true for individuals like Al Nicholas and Harry Pocock.

For others, though, the commitment reached a deeper level and became a life-long passion, a kind of religion. For them, education was not only important – it was the movement's life blood. During the early 1940s and most of the 1950s, the University of British Columbia played a vitally-important role in educating the people involved with credit unions. Its Extension workers organized study groups of 10 to 20 individuals within existing credit unions or among people interested in forming new ones. The first course introduced the clubs to the co-operative movement generally, and addressed such topics as "What's wrong with our existing social order?", "The co-operative alternative", "The farmer and co-operation" and "The trade unionist and the movement." The second course examined credit unions more specifically by looking at their possibilities, achievements, operation and organization.[9]

The field workers from the Extension Department assumed high profiles within the fledgling B.C. movement. The first fieldman, Arthur Wirick, was hired in August, 1939. He soon established that the major problem confronting the credit unions that had been – or were being – formed was a lack of knowledge in bookkeeping. He prepared a simple manual, designed in part with the wives of fishermen in mind, since they often tended the books for the small credit unions scattered along the coasts of Vancouver Island and the mainland.[10] Like the other Extension workers, Wirick often directly and continuously helped credit unions, even after their leaders were no longer taking courses. Thus, once a month for nearly three years, he would call on treasurers of local credit unions, often enjoying – or enduring – a Kraft dinner, and draw up the month's statement. It was partly on that experience that Wirick drew when he prepared his booklet, which would be a standard for 15 years.

Of the other Extension workers, two played particularly important roles in the early 1940s. One was Breen Melvin, who organized several credit unions and co-operatives, particularly in northern British Columbia. A gentle, unassuming and committed co-operator, he worked for the Extension Department from 1942 to 1944. Afterward, he began a long co-operative career that would be spent largely in the Co-operative Union of Canada and Co-operators Insurance Services (later Co-operators Insurance). In both these positions, he would continue to promote the co-operative dimension of credit unionism in B.C. throughout his long career.

The other principal field worker was Lin Brown, who joined Extension in 1943. She too organized many credit unions during the 1940s, especially along the coast. An enthusiastic, committed and popular individual, she went on to become an important writer and organizer in the fishing trade unions. While she worked with credit unions, she played another important role by encouraging women to accept responsibilities on boards and committees and as secretary-treasurers.

A feature of the Extension Department's program was the extensive use of film and radio. By 1942 the Department was showing films about co-operatives in the United States, Nova Scotia (a silent film), and Sweden. It also showed film slides and lantern slides on the movement in Nova Scotia and among the B.C. fishing communities.[11]

9. See "Educational Services: Co-operatives and Credit Unions," University of British Columbia, Department of Extension, undated (but intended for the 1942-43 academic year), Vancouver City Archives, Army of the Common Good Papers.

10. Wirick interview.

11. "Educational Services: Co-operatives and Credit Unions," University of British Columbia.

A Boy Makes Good

Several years ago a school boy joined the C.G. Credit Union. By delivering milk, morning and evenings for another C.G. member, he learned to save a small amount regularly each month in the Credit Union. The following Spring he left school and secured a job on a fish packer – picking up fish along the B.C. coast. He was earning good wages, but because he had learned the art of saving, he now began in earnest to put his money in the Credit Union.

By November this lad had sufficient savings accumulated to allow him to quit his job and to enroll at a Wireless School in Vancouver. Each month the Credit Union sent a cheque from his savings account for his tuition fees. He has now graduated with high marks and is serving as a wireless operator in the merchant marine navy.

This boy's success symbolizes the success of the C.G. in helping the members to help themselves.

Article, B.C. Credit Unionist, *January, 1945*

12. *B.C. Credit Unionist*, June, 1945, p. 15.
13. Ibid.
14. *B.C. Credit Unionist*, November, 1943, p. 6.
15. A.J. Wirick, "A Rural Credit Union," *B.C. Credit Unionist*, February, 1943, p. 10.
16. Ibid.

In 1943, it started to co-ordinate its activities with Farm Radio Forum, a CBC weekly series built around study clubs that gathered in homes, listened to weekly programs, and answered study questions based on those programs. Another support agency, one that was to be more important in the long run, was the Inspector's Office. DeBeck was directly involved in the inspection of several credit unions each year, although increasingly that responsibility was taken over by his deputy, Tom Switzer, who was appointed in 1943. Their annual visits exposed the kinds of problems the credit unions were encountering; their monitoring of the Act contributed significantly to its frequent reform and better application. They were also involved in encouraging the formation of credit unions, particularly among public servants. Switzer, in fact, would later be credited with having helped directly in the formation of over 80 credit unions. Largely because of his efforts, Victoria became an important centre for the provincial movement during the 1940s and 1950s.

By using the networks that had been formed in the 1930s, by drawing on the experiences of CUNA, and by taking advantage of the services of UBC and the Inspector's Office, the credit union movement expanded steadily between 1940 and the end of 1943. At the latter date, there were 129 credit unions in operation (15 having gone out of business). The operating credit unions had 15,500 members and nearly $1-million in assets.[12] By 1944, too, the movement had significantly expanded from its original Vancouver, Victoria and coastal bases; there were 13 in New Westminster and 33 in "interior points."[13]

Nevertheless, the movement had a strong urban – or at least town – bias. Over 80% of the credit unions formed to the end of 1943 were in communities classified as urban.[14] In fact, some people in British Columbia questioned whether credit unions could function effectively in rural areas where comparatively few people had regular, dependable incomes – according to one perspective, an essential requirement for solid credit union growth.[15] This urban focus would contrast strikingly with the attitudes emanating generally from credit unions in other provinces, 60% of which were rural.[16] It would be a major reason why the B.C. movement became somewhat different from the others.

Wherever they were located, however, B.C. credit unions in the early 1940s were involved in making very small loans for buying cars, consolidating debts, or purchasing supplies. The experience of the Powell River credit union in 1941 seems to have been typical. In that year, it made loans worth $10,462 to 111 borrowers: 25 of the loans were for furniture and house repairs; 15 were for the consolidation of debts; 10 were for medical expenses or funerals; eight were for insurance; and the remainder were for car expenses, construction and

Top Rate Security

by Clarence Morin

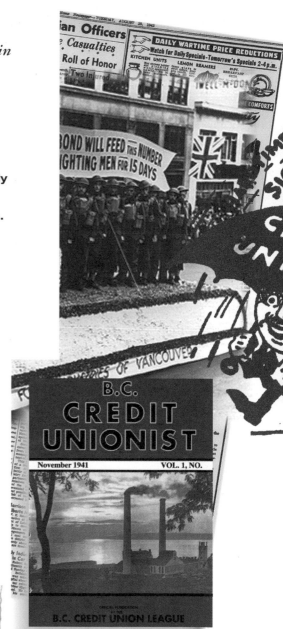

Credit unions have always boasted about their liberal lending policies and how a person's character was a key factor considered when granting loans, but few applied the theory as rigidly as Richmond Savings Credit Union when it granted its first loan.

With a few deposits on hand, the time came to earn some income. To get things moving and to see how loan granting worked, the president of the board of directors filed the first loan application. The credit committee, whose approval was required, looked it over very carefully and decided more security was needed. After much discussion at both the committee and board levels, it was decided the loan could be granted only if Father Patrick McEvoy, the parish priest and founder of the credit union, co-signed the president's application and accepted responsibility for payment if anything went wrong.

Father McEvoy agreed; there were no problems. The loan was repaid as scheduled.

Louis van der Gracht, who served as treasurer of the credit union for 32 years, said the credit union's officers learned many things from that first loan: loans could be granted with only a person's character as security, the president was an honest man, and credit union theories of saving and lending actually did work.

The credit union went on to become one of the largest in the province; by 1994 its assets were well over $1-billion.

vacations. There was no delinquency and the credit union paid a patronage dividend of 5% and a share dividend of 3%.[17]

From the vantage point of the 1990s, it is perhaps easy to underestimate the value of such small lending activities. To appreciate it, though, one must understand that most members would have had great difficulty securing a loan elsewhere or would have had to pay exorbitant rates to do so; that it was easier to apply for credit in a credit union than anywhere else; that the application was probably dealt with quickly; and that the terms of payment were negotiable. Moreover, the dividends would possibly have been among the first interest payments some of the members would ever have earned – and the rate of return exceeded bank interest.

Credit unions also provided their members with a range of services they could not secure elsewhere. Many of them developed and promoted monthly savings plans. Most of them also offered their members insurance policies on loans and deposits, provided by CUNA Mutual Insurance. Under these policies, loans would be paid off and any deposits would be doubled upon the borrower's death, for the benefit of heirs. Given the cost of insurance at the time, this could be a significant benefit. Credit unions also took pains to encourage their members to save – thus the inclusion of the word "Savings" in the official name of many of the credit unions at this time.

Regular saving also became viewed as an indicator of character, so that, if a member had a good saving record, it would be viewed positively when he or she applied for a loan. In 1943, for example, the Common Good Credit Union turned down only two applicants for loans – in both cases members who had not lived up to previously-made saving commitments.[18] It also may have been important that credit unions would lend to women, at a time when few financial institutions would do so – although, thus far, no records have been found to show that women took much advantage of this opportunity.

There were, however, problems within the credit unions as they grew during the early 1940s. On rare occasions there were the problems of human frailty. In one instance, the president of a credit union ran off with the secretary, fortunately leaving all the deposits behind. In a handful of other instances, secretary-treasurers "borrowed" funds without applying for loans.

But such human problems seem to have been the exception. The chief difficulties concerned the business operations of the credit union. One of the most basic problems was the training of the secretary-treasurer, the most important official in the routine operations of the credit union. The secretary-treasurer's main duty was bookkeeping, a set of tasks for which most had no training. There were also problems in deciding on what records should be kept and in dealing with the rare

17. "Co-op News Letter," April, 1942, pp. 2-3, Vancouver City Archives, Army of the Common Good Papers.

18. "C.G. Credit Union, Mid-Year Progress Report," August 31, 1944, Vancouver City Archives, Army of the Common Good Papers.

but troublesome delinquent loans. While representatives from the Inspector's Office could help and there was always advice at the annual meetings, these opportunities were too infrequent – or too late – to be useful in every case. That is why leaders of local credit unions sought the help and consolation of colleagues facing similar situations.

Many credit union directors were also confronted by perplexities in conforming with the requirements of the Credit Union Act. Most of them had to learn the meaning of "reserves" under the Act. Before the creation of B.C. Central Credit Union, they had to reach an understanding of what it meant to deposit the funds of the credit union in a bank "at the earliest possible moment." (For too many, it seemed to mean "whenever it was convenient.") They had to learn how to audit passbooks on an annual basis, and how to adopt a bookkeeping system, usually the one provided by CUNA. As early as the summer of 1941 it was possible to establish a list of authorities, at least in Vancouver, drawn from Stry, Van-Tel, Danish and Westminster credit unions – individuals with sufficient experience and training to help neophyte directors and secretary-treasurers.[19] That was not possible in most other areas of the province, and even in Vancouver more systematic assistance would soon be necessary.

Thus the practice began of leaders from credit unions in the same, or nearby, areas getting together on a regular basis. One of the first efforts of this kind took place in New Westminster. In 1941 and 1942 three credit unions were organized by employees at the Provincial Mental Hospital, the B.C. Penitentiary and Canadian National Railways; they joined three already in existence in and around New Westminster. In September, 1942, leaders from these credit unions, along with leaders from the Common Good Credit Union, started to meet informally on a monthly basis to share information.[20] In time, the credit unions in New Westminster would become one of the most dynamic and innovative groupings in the province.

The first formal grouping of credit unions on a regional basis took place in Victoria in early 1942. It brought together seven credit unions, the most prominent being those organized among public servants and by the Catholic Church. They formed a chapter based on a structure widely used in the United States; it was the first of several such chapters in British Columbia.

The Victoria chapter ran monthly information meetings, encouraged member credit unions to pool orders for supplies, and helped secretary-treasurers learn their jobs. The New Westminster credit unions soon followed the lead of Victoria and organized a chapter in late 1942. Another was formed in Vancouver in 1943, followed by one for credit unions on central Vancouver Island and the nearby Gulf Islands in the summer of 1944.

19. *B.C. Credit Unionist*, November, 1941, p. 3.
20. Ibid., November, 1942, p. 6.

These chapters were vitally important for nurturing the movement in the early years. Long-distance travel was often awkward, expensive and inconvenient in those days before extensive paved highway systems, frequent ferries and local air lines. The chapters, therefore, provided opportunities for the enthusiasts and the office-holders to learn how to meet their responsibilities. It was an early, vital link in what was one of the great contributions that credit unions were to make to the development of British Columbia: the training of thousands of people in how to run organizations and operate businesses. Like all co-operatives, B.C. credit unions, even if they would eventually lose much of their adult education heritage, would never be able to ignore the training of their leaders. It was a tradition that the chapters – and the League – helped to cement in the early 1940s.

Between its creation in June, 1940, and its fourth annual meeting in June, 1944, the League made steady – if sometimes difficult – progress. Its most public activity was the publication of a monthly journal, *The B.C. Credit Unionist*. Produced entirely by volunteers until the early 1950s, it publicized the successes of credit unionism – and, in the early days, co-operativism – and summoned its troops, both absolutely vital tasks for any growing movement.

The first editor was George Gallagher, who had been involved in the early credit union discussions among postal workers in 1938; in fact, he was the first president of Amalgamated Civil Servants of Canada Credit Union. In publishing the *Unionist*, he was assisted and directed by an editorial committee called the Control Board, made up of people drawn from Vancouver-area credit unions and the UBC Extension Department. Preparing and publishing the journal was a heavy task for volunteers to sustain, and it was not done without considerable strain, including one extensive reorganization of the volunteers in the summer of 1942. For the magazine's early years, however, some members of the Control Board wrote, or collected, all the information for sections of the journal. Others were responsible for encouraging credit unionists around the province to take out subscriptions, while others were responsible for selling advertising, on which the magazine depended for essential funds.

Despite the problems, producing the *B.C. Credit Unionist* appears to have been a labour of love for all those involved. George Gallagher seems to have caught their idealism well in his first editorial:

> Out of the challenge to democracy one fact is emerging. It is plain for those who have eyes to see that people, even common people like you and I, are the only real wealth of any nation – the whole world.
>
> With its roots in the soil and deep within the common people of the world, there is no reason why the Credit Union movement should not become world-wide in its scope, and all powerful in its effect on

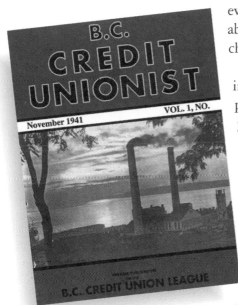

The B.C. credit union movement has a long history of publishing award-winning magazines. The first was the *B.C. Credit Unionist*. It began publication in 1941 and was prepared by volunteers until the early 1950s. It won several awards from the international movement for its articles and commentaries.

the upward surge of the future. For we must remember that there shall be no standing still. We must either go forward or backward.

Having no barriers of race, creed, nor colour, Credit Unionism has all the ingredients to become the most vital motivating power of Tomorrow's Forward March.

Are we, as Credit Unionists, aware of the awful power that lies within our grasp?[21]

The magazine was part of an extensive educational program that the League's leaders embraced with enthusiasm. An Educational Committee was established at the 1942 meetings, where a resolution was also passed advocating that credit unions allocate 5% of their earnings to the education of members. Another motion at the same meeting called upon the provincial Department of Education to provide for education about co-operatives and credit unions in the schools and colleges.[22]

In addition to these educational activities, the League provided several services for local credit unions. It ran a supply service that was staffed by volunteers until the late 1940s. Even in their early days, credit unions required considerable supplies: ledger books, passbooks, calendars, savings banks and memorabilia. Most of the items came from CUNA Supply in Madison, the supply co-operative owned by CUNA Leagues. Local credit unions, however, did not automatically assume that CUNA Supply was the least expensive or best source, and there was a continuous challenging of that connection, a challenge that probably ensured good value.

The League also played a significant role in the creation of credit unions. There were 18 members of the board in this period, at least six of them from credit unions outside the Vancouver metropolitan area. Board members were looked upon as leaders for their regions or communities as well as for their credit unions. In the early forties, no one questioned the advisability of forming credit unions whenever and wherever possible, and so board members were expected to promote the formation of credit unions in their districts.

The president, Al Nicholas, and the treasurer, Harry Pocock, were both particularly active in this regard. They visited several groups in the Lower Mainland and the Okanagan. Board members on Vancouver Island similarly advised on the formation of several credit unions. One minor but well-publicized dimension of this organizational enthusiasm was a competition among board members for the coveted "founder's pin," given by CUNA to any individual who could claim a crucial role in the starting of a credit union.

Throughout the early forties, too, the League was deeply involved in negotiating changes in legislation with the provincial government. During this period, Dorothy Steeves continued to play a prominent

Until the later 1960s the leaders of the B.C. movement — and indeed the international movement — judged growth largely in terms of the number of credit unions. Helping to start a credit union, therefore, was a prized activity; those who did so were rewarded with a "founder's pin," worn proudly by many of the pioneers of the B.C. movement.

21. As quoted, *Enterprise*, 50th Anniversary Special, March-April, 1991, p. 3.
22. Minutes, BCCUL Annual Meeting, June 26-27, 1942, BCCCU Archives.

role in these efforts, but gradually a group of informed credit union lobbyists began to emerge from the ranks of the credit unions. They were concerned about a wide range of issues, including definitions of membership, joint spousal shares, appeal systems for members who felt aggrieved, the make-up of boards, and the terms of directors.

To meet the growing lobbying issues, the League struck a Legislative Committee in 1943, and it worked closely with Vancouver lawyer Bob McMaster. He had become interested in credit union and co-operative legislation in the late 1930s: he would play a long and significant role in the B.C. co-operative and credit movements. Indeed, McMaster was one of a handful of lawyers who were adequately informed about co-operative law, a specialty that had been well developed in Europe but generally ignored in North America. The result was that he was a guiding hand behind legislation in the province until his death in 1971. Beginning in 1944, he would also significantly influence co-operative legislation at the national level, a daunting task given the federal-provincial division of responsibilities for co-operatives.

But the main challenge confronting the League in the early 1940s was the rapid growth of credit unions. As each credit union emerged, the League was asked to assist in training the new officers and members. The League's own officers, who contributed most of their time in the evenings and on weekends, were soon pushed to their limits – and their families' limits. When Harry Pocock was called on to make the secretary-treasurer's report at the 1942 annual meeting, he is said to have remarked laconically that he "had nothing to report but work."[23]

The growth of the movement was reflected in the numbers of credit unions reported in existence at each annual meeting. At the time of the 1941 meeting, there were 62. That figure grew to 81 in 1942, and 98 in 1943. By the time the 1944 meeting rolled around, the total had reached 122.[24]

The numbers were frightening – for two reasons. First, there had been 11 credit union failures – although none of these had cost their members any money. Preventing such failures, however, became a

The structure of the North American credit union movement was depicted in this CUNA publication of the 1940s.

23. Minutes, BCCUL Annual Meeting, June 23-24, 1944, p. 20.
24. Ibid., p. 15.

preoccupation for the League, as it did for government officials, and one way of doing so was to improve the quality of the advice given to organizers. The second problem was that eight of the existing credit unions did not join the League, some because they felt they could not afford its dues, others because they were not impressed with its services.

At the same time, several credit unions were growing large enough that they either had more money than their members wanted to borrow or, conversely, they did not have enough money to meet their members' demands for loans.

One type of member in particular need of funds was other co-operatives. In the 1938 Act, co-operatives were one of the few kinds of organizations allowed to become members of a credit union. During the early 1940s, groups associated with credit unions were involved in forming, or at least considering, several new consumer co-operatives as well as a few housing co-ops and worker co-ops. Although restricted in development by the regulations governing economic growth in wartime, they nevertheless made frequent applications for loans from the fledgling credit unions, requests that might more easily be granted if the resources of several credit unions could be pooled.

There were several reasons, therefore, why B.C. credit unions began to consider creating a central credit union – or central bank, as it was usually called at the time – in the early forties. Not that it was a new idea. In 1941, Saskatchewan credit unions had created such a central, the Saskatchewan Co-operative Credit Society, to spread risks between rural and urban credit unions, to make maximum use of credit in the province, and to meet the financial needs of co-operatives.[25] In 1942, Nova Scotia credit unions and co-operatives had followed suit and created a central credit union to meet similar objectives. During the winter of 1942-43, New Westminster credit unions met with nearby co-operatives and considered forming a regional central to meet their needs. Aware of what had happened in Saskatchewan and Nova Scotia, they decided that such activities were better undertaken at the provincial level.

The idea was soon picked up by members of the board of the British Columbia League, some of whom must also have already been intrigued by what they had heard about experiments with "central banks" in other provinces. The board appointed a committee, chaired initially by Dorothy Steeves, to explore the idea. Most of the members of the committee came from the Burnaby–New Westminster area. One of the members was Les Wilson, the night foreman of the Westminster Paper Mill, and the committee frequently met in his company's board-room in the evening, Wilson excusing himself periodically to make his rounds of the premises.[26]

25. Christine Purden, *Agents for Change: Credit Unions in Saskatchewan* [Regina: Credit Union Central (Saskatchewan), 1980], p. 59.

26. Holtby interview.

The committee reported to the 1943 League annual meeting held in the Knights of Columbus Hall in Victoria. It recommended that a central credit union be incorporated under the Credit Union Act. It could be organized by any 10 credit unions, would have its capital subscribed by member credit unions and co-operatives, and would require member credit unions to deposit 25% of all their members' deposits.[27] After much discussion, the delegates approved the idea, and the committee was requested to prepare by-laws.

At the same meeting, the delegates instructed the board to formally incorporate the League, which to that time had been operating only on informal understandings and goodwill. Given the size and extent of its commitments, this was no longer desirable, and a committee was appointed to prepare for incorporation of the League under the provincial co-operatives act. The committee worked expeditiously, and the League was incorporated in April, 1944. This was just in time for the next annual meeting, which was held, auspiciously enough, in the Hotel Georgia in Vancouver.

Most of that meeting was given over to discussion of the by-laws for the new Central. There was considerable debate – more than 50 resolutions were put forward concerning the proposed by-laws – but the proposal was carried with great enthusiasm by the delegates. The structure and the purposes were essentially in line with the proposals brought to the Victoria convention a year earlier. The new organization was incorporated immediately after the meeting, with Gordon Holtby, whose involvement in credit unions went back to the Common Good in the 1930s, as its first president.

With the formal creation of the two central organizations, the B.C. credit union movement had reached the end of the beginning. The structures were now in place – the League to spark growth, the Central to grasp business opportunities, the government officials to provide guidance – to propel the movement rapidly forward.

27. Minutes, BCCUL Annual Meeting, June 25-26, 1943.

CHILLIWACK SEES
BEST IN CATTLE

B.C. CREDIT UNIONIST
Vol. VIII, No. 5   PUBLISHED IN VANCOUVER B.C.   May, 1949
SOME PIONEERS OF CREDIT UNIONISM IN B.C.

OFFICIAL PUBLICATION
OF THE
B.C. CREDIT UNION LEAGUE

CREDIT UNION
ANNUAL
CREDIT UNION
ORGANIZATION AWARD

VARIETY SHOW
DWIGHT HALL - 8 p.m. - SATURDAY, OCTOBER 7

Supported by
The Powell
River Credit
Union Choir

Supported by
Radio Station
P.R.C.U.
Broadcast of
"My Dad's
Family"

Winners of the
Powell River
and District
Musical Festival
Junior Trophy

Fun and Frolic
with the
Craziest People

The Edelweiss Schuh Platter Dance Team
(A Group of Sixteen)

DANCING STARS OF *Bing Crosby's* MOTION PICTURE
The Emperor Waltz

THESE ALPEN DANCERS THRILLED LARGE CROWDS AT VANCOUVER'S P.N.E. AND PLAYED
TO CAPACITY AUDIENCES IN THE OKANAGAN VALLEY LAST WINTER. THEIR COSTUMES
ARE IMPORTED DIRECT FROM VIENNA WHILE THE DANCERS THEMSELVES ARE THIRD AND
FOURTH GENERATION CENTRAL EUROPEANS AND FOR THE MOST PART MEMBERS OF THE
EDELWEISS CREDIT UNION (VANCOUVER)

Reserved Seat $1.00 on Sale Sept. 21st at Otto Peterson's
(No Reservations by Phone Please)

General Admission 75c on Sale Now at the Credit Union Office, Otto Peterson's, Westview
Jewellers and Jack Fletcher's, Westview and Cranberry

Two Hours of Superb Variety Entertainment

We must find a better system,
And I'm very sure we can.
Where mankind now serves the dollars,
Dollars then must serve the man

You should join your Credit Union,
And then boost it all you can;
Then you'll make our money system
Servant of the common man

If you join your Credit Union
And then boost it to the sky;
You will find life more worth living,
As the years go slipping by.

Vera Loucks,
Baldonnel Credit Union[1]

1. *B.C. Credit Unionist*, March, 1944, p. 13.
2. *B.C. Credit Unionist*, June, 1945, p. 19.
3. Ibid., April, 1949, p. 13.

*I*N 1944, WORLD WAR TWO ENTERED ITS FINAL PHASE. IN JUNE, the Allies opened their second front in Europe when they landed in Normandy. In October, the tide clearly turned in the Pacific when the Americans destroyed the Japanese fleet at the battle of Leyte Gulf and began their assault on the Philippines. The horror would not be over until the summer of 1945, but for the first time in four years the future did not appear to be so ominous.

The war irreversibly changed British Columbia. Vancouver became a major Canadian metropolis, the country's gateway to the increasingly important Pacific region. Victoria, its Esquimalt harbour suddenly a vital military resource, once again became a major industrial city – as it had been at the turn of the century. Mines in the interior and the north worked at full capacity to build and fuel the steam engines on land and sea that made fighting the war possible. Above all, the forest industries boomed, providing lumber for new buildings, ties for new railways, and sitka spruce for airplanes. Even the agricultural industries, so devastated by the Depression, rebounded. Indeed, they were limited in their expansion only by the shortages of farm labour in the Okanagan and the Fraser Valley – an ironic change from the days of too many workers and not enough markets, which had characterized the 1930s.

The credit union movement was one of the beneficiaries of this economic growth. With unemployment virtually non-existent, income levels rising, and consumer demand escalating (if restricted by wartime controls), the saving and lending needs of working-class people, farmers, and the lower middle class became increasingly more important. Between December, 1944, and December, 1948, the number of issued credit union charters grew from 134[2] to 195[3]; indeed, in the latter year, British Columbia had the fastest growing credit union movement in both the United States and Canada. This growth would strain the resources, though hardly the ingenuity, of those leading the central credit union/co-operative organizations of the province. In fact, the mid-1940s would be perhaps the most creative and exhilarating period in the history of the B.C. movement.

In the case of the League, the main pressures emanated from the training, supply and legislative needs of credit unions scattered around the province. In the case of the Central, the main issues were to establish its roles, to define its policies, and to attract the support of sufficient credit unions and co-operatives to be viable. Both organizations were hard pressed to meet these objectives; both were struggling to lead a movement that, in many respects, was growing too fast to be easily co-ordinated.

Nevertheless, the main trends of the period were nearly all positive. Credit unions benefited from the virtually full employment resulting from the seemingly insatiable demand for workers, particularly in Vancouver, who were needed to maintain the war effort. Along with the Golden Horseshoe in Ontario and the Montreal area in Quebec, Vancouver was among the chief beneficiaries of the industrialization associated with the war effort.

Vancouver's dockyards boomed as never before and alone employed more than 25,000 people. Factories to manufacture the uniforms, ammunition and armaments needed for the fight in the Pacific were built and expanded rapidly in the city's core, on the shores of North Vancouver, along False Creek, and, increasingly, in what once had been farm lands in Richmond. The airport, to that time a modest facility serving a few small planes, suddenly became vitally important. So, too, did the aircraft industry: at its height, Boeing would employ 5,000 people in its Richmond plant.[4] Dominion Bridge grew to employ 2,000 workers as it converted from the production of bridges to the manufacture of tanks.[5]

Indeed, there seemed to be no shortage of jobs for both men and women. Although women had been an important element of the work force long before 1939, the war opened up jobs in both light and heavy industry from which they had been previously excluded. In fact, by 1944, some 57,500 women were employed, including numerous housewives.[6] Many within this burgeoning work force would be susceptible to the credit union message and, during the 1940s, women would play an important role in credit unions: they would serve on boards and supervisory committees, and some would be secretary-treasurers on either a voluntary or part-time basis. And in many credit unions in the mid-forties, much of the often unrecognized but important volunteer work – attracting members, maintaining member lists, providing refreshments for meetings – would be done by women.

But it was not only that there were more jobs for men and women; there were also more better-paying jobs. By 1945, the average weekly wage for male workers in B.C. had risen to nearly $35 ($21 for females),[7] and many men in the resource industries were earning over $75 per week. This greater prosperity resulted in part from the growth of trade unionism.

In 1944, the federal government, influenced by the Wagner Act in the United States and concerned about the growth of radicalism in the Canadian labour force, introduced legislation that facilitated the formation of unions and company associations. This legislation

4. Ibid.

5. Ibid.

6. *The Labour Gazette*, December, 1946, p. 1863.

7. Ibid., December, 1946, p. 1862.

8. Paul Phillips, *No Power Greater: A Century of Labour in British Columbia* (Vancouver: British Columbia Federation of Labour, 1967), pp. 127 and 143.

contributed significantly to the process of unionization already underway. The cumulative impact was dramatic: by 1945, one worker in three in the province would be a trade union member (compared to one in eight in 1939). In absolute terms, union membership increased in those years from 34,387 to 83,823.[8] In fact, the major industries of forestry, paper, pulp, mining, fishing, construction and shipbuilding were almost completely unionized.

These workplace associations were important for the development of credit unions, at least until the later 1950s. By 1946, 52 of the 150 credit unions that had been granted charters were occupational, many of them the result of a growing sense of cohesiveness among workers in the province during the wartime period. In Vancouver, the associations were particularly important: nearly 70% of the credit unions in existence in 1946 were closed-bond, employee-based credit unions. Moreover, many of the community credit unions in single-resource towns – such as Port Alberni, Trail, and Kyuquot – were originally organized primarily among wage workers, be they in the forests, in the mines, or on the fishing boats.

This strong working-class base, often associated with trade unions and left-wing political movements, helped create an impression – encouraged by the very use of the word "union" in "credit union" – that credit unions were an extension of trade unionism, an impression that in later years some believed discouraged the support of more middle-class and conservative groups in society.

Not even in the mid-forties was this accurate. In reality, there were several British Columbias at that time and, as in all the succeeding periods, the credit unions immediately reflected that diversity. The Lower Mainland and the southern third of Vancouver Island formed something of an urban unit, but it was significantly separated from the remainder of the province, both geographically and emotionally.

Partly, the separation was the result of difficult communications. The connections between Vancouver, the Okanagan and the Kootenays were by railway or over roads that were difficult at many times during the year. Going to Victoria required an overnight ferry trip for most; travelling the same route by airplane was expensive and infrequent – in fact, so rare that it warranted comment in the *Credit Unionist*. Driving from Vancouver to Lillooet took two days by car, not much longer than it often took to go from Port Alberni to Victoria by road. In the North, the links went along the Canadian National Railways line from Prince Rupert to the Alberta border; travelling on the roads then in existence was still an adventure … in winter, it could be a terror.

There was also a psychological split between the urban southwest and the remainder of the province. Even by the mid-1940s, therefore, distinct regional groupings began to emerge, groupings associated

"What do I do with the money?"

by Clarence Morin

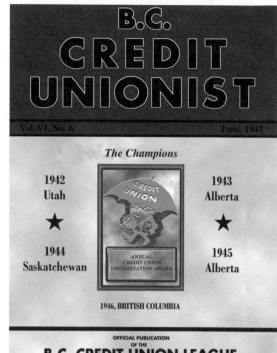

In 1944, a group of Summerland orchardists and their friends formed a credit union study club. After much reading and discussion, they invited the Superintendent of Credit Unions, Tom Switzer, to a meeting. Being a cautious group, they were looking for a question and answer session. But Switzer had other ideas. He decided it was time to get things moving. On July 11, 1944, he and Louis Ball, the manager of Oliver Credit Union (now known as Okanagan Savings), met the Summerland contingent and plunged into discussions. Then Switzer gave them an application for incorporation, told them to complete it, witnessed their signatures and collected $17.50 share capital.

This was a surprise for newly-appointed treasurer, Walter Bleasdale, who asked: "What do I do with the money?"

"Take it home," advised Switzer. Bleasdale did, and Summerland and District Credit Union was on its way.

Next morning, Bleasdale and two other newly elected officers opened an account for the credit union at the local Bank of Montreal, with the three as signing officers.

Three years later, the credit union had its own office building, two blocks east of the bank. In 1968, it opened new, larger offices across the street from the bank. By 1980, it needed even more space and moved a block north to its third building, a very large attractive facility.

Fifty years after incorporation, Summerland and District Credit Union is clearly the area's leading financial institution under manager Lou Campana — a former employee of the bank.

Tom Switzer, who served as Superintendent of Credit Unions from 1943 to 1958, was one of the most beloved of the early credit union leaders in the province.

The number of credit unions in B.C. grew faster than in any other province or state in 1946, as depicted on this cover of the *B.C. Credit Unionist.* It is interesting to note how rapidly the Canadian movement was growing in other provinces during the mid-1940s.

Lakeview (later spelled Lake View) Credit Union became symbolic of credit union "grit and determination" when it recovered from a disastrous fire in February, 1948.

9. *B.C. Credit Unionist*, February, 1948, pp. 3 and 20.

with Vancouver, Vancouver Island (where arguably at times two might be found – one in Victoria, the other in the rest of the Island), the Okanagan, the Kootenays and the North.

One of the most distinctive of the regional groupings was in the North. It was made up of credit unions located in communities stretching from Prince Rupert in the west to Dawson Creek in the east. This group became known as the Northline because of the importance of the railway line in communications. In reality, though, there were at least three "Norths"; they appeared as one only because they met together throughout the year and because they shared a general suspicion of anything – even credit unions – that came from Vancouver.

One group of northern credit unions emerged along the Pacific Coast, an outgrowth of the co-operative movement associated with the fishing industry in Prince Rupert. A second developed in the Interior where several credit unions were being formed – in places like Prince George and Terrace – to serve the lumber and agricultural communities that prospered during the war. In the northeast, arguably more like Alberta than the rest of B.C., groups in prosperous rural communities formed several credit unions. A particularly important community from the beginning was Dawson Creek, where a vibrant credit union emerged out of a strong co-operative store during the mid-1940s.

Indeed, in 1948, Lakeview Credit Union in Dawson Creek became a symbol of credit union resilience and member loyalty. Early on Sunday morning, February 10, a fire broke out in the second-floor apartments of the Co-operative Union block. The 10 tenants escaped, but the Co-op store and the credit union offices, also on the second floor, were destroyed. So too were many of the credit union's records. Member support among farmers and townspeople who had endured the ravages of the Great Depression, however, was strong enough to rebuild almost immediately. Help was also extended by credit unions in other parts of the province, but, most amazingly, the volunteer officers of the credit union were able to recall – to the known satisfaction of everyone – how much each member had on deposit or had borrowed.9 The credit union rebuilt immediately and soon became one of the most important leaders of the Northline and a significant, forceful contributor to Central meetings in Vancouver; it even placed an advertisement in the *B.C. Credit Unionist* two months after the fire, wishing good luck to the delegates attending the forthcoming credit union conventions.

There were other credit unions in the North that attracted considerable interest on the pages of the *B.C. Credit Unionist* in the mid-forties. One was in Baldonnel, which briefly played an important role in the debates of the period. Another one, in Tate Creek, attracted considerable sympathy because it was formed among German immigrants who had fled Hitler during the 1930s with the assistance of British and Canadian co-operators.[10] Some of the Tate Creek credit unionists, in fact, had been very active in co-operatives in Germany and brought considerable experience to their efforts in Canada. The ancestors of a few of them had been active in the Raiffeisen co-operative banks in the nineteenth century.

These credit unions joined a regional grouping that, despite the differences in socio-economic background and geographic location, quickly developed a distinct perspective. Collectively, they possessed attitudes that tended to be critical of decisions made in the south; that had strong community commitments; and that strongly favoured co-operative development. These attitudes and loyalties would contribute to the diversity

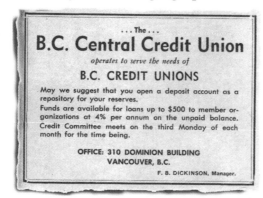

... The ...
B.C. Central Credit Union
operates to serve the needs of
B.C. CREDIT UNIONS
May we suggest that you open a deposit account as a repository for your reserves.
Funds are available for loans up to $500 to member organizations at 4% per annum on the unpaid balance.
Credit Committee meets on the third Monday of each month for the time being.

OFFICE: 310 DOMINION BUILDING
VANCOUVER, B.C.

F. B. DICKINSON, Manager.

that would become — on balance — a significant source of innovation in the movement. They would also contribute to the debates and divisions that would periodically disrupt the provincial organizations, at first the League and then Central.

In its first few years, B.C. Central Credit Union searched for its role amid such diversity. Most of the energy devoted to the provincial movement by the growing band of credit union enthusiasts was focused on the League. With its primary emphasis on educating directors and members and its important secondary role of government liaison, the League was central to the expansion of the period. In 1944, the League hired its first field worker – J.W. Burns – to work with groups organizing credit unions. Members of the League's board continued to be heavily involved in helping new credit unions, as did a significant number of directors of local credit unions. The creation of credit unions was one of the main tasks the League assumed – with the help and encouragement of the Inspector's Office – and, for many years, few credit union leaders would question the wisdom of forming so many small credit unions.

B.C. Central experienced slow but steady progress in its early years. During its first year of operation, Central attracted 70 credit unions and co-operatives to its membership and by year-end they had invested $21,000 in shares and deposits. Central used these funds to make loans that totalled close to $30,000.

10. Ibid., December, 1944, p. 12.

The League also undertook a variety of tasks on behalf of credit unions. Most were performed largely by volunteer enthusiasts, although by the end of the War, the League was employing four people, each on a part-time basis. The tasks included the operation of a Supply Department; the publication of the *B.C. Credit Unionist*; the development of educational materials and the promotion of credit unionism among young people; and the continuing negotiations with the B.C. government over legislative changes.

As for B.C. Central, it experienced slow but steady progress in its early years. During its first year of operation, Central attracted 70 credit unions and co-operatives to its membership and by year-end they had invested $21,000 in shares and deposits in Central. Central used these funds to make loans that totalled close to $30,000.[11] Most of the loans were in the range of a few hundred dollars, made to credit unions, mostly for the purchase of equipment or the improvement of premises. Credit unions expanded considerably during this period, although expansion was restricted by the fact that, under the Credit Union Act, they could only borrow up to 25% of their assets. Since most of them had only a few thousand dollars in assets, this meant they could borrow only very small amounts.

The larger loans, with one exception – Prince Rupert Fishermen's Co-op – typically totalled $1,000 to $3,000. They were made mostly to co-operatives for the development of stores or the purchase of supplies. Because of the size of these loans relative to the small asset base of Central, they required the approval of the Inspector's Office. This was a process that could take time and it increasingly perturbed the Inspector, who tended to be preoccupied with credit unions, not co-operatives, which were, in any event, not under his jurisdiction.

Even at this early stage, there was some controversy over lending to co-operatives. Some lawyers in Vancouver questioned the legality of co-operatives being admitted as members to Central, but their objection was short-lived.[12] More seriously, a segment within the movement, particularly some leaders of closed-bond, employee-based credit unions, preferred that all money pooled in the Central be used exclusively for the development of credit unions. Their concern stemmed from the fact that the credit unions they knew best were often hard pressed to meet member needs, although those needs did tend to have cyclical variations throughout the year.

The reality, though, was that Central for several years would depend heavily on loans to co-operatives since the loan demand from credit unions varied significantly throughout the year, from year to year, and from credit union to credit union. Moreover, despite the wishes of those who wanted all of Central's funds to be devoted to

11. Ibid., June, 1945, p. 18.
12. Ibid.

credit unions, the loan demand from credit unions until the fifties was rarely sufficient to require all the funds Central had available.

Nor were there profitable ways to deposit money in other institutions; in particular, depositing funds in banks would earn an extremely low rate of return. Moreover, while there was strong support for Central among several credit unions, there was considerable skepticism in many others, and that skepticism would last for many years. As a result, Central would have to search continually for ways to be profitable: it would never be able to count on the automatic support of all credit unions.

On the other hand, the vast majority of co-op loans were profitable and posed no difficulties. Some co-operatives were also important to Central because their needs were for large short-term deposits at different times throughout the year. By far the most significant of these was the Prince Rupert Fishermen's Co-operative. The mid-1940s were profitable years for the Euro-Canadian fishermen of the Pacific Coast. Technology had made canned salmon inexpensive and safe to produce; the war had stimulated demand to historic highs; and the removal of the Japanese from the industry had created extremely profitable opportunities. Prince Rupert boomed, as did the other fishing communities along the coast.

Of particular importance for the development of Central was a generation of leadership in the Prince Rupert co-operative community. It was a generation that included many Scandinavian people and it was determined to build a flourishing, integrated co-operative economy. In the early 1930s the fishing people of Prince Rupert had started a fishing co-operative. It grew steadily and constructed a cold storage and ice plant that, in the 1940s, was one of the province's largest. It also operated a store on the waterfront to provide gear and supplies to the fishermen. It fostered the development of a co-operative store, Kaien Consumers' Co-op, and it ran a bakery – "the largest and most up to date in town."[13] The employees of these various enterprises sponsored the Co-operative Welfare and Educational Association, which undertook educational activities, particularly on behalf of consumer co-operatives and credit unions in Prince Rupert and among the communities of the Skeena and Bulkley valleys.

From its beginnings in 1940, the Prince Rupert Fishermen's Credit Union was an important part of this co-operative nexus. The credit union was located in space provided by the fishing co-op, and its first (part-time) treasurer was an employee of the co-op. This meant that the credit union was, in effect, open at least five days a week during the co-op's office hours. It was also located close to where the fishing people docked their boats and unloaded their catches. Consequently, it soon became convenient for members to use the credit union much like

For many years the League honoured credit unions that were judged to be making the best progress. In 1945, Prince Rupert Fishermen's Credit Union was recognized. Its general manager, George Viereck, is shown here receiving the plaque for that year. Viereck, one of the main leaders in the powerful Prince Rupert co-operative movement, would play a key role among B.C. and national credit unions for nearly 50 years.

13. Ibid., July, 1947, p. 15.

they would use a bank. In fact, the credit union was one of the first to develop two kinds of accounts. One was for shares, the kind of account all credit unions had; indeed, the only kind of account most credit unions had for their members. The second was a deposit account that by 1948 had nearly $200,000 in member deposits, an amount that made the credit union the largest in British Columbia.

George Viereck, who became secretary-treasurer of the fishermen's credit union in 1943, was perhaps the most determined and the most co-operatively-oriented of the co-operative enthusiasts in Prince Rupert. From his early involvement in credit unions in 1940 until his death in 1993, he embraced the total co-operative perspective, one that would work for the establishment of a group of co-operatives – in Prince Rupert, throughout British Columbia, and ultimately across Canada – that could meet all economic and most social needs. In the early days of Central, his loyalty would mean that the Fishermen's Co-op and its credit union would strive to find ways to deposit in, and to borrow from, Central and other co-operative institutions whenever possible. Perhaps just as important, they would not insist that Central pay the very best rate.

The demands of the fishing industry placed considerable pressures on Central, while opening up attractive opportunities. During the winter and early spring, fishing people needed funds to refurbish their boats and to prepare for the coming season. In the summer and autumn, they usually earned a large surplus of short-term money to be invested, a surplus that was too large for the local credit union to use effectively. In taking deposits from Prince Rupert or returning them, the challenge for Central was to manage its funds effectively as it moved from periods when it had too much money to the longer periods when it did not have enough.

Up until August, 1945, Central was managed entirely by volunteers. In that month H.H. ("Harry") Brown became a part-time manager, a post he held until November, 1947. Much of the work, however, continued to be done by a small group of committed volunteers, particularly a few who lived in Vancouver. For the most part, they came from two credit unions. One was the Amalgamated Civil Servants of Canada Credit Union. Leaders from this credit union, many

When credit unions began, the consumer co-operative movement was well established and several credit unions began as adjuncts to their activities. Moreover, the financially-strongest and largest organizations in the League were fishing and consumer co-operatives. The *B.C. Credit Unionist*, therefore, carried many advertisements extolling the virtues of co-operative products.

of whom were on shift work with the government or were given time off to help with the development of credit unions, played vitally important roles in the early history of Central and the League. The most important of these were A.L. Nicholas, Harold Pocock and George Gallagher.

The other particularly important credit union for the early operations of the provincial organizations was Stry Credit Union. It had been formed among Street Railway workers in 1940 after an extensive period of study, led in part by Dorothy Steeves. Stry was strongly committed to the development of the movement on a provincial level. Among its prominent leaders who played crucial roles in the early history of Central and the League were Farley Dickinson, Jack Burns and Dick Monrufet.

In addition to these volunteers, the Inspector, Ed DeBeck, played a continuous, important role in Central and, to a lesser degree, the League. DeBeck, however, was not the strongest advocate of Central during the mid-forties because he did not believe that the movement was ready for a strong central financial organization. He did not think that the movement had the expertise to deal effectively with large pools of money, and he tended to prefer closed-bond credit unions, especially those associated with the workplace. He was particularly concerned with the growing importance of loans to co-operatives at the Central level. For that reason, he was continually watchful, particularly to ensure that all the loans made by Central were well-secured.

One of the questions that confronted Central's board from the beginning was the demand for services that would give credit union members easier access to cash. One dimension of this demand was a protracted discussion over the introduction of chequing services. The first known discussion of this topic actually pre-dated the formation of Central and occurred in early 1943. During 1944 and 1945, the matter was raised frequently but, although the Inspector had no objections, the leadership of Central could not make the necessary arrangements with the banks to secure chequing services.

Another dimension of the demand was a request for travellers' cheques. In 1946 Central was successful in making arrangements, through a branch of the Bank of Commerce in Vancouver's Mount Pleasant district, to retail travellers' cheques through local credit unions. This service proved to be useful for a short period for a few credit unions, but it fell far short of the needs most credit union members were beginning to feel for a full-fledged chequing service. Nevertheless, it was the beginning of what would be a major change in the movement: a switch from an essentially savings and loan business to the provision of banking services for credit union members.

This developing demand for more member services, however, was not a part of some carefully-thought-out business strategy. Rather, it was a manifestation of what might be called co-operative entrepreneurship. The mid-forties arguably witnessed the richest flowering of co-operative enthusiasms and vision in the history of the B.C. co-operative movement. The wartime theme of the "struggle for democracy" encouraged many to think that fully democratic societies would be created only when the economy as well as the formal political structure were controlled democratically. The growth of the welfare state also led many to consider how voluntary associations – such as co-operatives – might meet more human needs. The celebration, in 1944, of the 100th anniversary of the founding of the Rochdale store also made many people aware of how extensive, viable and important the international movement had become. In that sense, British Columbia participated in an international revival of co-operative enthusiasms.

Attacks on co-operatives, ironically, also helped. In 1943 and 1944 private enterprise groups, particularly in the insurance and retailing industries, launched anti-co-operative campaigns in both the United States and Canada. On the one hand, they sought to identify co-operatives with extreme socialism; on the other, they sought to change current taxation policies that allowed co-operatives to distribute surpluses as though they were rebates – and therefore not taxable.

In Canada, this campaign led to the appointment of a federal Royal Commission, the McDougall Commission. The commission systematically toured the country to hear from co-operative groups and their competitors. In Vancouver it heard from League representatives, along with individuals representing the fishing, consumer and agricultural co-operatives. The most impressive submission, though, was made by Mrs. S.L. Simpson of the Masset Clam Co-operative on the Queen Charlotte Islands; she poignantly described how co-operative techniques could be used to improve significantly the standard of living of even very poor people. Her appeal gave a contemporary, human dimension to the rather statistical and historical presentations of others (including the credit union representatives) who made submissions on co-operatives across Canada.

The commission's findings, which made some of the distributed surpluses taxable but left most untaxed, was a partial victory. The important result, though, was that it encouraged co-operators in the province to start working more closely together. Each year during the mid- and late-1940s, joint meetings were held involving co-operators from consumer, credit union, fishing and agricultural co-operatives. Many of them attracted 200 or more co-operators, who collectively saw few limits to the development of co-operative enterprise.

Evidence of these co-operative enthusiasms abound in the records that survive. The first efforts in co-operative housing took place in the mid-forties, as did the first attempts to develop worker co-operatives, and in both cases credit union enthusiasts were involved. In the rural areas – for example, Surrey, Penticton, Nanaimo, Comox and Alberni – strong associations emerged between co-operatives and credit unions. The most important blending of interests, however, occurred in the field of health care.

The Depression had been a watershed for the evolution of Canadian health policy. Poor diets, especially during the 1930s, had led to bad health; the lack of cash had meant that the poor could not afford doctors. When World War Two broke out, and the needs of war escalated, the extent of bad health among the Canadian people once more became obvious – as it had done during World War One – and many Canadians became convinced of the need for health-care reform.

Health-care co-operatives were a possible solution to these problems. There had been experiments, in Oklahoma (starting in the 1920s) and on the Prairies in the late 1920s and the 1930s, with co-operative community clinics based on monthly membership fees and salaried doctors. Then, during the war, Canadians became impressed with how effectively health services had been organized to meet the needs of the armed forces; they wondered why similar methods of organization could not be used within co-operative structures to bring universal health care to the entire population.

A few individuals in British Columbia, most notably John Hunter, a transplanted, experienced Prairie co-operator, were aware of the earlier efforts and were involved in the contemporary debate over health care.[14] Another was Howard Hunter of Vancouver Firefighters Credit Union. At the 1944 League annual meeting, they proposed that credit unions explore the possibility of developing a health insurance program. The intent was to provide a way in which British Columbians could subscribe to a health insurance program that would pay the cost of most medical needs.

The idea aroused interest and a committee, chaired by John Hunter, was appointed. It reported to the 1945 convention, held in Vancouver, and the 1946 convention, held in Powell River. It recommended the formation of a province-wide co-operative, to be named CU&C (for "credit union and co-operative"), which would be fostered by the leadership and members of the province's credit unions and co-operatives. The idea was enthusiastically received, and a sister movement was born.

The new health co-operative was also closely tied to the consumer and, to a lesser extent, the producer movements. The affinity was demonstrable in many ways. Many of the same people were involved as

John Hunter, one of the early leaders of CU&C health co-operative, an organization started by credit union and other co-op leaders in the mid-1940s as a way to meet health-care needs through co-operative enterprise.

14. See "In Sickness and in Health: the Story of CU&C Health Services Society," CU&C: undated pamphlet, pp. 3-4, and Minutes, Sixth Annual Convention, B.C. Credit Union League, 1945, pp. 37-41.

The Nanaimo and District Credit Union played a major role in the provincial credit union and co-operative movement from 1950 to 1980. Pictured at left is the board of that credit union in the early 1950s. Its most dynamic member was Rod Glen *(second from the left, front row)*.

Roy Bergengren was the chief builder of the Credit Union National Association in the United States. From the mid-1930s until his death in 1955, Bergengren assisted many credit union groups in Canada, including British Columbia. He is generally acknowledged as the first important individual to grasp the possibilities of credit unions as an international movement.

elected officials in the four movements. The consumer wholesale (B.C. Co-operative Wholesale), CU&C, the League and Central arranged to hold their annual meetings on four consecutive days in June each year. This meant that individuals involved in more than one organization could schedule the time required for their participation in annual meetings more efficiently. It was an arrangement that would last until 1973.

The commitment to working together was also seen in how the various organizations sought to meet their building needs. In 1948, Central, the League and CU&C, along with Stry Credit Union, entered into a partnership to purchase and operate a building at the corner of Quebec Street and Broadway in Vancouver. For years that building would be the heart of the provincial co-operative movement, a place where co-operative enthusiasts worked, met for lunch, and held evening and weekend meetings. This arrangement symbolized the mingling of interests and ambitions that characterized the co-operative movement in the mid-forties.

The close ties between credit unions and co-operatives, however, was not without controversy. Some misread the development and interpreted it as largely a left-wing initiative. The reality was more complex, since the co-operative enthusiasms involved many who were on the right of the political spectrum, but the impression nevertheless became accepted truth. Government officials were also lukewarm. Partly, they feared that involvement with co-operatives could lead to bad investments by credit unions at both the local and Central level. Partly, too, they resented the time they had to devote – in personal schedules that were already full – to review the co-operative loans handled by Central and local credit unions. In at least one instance – with North Shore Credit Union in 1948 – a special general meeting had to be called before the Inspector would be reassured that the membership supported making loans to a co-operative.

But the most vigorous questioning of the co-operative connection came from the Credit Union National Association in the United States. There the issue of the influence of left-wing politics was a long-standing debate triggered by the role of communists within co-operative/credit union circles in Minnesota and Wisconsin. The suspicion that communists were active, even dominant, in co-operatives had been planted in American credit unions during the 1920s. It persisted, and in some areas was exacerbated, during the 1930s when communists sought to engage co-operatives and credit unions in the political turmoil of the fight for trade union recognition.

In the 1940s, the issue moved beyond rhetoric when it became directly embroiled in a struggle for leadership within the Credit Union National Association and Credit Union Mutual. The executive director of CUNA, Roy Bergengren, had held office since 1935. An outgoing, deeply-committed, and effective enthusiast and organizer, he was somewhat less successful as an administrator. He also had a rival – Tom Doig, the vice-president – who had gained the admiration of many board members of the two organizations. The two men were on a collision course by the mid-1940s.

The communism issue surfaced amid this rivalry because Bergengren, although hardly sympathetic to communism, was more tolerant of communists and indeed all kinds of political views than Doig and the elected leadership of the American movement. Bergengren strongly resisted the idea that he was too tolerant of communists, but he was increasingly losing the confidence of the CUNA board, partly over the communism issue, but largely because of the management issue. In 1946, the long-simmering controversy erupted; the board removed Roy Bergengren from his executive director post – although he remained as a kind of roving ambassador – and replaced him with Tom Doig.

Thus American credit unionists, as they became more interested in the B.C. movement in the mid-1940s, reflected a suspicion of co-operatives generally and a fear of communists particularly. The Americans were also faced by a growing and threatening Canadian interest in co-operative insurance. This was not a minor irritant: CUNA Mutual Insurance was the financial heart of the American credit union movement. It offered credit unions insurance coverage on both member deposits and loans. It did so on a competitive basis, but it had also built up a very successful business by the mid-1940s. It invested its reserves conservatively, for the most part in stable American companies; it rarely invested them in co-operatives. In other words, in its investment policies, it tended to act like any other insurance company. All of these factors – that it was American, that it did not invest in co-operatives, and that it invested like other insurance companies – started to become major issues in Canadian credit union/co-operative circles in 1946. They would remain so for decades.

These issues had begun to surface as early as 1945, a year that found the Canadian co-operative movement in an optimistic and expansionist frame of mind. It had successfully defended itself from the attacks of private insurance companies and retailers that had culminated in the McDougall Commission. Many co-operatives were affluent. They had accumulated funds amid the prosperity of the War when they had been unable to expand owing to restrictions on construction. A new generation of leaders had begun to emerge, bound together by the fight over taxation and a restructuring of the Co-operative Union of Canada. Many of them drew inspiration from the widespread commitment to build a better Canada, evidenced in

Reconstruction after the war, and they reflected a general desire among Canadians to create a society worthy of the sacrifices made in the struggle against fascism.

The main project growing out of this increased national commitment was an interest in developing a national financial co-operative system. In 1943, leaders of the caisse populaire and credit union movements met for the first time on an organized national basis at the Quebec Congress of the Co-operative Union of Canada. They discussed essentially two main projects: the creation of a national organization for credit unions, possibly including the caisses populaires, and the development of insurance companies. The Quebec leadership soon withdrew from these discussions, but the leaders from English Canada retained their enthusiasm. In 1945, co-operative organizations on the Prairies started Co-operative Life Insurance Company, which they hoped would become a national company. The following year, Ontario co-operative and farm leaders established Co-operators Fidelity and Guarantee Association, initially as a bonding company but soon to become a general insurance company. Both of these initiatives attested to the desires of Canadian co-operative leaders to develop a national insurance program, one that ultimately would compete with CUNA Mutual. In time, it would become a particularly difficult issue in British Columbia.

The creation of a national credit union organization was another, yet related, matter. Discussions on this possibility were resumed at the 1945 Congress of the Co-operative Union of Canada, held in Winnipeg. Jack Burns, one of two B.C. credit union representatives at the meeting, played a particularly important role in these discussions. He was, at that time, a strong advocate of a national organization, and he helped spark the formation of the Canadian Federation of Credit Unions. He was one of three elected to its founding executive committee, and he was primarily responsible for devising its initial constitution, control structure and funding formula.[15] The Federation's main tasks were: to compile statistics on Canadian credit unions; to assist in lobbying for more effective credit union legislation; to assist in educational programs on behalf of credit unions; to encourage Leagues to affiliate with provincial sections of the Co-operative Union of Canada; and to act as an agent for CUNA Mutual Insurance Company.

The connection to CUNA Mutual would become an issue in time as Canadian co-operative leaders struggled to develop their own insurance program. It also raised the more general problem of how the Canadian credit unions would associate with the credit union movement in the United States. This was a problem on both sides of the border. In Canada, of course, it raised nationalist issues and stirred those who wanted to build a distinctively Canadian movement,

15. For details on the Federation's structure and purposes, see Report on the Canadian Federation, BCCCU Archives.

69

reflecting Canadian values, needs and priorities. In the United States, the emergence of the Canadian movement created a structural problem for CUNA and CUNA Mutual: how could the organization, which had been developed to meet credit union needs essentially at a state level within the American federal system, be adjusted to meet the needs of an international movement? They were two sets of issues that often conflicted with each other and would not be resolved for many years. In particular, they would become significant issues for the B.C. movement – for the League and for Central – until the 1980s.

In the mid-forties, though, the key developments in B.C. credit unions did not take place at the comparatively heady level of national and international organizations. They took place on the local level, where the priorities and needs of the B.C. movement were being established by the more than 2,000 volunteers elected to boards of directors, supervisory committees, and credit committees. By the end of 1948, a total of 195 credit unions had been organized in the province, of which 162 were still active: 77 community, 65 occupational, nine religious (all Catholic), seven organizational (mostly branches of the Royal Canadian Legion) and two ethnic (Danish and German). The inactive 33 were mostly credit unions that had been chartered but had never become active; a few had been amalgamated, most particularly several credit unions among federal public servants.

There was a kind of amateur enthusiasm that pervaded most of the credit unions at this time. Essentially, they were made up of neighbours or members of groups joining together to help each other. Most of them had monthly meetings, usually held in the evenings, and those meetings were as much given over to social activities as they were to discussions of lending policies. Volunteers who served on the board or on the committees often became friends and in many instances kept up their friendships for years. Committee and board meetings were partly social functions; annual meetings were community gatherings; many credit unions sponsored bowling teams and held dances; at least one – Danish Credit Union – sponsored a dance band for several years; another – Stry – even built a bowling alley for its members and the members of other credit unions; and many operated extensive educational programs for their members.

Similarly, annual meetings of the League and Central were nearly as much social events as they were business meetings. Until the end of the War, the annual meetings of the League and Central were generally held in Vancouver. Starting in 1946, the meetings were alternated between Vancouver and other southern B.C. communities, such as Powell River and Victoria. They were major events for many who served as volunteers. For some, these were the only large conventions they attended. For others, they were rare opportunities to travel from

Edelweiss Credit Union, organized in 1943, became best known for its sponsorship of the Schuhplattlers dancers. Their name came from the Alpen woodworkers who developed a dance from their practice of "jumping around and slapping themselves, their legs, their shoes, etc., in order to keep warm." The band was so successful that it was employed to perform the Alpen dances in the Bing Crosby film "The Emperor Waltz", shot in Jasper Park in 1947.

VARIETY SHOW
DWIGHT HALL - 8 p.m. - SATURDAY, OCTOBER 7

Supported by

The Powell River Credit Union Choir

Winners of the Powell River and District Musical Festival Junior Trophy

Supported by

Radio Station P.R.C.U.

Broadcast of "My Dad's Family"

Fun and Frolic with the Craziest People

The Edelweiss Schuh Platter Dance Team
(A Group of Sixteen)

DANCING STARS OF **Bing Crosby's** MOTION PICTURE

The Emperor Waltz

THESE ALPEN DANCERS THRILLED LARGE CROWDS AT VANCOUVER'S P.N.E. AND PLAYED TO CAPACITY AUDIENCES IN THE OKANAGAN VALLEY LAST WINTER. THEIR COSTUMES ARE IMPORTED DIRECT FROM VIENNA WHILE THE DANCERS THEMSELVES ARE THIRD AND FOURTH GENERATION CENTRAL EUROPEANS AND FOR THE MOST PART MEMBERS OF THE EDELWEISS CREDIT UNION (VANCOUVER)

Reserved Seat $1.00 on Sale Sept. 21st at Otto Peterson's
(No Reservations by Phone Please)

General Admission 75c on Sale Now at the Credit Union Office, Otto Peterson's, Westview Jewellers and Jack Fletcher's, Westview and Cranberry

Two Hours of Superb Variety Entertainment

small towns and rural communities to other parts of B.C. over roads that were often difficult.

The meetings, too, shared in the high-jinks typical of most conventions of the period. Sometimes sombre discussions on lending policy were punctuated by skits; occasionally, co-operative and credit union songs livened up the openings. On at least one night at conventions (sometimes two) there were dances. Always there were memorable meals in good restaurants or in church halls. During the time that was left over – for those who drank alcohol – there were bars or shared bottles at hotel room parties. When the conventions were held in small communities, accommodations could mean being billeted in homes of local credit unionists – and often the beginnings of long friendships. From such gatherings came alliances and bonds that would provide much of the glue – and more than a few of the disagreements – that would shape the movement over the years.

One of the most obvious characteristics of credit unions in those – and later – years was the way in which they reflected the groups and communities whence they came. Credit unions in fishing villages reflected the various ethnic groups and political allegiances of those communities: Scandinavian, aboriginal, and German; Marxist, social democratic, and liberal. Rural credit unions reflected the quiet desperation, canniness and financial conservatism that characterized those who were able to survive the limitations imposed by rapid rural change. Credit unions in the Fraser Valley reflected the influence of the deeply-held conservative religious values of their rural members. Credit unions among the Okanagan and Peace River farmers reflected the co-operative ethos that many rural people in those regions adopted as an economic and social strategy for survival.

In contrast, credit unions in lumber towns had memberships that were more boisterous, a blunt way of identifying issues, and an obvious indebtedness to the trade union movement.

Similarly, in the mining towns around the province, much of the early interest tended to be among trade unionists, usually among the locals, and was often accompanied by strong feelings of solidarity. In many places, such as the Kootenays, the leaders could be inward-looking and suspicious of their community credit union counterparts from the cities, especially Vancouver.

The credit unions among public servants appear to have had the most orderly meetings and they were probably the most conservatively operated. Certainly, the public service credit unions seemed to have the most directors with some understanding of accounting practices. For that reason, leaders from the public service credit unions, particularly Vancouver Federal Credit Union, played perhaps the most important role in improving standards of operation among credit unions during the 1940s. The public service credit unions also had the highest percentage of members with high educational levels and experience in dealing with governments – and politicians. Accordingly, they took the lead in arranging meetings with the Inspector and the Minister over legislation.

Then there were the credit unions that reflected a common ethnic or religious base. The Danish Credit Union in Vancouver was one of these. Its roots went back to the deep Danish commitment to co-operatives, a commitment that had made the Danish movement (perhaps as much as the more popularized British movement) an international model for co-operative development. Started in 1940, the Danish Credit Union grew rapidly and innovatively. At its prompting, six other credit unions banded together with Danish in 1948 to open a jointly-operated office under the management of a single treasurer. Danish was among the first credit unions in the province to use radio broadcasts to publicize its activities. The organization's social gatherings, usually featuring its own band, were popular events for many credit unionists in Vancouver.

Another prominent "ethnic" credit union was Edelweiss Credit Union, organized by German Canadians in 1943. Among the early leaders was Mathius Wurzhuber, whose grandparents had heard Raiffeisen and whose grandfather had been president of a Raiffeisen co-operative bank a few kilometres from Raiffeisen's home. Like the Danish Credit Union, Edelweiss had a strong social commitment. It became best known for its sponsorship of the Schuhplattlers dancers. Their name came from the Alpen woodworkers who developed a dance from their practice of "jumping around and slapping themselves, their legs, their shoes, etc., in order to keep warm."[16] The band was so successful that it was employed to perform the Alpen dances in the Bing Crosby film "The Emperor Waltz", shot in Jasper Park in 1947.

Most of the credit unions in the mid-1940s had much the same problems. Perhaps the most common of these was a need – evident since the start of the decade – for the training of directors and members of the various committees, especially the credit committee. This was a problem that also perplexed the Inspector's Office. Very few of the elected leaders of the credit unions had experience in providing direction for community organizations; fewer still had training in even preliminary accounting. Consequently, the books and records for many credit unions were not kept properly and mistakes were too frequent – particularly for the Inspector's liking.

As in the past, the most common way of dealing with the bookkeeping problem was to enlist the assistance of more experienced leaders in helping nearby credit unions. This approach was particularly successful wherever there were several credit unions reasonably close

16. *B.C. Credit Unionist*, April, 1948, p. 12.

together, and it was aided by the effective use of chapters. By 1949, five chapters had been created – in Vancouver, New Westminster, Victoria, the South Okanagan and Northern Vancouver Island (including Powell River) – and credit unions in the north had joined with co-operatives that year to form the Northern Co-op Council. The most important task undertaken by all these organizations was to encourage credit union leaders to understand their roles and responsibilities.

Still more, however, was needed. In 1947, Ed DeBeck, the Inspector, approached the Director of High School Correspondence and, with the help of the Credit Union League, arranged to have a correspondence course developed. The course, distributed by the provincial Department of Education, relied upon manuals that had been prepared by the League a year or so earlier (mostly through the efforts of George Cockburn), but were inadequately used. The new program required 120 hours of study and covered general bookkeeping principles as well as the specific needs of credit unions. For $13, a student would submit seven papers based on course materials and receive a certificate upon successful completion.

By 1949, hundreds of credit unionists in British Columbia had taken this course, and it was in the process of being adapted for use by the international credit union movement. It had quickly become – and in various editions would continue to be – a significant factor in making B.C. credit unions steadily more efficient and effective. Indirectly, too, of course, it helped ultimately thousands of British Columbians learn the complexities of financial management, to the immeasurable benefit of the provincial economy.

The individual who played the most important role in determining the success of the local credit union was the secretary-treasurer. He or she was responsible for the daily operations of the credit union, for the preparation of information for board and committee meetings, most of the correspondence to Central, the League and the Inspector's Office, and the preparation of annual statements. Many credit unions, especially the very small ones, expected their secretary to carry out his or her work for no compensation. The larger ones paid an annual honorarium of between $5 and $15. By 1949, a growing number – perhaps 15 or 20 – started to pay their secretary-treasurers 25% of the credit union's interest income (20% if the credit union rented premises). In two or three credit unions, secretary-treasurers were paid salaries – although this practice was frowned upon. As the League's manager, Jack Burns, wrote: "The most serious mistake a credit union can make is to set aside a monthly partial wage in advance each year. The natural tendency of most people, unless they are completely idealistic by nature, is to give a fair return only for their wage."[17] In other words, even in credit unions, it was all right to trust people – but not too much.

The early credit union leaders in British Columbia believed they were starting an historic movement that could significantly alter the course of the province's history. By as early as 1949, they were honouring their "pioneers."

B.C. CREDIT UNIONIST

Vol. VIII, No. 5   PUBLISHED IN VANCOUVER B.C.   May, 1949

SOME PIONEERS OF CREDIT UNIONISM IN B.C.

OFFICIAL PUBLICATION
OF THE
B.C. CREDIT UNION LEAGUE

17. J. Burns, "Managing Director's Column," *B.C. Credit Unionist*, November, 1948, p. 9.

The conventions of the 1940s were boisterous, happy affairs, punctuated by vibrant debates and characterized by good humour. They were remembered fondly for years afterward.

This differential in how credit unions acknowledged the contributions of their secretary-treasurers reflected a growing complexity within many credit unions – and the beginnings of differences among them. So too would the chequing issue. B.C. credit unionists discussed the possibility of developing chequing services as early as 1943; in fact, it was one of the reasons why Central had been formed. At about the same time, British Columbia's leaders were finding out about the chequing services that caisses populaires in Quebec had been offering their members for years; the Quebec experience, in fact, became the model the provincial movement would ultimately emulate.[18]

The matter was first addressed formally at the 1946 convention in Powell River when a number of delegates complained about not being able to cash cheques easily. A year later, at the convention held in Vancouver, Arthur Fitzpatrick, Supervisor of Credit Unions in Alberta, reported on a small but successful experiment with chequing initiated by francophone members of St. Albert Credit Union. In collaboration with an Alberta Treasury Branch, they had successfully cashed some 60 cheques, including one in Vancouver. Having demonstrated that it could be done, members of several Albertan credit unions in the Edmonton area had started to use cheques extensively. Buoyed by this success against the "Eastern Capitalists", as Fitzpatrick called the banks, the B.C. Central delegates appointed a committee to pursue the chequing issue. It included Central's manager, Harry Brown, and two board members: President Farley Dickinson and Gordon Holtby. They met nearly every week during the summer. Their initial hope was that Central could become an associate, direct member of the Vancouver cheque clearing-house, but they soon found out that Central would not be accepted.

During late 1947, following a special meeting of Central's member credit unions in October, the committee then negotiated an arrangement with three banks, only to find out that this was also unacceptable to the clearing-house. The committee then turned to the Imperial Bank alone and negotiated an exclusive contract. The arrangement it reached (which was accepted by Central) was that Central and its members would be able to use negotiable instruments, whereby the bank would be able to collect amounts of money from Central (rather than chequing, which would have required Central to "pay").[19]

This system of "primary chequing", as it came to be called, was an important step forward. It was introduced on May 31, 1948. Although it could be used only by Central and its member organizations, it contributed significantly to bringing the system together. In particular, it facilitated the inexpensive flow of funds between Central and its members. At first, arrangements could be made only for credit unions and co-operatives in the Vancouver area, but by September, 1949,

18. Interview with J.R. "Rip" Robinson by Schroeder and McTiernan, June 2, 1976, BCCCU Archives, typescript, p. 5.

19. *B.C. Credit Unionist*, June, 1948, pp. 9-11.

coverage was extended to virtually all member credit unions and co-operatives across British Columbia.

Primary chequing, however, did not serve the individual member. This meant that virtually all credit unions remained as savings and loans institutions. Most had one class of deposit – shares – and

members had to deposit or withdraw funds or make a loan payment in person. They did so by meeting with the treasurer, who typically was available for only limited times during the week. Obviously, as credit unions grew, and as more members wanted to use their credit union more extensively, this system was unsatisfactory. By 1948, a few credit unions were finding ways to improve upon it. Most particularly, Prince Rupert Fishermen's Credit Union, with deposits of over $250,000, was becoming a large organization serving some 1,100 members. Its contact with the Fishermen's Co-op and the co-op store led it to experiment with its own internal cheques, which credit union members could use to buy goods from the store. The cheques soon found their way into other stores in the community and through them to the desk of the local manager of the Royal Bank. Not wishing to antagonize the large proportion of the community associated with the co-op organizations – and the Fishermen's Co-op, which used the bank for services the credit union could not provide – the manager agreed to honour the cheques for a monthly fee. It was the start of personal chequing in the B.C. movement, and ultimately a major step in the movement's history.

"Rip" Robinson served the movement as B.C. Central's general manager from 1948 to 1965, followed by five years as manager of the Credit Union Reserve Board. Here he is seen in 1954 on a tour of the Cominco smelter in Trail.

In 1949, the B.C. movement celebrated its 10th anniversary. They had been remarkable years: 206 credit unions had been organized; they had nearly 45,000 members and over $10-million in assets.[20] Two strong provincial organizations had been created; initiatives had been undertaken to create new sister organizations within the provincial co-operative movement; B.C. credit unionists were playing prominent roles within the national and international credit union and co-operative movements. A strong leadership cadre had appeared; most local credit unions were efficiently operated; and the provincial government was supportive. The future was full of promise.

20. Appendix, B.C. Credit Union League Annual Report, Eleventh Annual Convention, June 23-24, 1950, p. 5.

Growing
1950-1957

I never had two nickels in my life until I was forced to buy a home and the credit union loaned me the money for it, and then I could pay it off as fast as I liked, and I have to give the credit union all the credit for making it possible for me to own a home.

Dairyland Credit Union member, as recalled by J. "Rip" Robinson[1]

1. Robinson interview, p. 3.

2. Statistical Summaries, Annual Report, B.C. Credit Union League, 1950, unpaged, BCCCU Archives.

3. The enlarged building held the offices of the League, Central and CU&C Health Services in one unit; in the other unit were offices for eight credit unions – Vancouver City Savings; Civic Employees; Vancouver & District Danish; IWA Local 1-217; Canadian Express, Railway & Steamship Employees; Electrical Trades; Plumbers & Steamfitters; and City Hall & Hospital Employees. *B.C. Credit Unionist*, October, 1951, p. 4.

4. Minutes, Eleventh Annual Convention, 1950, Penticton, June 23-24, 1950, p. 28.

*I*N LATE JUNE, 1950, SOME 125 DELEGATES AND observers gathered in Penticton for the League, Central and CU&C annual meetings. It was the first time the organizations had held their integrated conventions in the Okanagan, and it was a time for celebration.

During the previous year, the 200th credit union charter in British Columbia had been granted to Abbotsford Credit Union. During the previous year, too – only 10 years since the first legislation had been passed – the total provincial membership exceeded 45,000 and total assets went over $10-million.[2] Prince Rupert Fishermen's Credit Union alone was nearing the $1-million mark in assets at year-end and four credit unions (Vancouver Federal Employees, Stry, Van-Tel, and Lakeview) had more than 2,000 members. Central's primary chequing service – the service it ran for its member organizations – was functioning well, and several credit unions, following Prince Rupert's example, had managed to establish secondary chequing services for their members. Central was also planning a substantial expansion in its offices on Broadway in Vancouver, an expansion that would take place the following August.[3]

The B.C. movement, however, was not an easy one to lead. In fact, Central and the League were very much like a farm couple trying to herd a large flock of chickens: if they pushed too hard from behind, the chickens tended to scatter left and right; if they got too far in front, no matter what enticements they spread, a few would forage among the weeds in nearby fields. Such tensions between central and local organizations were not easily resolved – nor would they be in the future. Indeed, they are endemic – in some ways maybe even beneficial – to any federated co-operative structure. They are the public manifestations of the local autonomy and pooled resources that are simultaneously the great strength – and a major weakness – of any co-operative movement.

Central, nevertheless, was generally in good shape. The introduction of primary chequing had transformed the organization. Between 1948 and 1950, more than $8-million had been circulated through the primary chequing activities, thereby significantly increasing the capacity of several credit unions and co-operatives to meet the needs of their members.[4]

Moreover, more credit unions had deposited surplus funds in Central as a result of the chequing system, meaning that the organization had a more stable pool of funds with which to make loans to credit unions and co-operatives. Most of the loans were short-term, for seasonal purposes or to meet temporary pressures. Some credit unions, however, were soon demanding long-term loans in order to meet growing mortgage needs among their members, a demand that Central initially resisted amid some controversy.[5]

Central charged a going rate of 4.5% on the loans that it did make. The funds thus earned were used to pay some of the costs incurred in running Central, to build a reserve fund, and to pay, in part, a dividend on the deposits credit unions had made in Central. During the early 1950s, Central was able to pay out between $27,000 and $50,000 in interest on these deposits. Central's board and management, however, had growing concerns that the reserves were not being built up fast enough. As a result, they became very conservative in accepting loan risk, a frustrating situation for many credit union and co-operative leaders. Nor were there always sufficient funds to meet the short-term needs of credit unions. On at least two occasions, it was only by prematurely calling large short-term loans from Prince Rupert Fishermen's Co-op that Central was able to meet pressing credit union needs. For that reason, the loans to the Co-op were particularly beneficial: not only were they profitable – in a pinch they were always available for other lending since the Co-op could easily replace them with loans from a bank.

The staff of B.C. Central Credit Union in the early 1950s pose for the camera with J. "Rip" Robinson, the general manager (back row centre).

Despite the pressures and limitations, Central made solid progress in the early 1950s. In early 1951, Central reached the $1-million level in total assets. One year later, rather remarkably, it reached $1.5-million and surpassed Prince Rupert Fishermen's as the largest credit union in the province. More than $840,000 of those assets were in chequing deposits, $530,000 were in term deposits, and $70,000 were in member shares.[6] The Board of Directors was held generally in high regard around the province, and any disputes that emerged were usually resolved quickly.

Central was also enjoying the benefits of stable management under the leadership of J. "Rip" Robinson. A Vancouver native, Robinson had started to work for Fraser Valley Milk Producers in 1930 and eventually became its paymaster. He helped form Dairyland Credit Union in 1941, becoming its first treasurer. Robinson was elected to Central's Supervisory Committee in 1946, and he joined Central on a half-time basis in 1947. The following year, he took over as treasurer (or general manager) from Harry Brown.

Robinson was a quiet, determined and resourceful person, diplomatic in his relations with the managers of the League and CU&C, with whom he had to work, and always respectful of the role of volunteers. As a former employee of Fraser Valley Milk Producers, he was

5. See B.C. Credit Unionist, September, 1950, p. 16.
6. Ibid., February, 1952, p. 14.

also knowledgeable about, and sympathetic to, co-operatives. Above all, he was transparently honest, and a man who always seemed to enjoy his work as manager of Central, a post he would hold from 1948 until 1965.

Robinson's main task at the beginning of his managerial career with Central was to develop the chequing systems. Indeed, much of his time between 1948 and 1951 was spent expanding credit union use of primary chequing and negotiating for secondary chequing. He was determined to develop Central's capacity in chequing because he realized that it was crucial to the future of Central and, indeed, the provincial movement. Unless Central was effective in developing that service, some credit unions – which, even in those days, tended to want to control their own affairs regardless of provincial consequences – would turn to banks. By 1951, with the help of his board, Robinson had succeeded in heading off this possibility by negotiating an arrangement with three national banks, and the future was assured.[7] Within a few months, Prince Rupert, Summerland and three Vancouver credit unions were offering this new service to their members, and many others were thinking of doing so.[8]

The move into chequing, however, was controversial. The American model of credit unionism, which had many admirers in British Columbia, did not favour provision of chequing services, just as it – or, at least its spokespersons sent to B.C. – had originally been suspicious of community bonds rather than workplace associations.

The main reason for these two positions was essentially the same: the American approach emphasized tight controls over credit based on workplace relationships. Thus, chequing, by giving members access to their funds in another way than directly through the secretary-treasurer, presented greater opportunities for fraud and misappropriation. At the same time, community bonds weakened the social influence workers could have over their colleagues – and, if necessary, compliant companies could have over the payrolls of employee/members. Chequing also meant that members would deposit less money in share accounts, meaning that there were fewer deposits for CUNA Mutual Insurance Company to insure.

As a result, those credit unions that were closely tied to CUNA – notably some in the Kootenays and some closed-bond operations in Vancouver – opposed the introduction of chequing. For some years, in fact, CUNA representatives spoke out publicly against credit unions providing that service to their members.[9] The struggle for chequing, therefore, was not easily won; nor would it be entirely over even when the arrangements were completed in the early 1950s. For nearly a decade, there would be some doubters who would prefer to deal with the banks.

7. Ibid.
8. Ibid.
9. Ibid.

During those same years, Robinson also concentrated on attracting more credit union investments in Central. Throughout the 1940s, credit union treasurers around the province, while making minimal deposits in Central, had deposited considerable funds in banks. They also invested significant amounts in government bonds, partly because of the patriotism engendered by the War and partly because it was convenient to do so. On the other hand, until the early fifties, many of them found it slow and expensive to invest in Central. Primary chequing helped overcome some of these problems, but there were still many treasurers who did not find it sufficiently attractive to invest funds in Central. Robinson therefore introduced term deposits at competitive rates and developed a pre-arranged loan program whereby qualifying credit unions could be granted immediate loans in multiples of $1,000 – in effect, a kind of overdraft.[10] All of these changes meant that Central was increasingly capable of becoming a genuine "bank" for the provincial movement.

The League also went through similar dynamic changes. Its primary responsibilities continued to be the development of new credit unions and the training of credit union leaders. In the spring of 1951, its manager, Jack Burns, resigned to become assistant manager with CUNA Mutual Insurance Company. Burns had been a successful manager for the League: patient with the inevitable frustrations in trying to bring together the disparate groups involved during the 1940s, tireless in moving about the province, and diplomatic amidst the tensions that had emerged.

When Burns had assumed the part-time management of the organization in 1945, it had 15 members whose assets amounted to only $100,000; it was almost entirely dependent on volunteer labour; and it had an annual budget of $4,000. When he left, the League had 190 members whose assets were over $12-million; it had four full-time and several part-time employees; and it had an annual budget of $55,000.[11]

Burns was replaced by Dick Monrufet, a native of England who had been raised in British Columbia. As a youngster in the 1920s, he had toured the United States with his family in a "housecar" built by his mechanic father; it was one of the first house trailers built in North America. Indeed, it was so unusual that the family earned some of its income for a few years selling blueprints to people who were attracted to it on the streets of American towns and cities. While in the United States, Monrufet had worked for a while on newspapers in Miami, an experience that would prove valuable when he became the League's manager. Monrufet had returned with his family (by then living on a

Dick Monrufet, who served as manager of the League from 1951 to 1970 and as Superintendent of Credit Unions from 1970 to 1976, was an important early leader through some of the most difficult years in the history of the provincial movement.

10. Ibid.

11. Statistics based on Twelfth Annual Convention, June 20-23, 1951, various reports, BCCCU Archives.

houseboat) to Vancouver in 1937. He found work as a streetcar conductor, became active in the union, and was one of the early supporters of Stry Credit Union – in fact, its first president.[12]

Monrufet played an important role in a variety of capacities on the boards of both the League and the Central during the 1940s; indeed, he had seconded the motion to create B.C. Central Credit Union in 1943. At the time he joined the League, he was president of the Vancouver Chapter. He had written several pieces for the *Credit Unionist* and he was an articulate, forceful speaker. He also knew British Columbia well, in those years a rare quality since travel around the province was so awkward and expensive.

When Monrufet assumed office in the summer of 1951, the League was in a modest deficit position of approximately $2,000, but support was generally good, and most of the deficit was attributable to inadequate support for the League's publications – hardly an issue of major concern. There were, however, only three other paid staff members at the time – meaning that Monrufet counted lawnmowing and fixing the plumbing among his tasks.

The League, nevertheless, was very active. It was continuously engaged in promoting credit unions through whatever means seemed appropriate – and could be afforded. One of the most popular ways to reach prospective members was by radio. In 1950, at least two credit unions – Powell River and Vancouver City Savings – started to broadcast messages over local radio stations. In 1951, the League, along with several Vancouver credit unions, sponsored a regular radio program over radio station CKNW in Vancouver. The program was devoted to 15-minute speeches by various credit union leaders, each addressing a specific credit union theme – history, theory, structure, co-op relations.

In early 1952, this homegrown show was replaced by "Lorne Greene's Notebook," a national program sponsored by CUNA and broadcast

From 1952 to 1954 Lorne Greene was the announcer for a regular series of radio programs on stations across Canada, sponsored by the national movement. The broadcasts did much to promote the credit union idea.

"Lorne Greene's Notebook"
SPONSORED BY YOUR

CREDIT UNION NATIONAL ASSOCIATION

12. Interview with Dick Monrufet, January 25, 1991.

IT PAYS TO ADVERTISE

* Are all your members alive?
* What about the sleepy ones?
* Why not save your breath and let these pamphlets talk for you?

PERTINENT
QUESTIONS
AND
ANSWERS
Concerning
Credit Unions

* The printed word is still the most powerful.
* Use it on that half-dead member.
* An informed member is a live member.

ORDER THESE TODAY!

THINGS YOU OUGHT TO KNOW
PERTINENT QUESTIONS AND ANSWERS
WHAT IS A CREDIT UNION?

A HANDFUL OF CHANGE
GOSH! ONLY A PENNY!
SAVE FROM THE TOP OF THE PILE

Above and Others May Be Obtained from League Supplies Dept.

over several stations in British Columbia and nearby stations in Alberta. It featured stories about "average" Canadians, written by Tommy Tweed, a brilliant broadcaster who became one of the most important figures in Canadian radio during the 1960s and 1970s. In those years, both Greene and Tweed were credit union members and many of their stories came from credit union backgrounds. The program lasted for nearly three years.

The heart of the League's work, though, was to find ways to improve the capacity of the local credit union leaders to better serve their memberships. In the autumn of 1952, the League hired its first full-time field representative, George Stirling. He was the first of several men – there were no women – who would travel the province over the next 20 years, trouble-shooting with credit unions in difficulty, attending board and membership meetings, offering training courses for board and committee members, and speaking to groups interested in starting credit unions.

The decision to hire a fieldman was motivated by the growing recognition that board members and the general manager could not meet all the needs of credit unions, and by a realization that the only effective way to train board and committee members sufficiently was to meet with them in their credit unions. It was no longer possible to rely largely on the training sessions of Chapters because they involved only a fraction of the volunteers in the movement.

Similarly, the Central and League conventions were inadequate for the training of directors and committee members. By the mid-fifties, the largest conventions attracted about 300 people, or approximately one-tenth of the volunteers associated with the province's credit unions. Moreover, educational activities had to compete with other interests and activities at the conventions as the provincial movement became more complex and diversified.

Nevertheless, education and training were major themes at conventions during the 1950s because it was growing increasingly difficult to preserve the kind of focus that had emerged during the movement's early years. With more than 200 credit unions scattered around the province, with a core of volunteers that conservatively would have numbered over 3,000 (including board and elected committee members), with credit unions operating in an amazing range of economic and social circumstances, the challenges of achieving agreement on common goals and of ensuring competence among the officials were intimidating. In some instances, they were becoming desperate. The main problem, as in the past, was that not enough elected leaders had the requisite background to make good decisions; it was a challenge that would continue for many years.

During the 1950s, the League's board was very active, as management relied on board members to maintain contact with the local credit unions. One of the most prominent directors in those years was Jean Archibald. She had first become active in the League in 1942 as the unpaid secretary; she had served in various posts thereafter, but most particularly as the writer of "Women's Point of View" in the *Credit Unionist*. In that column she – and her successor, Mary Maharg – highlighted the work of women in the credit unions, those who served on boards and the 20 to 30 who served as secretary-treasurers at any given time. A feisty person, "known to peel the paint off a barn door at forty paces,"[13] Archibald was a determined and widely-admired leader who became the League's unpaid Education Director in 1951.

The highlight of the year for the League was the annual general meeting, usually held in June, alternating yearly between Vancouver and other communities around the province. These meetings usually lasted a full two days and, when held in Vancouver, normally attracted about 300 delegates (as opposed to the 50 to 60 who typically attended Central's day-long meetings). The meetings devoted considerable attention to national co-operative issues, particularly the efforts to create a national co-operative financial system and to develop other national programs, usually connected to the activities of the Co-operative Union of Canada. At each annual meeting in the fifties, about one-third of the time was consumed by reports from various officials active in national and international organizations.

Those deliberations were all part of what the leaders of the day liked to call "the big picture" – a phrase introduced by Moses Coady during a visit in 1949 and widely used thereafter.

The "big picture" meant elevating the perspective of credit union leaders so they could envision the possibilities if all credit unions and co-operatives pulled together and, in turn, united their strengths with their compatriots within B.C. and across the country. For many, it was a way to create a fairer Canada; for some, it could change the world.

Debates at the League's meetings covered a wide range of other issues. One frequent topic in the early 1950s was the League's perennial deficit position. Even if the deficit was only a few hundred dollars, the situation always attracted some controversy. Moreover, the League was very much influenced by "out-of-town" delegates and board members – in striking contrast to the "in-town" (i.e., Vancouver-based) leaders prominent within Central.

The League, therefore, was the main carrier of the communitarian traditions of the co-operative movement. During its debates, the most stirring calls were made for further encouragement of the co-operative

13. *B.C. Credit Unionist*, May, 1951, p. 4.

movement as a way to address many of the province's social problems; they equally reflected eloquent affirmations – usually from Vancouver leaders – that credit unions should concentrate on improving their own financial health. It was a debate that was never resolved and always kindled sharp exchanges.

One of the favoured causes of those who reflected the communitarian tradition most deeply was the attraction of young people to the credit union movement. As early as 1939, credit union activists had been concerned about this issue. For them and their successors, attracting young people was crucial since, over the years, the young would carry on and expand the movement's larger goals; the young would also provide the kind of loyal support credit unions needed in order to overcome periodic adversity.

Many of the early leaders, too, were teachers, pressed into service in community credit unions – not to mention Teachers Credit Union, formed in 1942 – as secretaries or secretary-treasurers. In the post-war world, as many Canadians sought to create a more open society, many teachers saw in credit unionism a way to extend into economics the same democratic principles they believed should permeate the political process – supposedly, the issues on which World War Two had been fought.

During the 1940s, many credit unions had tried to encourage parents to open savings accounts for their children as "juvenile credit unionists." The first known juvenile member was enrolled in the North Kamloops Credit Union on September 1, 1941;[14] soon after, juvenile members were registered in Vancouver, and the practice became common in most credit unions throughout the decade.

The much preferred approach, however, was to organize school credit unions. An article explaining how they worked in Illinois, appeared in the September, 1942, issue of the *Credit Unionist*. Another was published in the September, 1947, issue, describing school credit unions developed by St. Brigid's Credit Union in Toronto. These articles sparked the formation of several savings clubs in local schools in British Columbia, although this often proved to be a controversial activity, opposed by local bank managers and viewed negatively by some parents. Not until a delegation of credit unionists met with the Minister of Education in 1952 would they be generally accepted – and even then several school boards remained suspicious.

The campaign for a systematic approach to the development of school savings clubs was a common topic at annual meetings and it became, in the late 1940s, a project for the League's Educational Committee. That committee had been formed at the 1943 annual meeting, but it had a rather frustrating experience throughout the 1940s since it had virtually no funds and very little staff support.

Jean Haynes (née Archibald) was a prominent leader of the provincial movement during the 1940s and 1950s, and a long-standing contributor to the *B.C. Credit Unionist*. An advocate of a larger role for women in the credit union movement, she was also one of the most vigorous and effective proponents of credit unions undertaking extensive educational programs.

14. Ibid., November, 1941, p. 2.

From the 1940s onward credit unions sponsored savings clubs in schools. The clubs depended upon the support of volunteers as well as teachers for their success. Pictured above is one of the clubs, at Sechelt School on the Sunshine Coast.

Hilary Brown, *right*, was one of the most colourful and dynamic leaders in the early history of the provincial movement. She lived on Hornby Island where she helped start a local credit union and one of the most remarkable consumer co-operatives in Western Canada. She consistently promoted educational activities and was one of the first B.C. leaders to advocate international involvement.

Instead of funding the work of this committee adequately, Central chose to use the funds it gathered in dues to support the *Credit Unionist*, to cover losses that often occurred in the operations of the Supply Department, to meet overhead and personnel costs, and to finance trips by League leaders to credit unions around the province.

In 1950, the Education Committee, somewhat resentful of the lack of educational activity, led a campaign that ended in a convention resolution instructing the board to give better support to educational programs. Shortly after the convention, Jean Archibald assumed her position as unpaid Education Director and she was given a modest budget for expanding educational activities.

One of the issues she took up was school credit unions. She had allies, the foremost of whom was Hilary Brown, a member of Central's board since 1947 and chair of the Educational Committee from 1949 to 1958. Brown was one of a number of influential women within the provincial movement in the early 1950s. A resident of Hornby Island, she was a native of Scotland's Clydeside. Educated in England and Geneva, she met her husband, Harrison Brown, a writer and correspondent, in Frankfurt in the mid-1930s. Bitterly opposed to the rise of fascism, they left Germany in 1937 to settle on Hornby Island. Hilary's family had been supporters of co-operatives and she had seen first-hand the large consumer co-ops in Germany. So when a credit union and a consumer co-operative were first proposed for Hornby Island in the early 1940s, she instantly became a supporter of the move.

Archibald and Brown found support in several credit unions for the idea of school credit unions or savings clubs. One of the first was Ivor Mills, who tried to start one toward the end of a teaching stint in Dawson Creek in the spring of 1951. The following year, after moving to teach in Port Alberni, he successfully organized a savings club within the local high school. Shortly thereafter, other savings clubs were organized in schools on Vancouver Island, particularly in Nanaimo and Duncan. In 1954, a School Savings Committee was formed within the League. One year later, there were 14 clubs in operation; they had 3,682 members, with savings of $63,305.[15]

The clubs relied on the voluntary efforts of teachers and parents to hold sessions at least weekly so students could deposit or withdraw funds. The money they deposited was kept in local credit unions, where it was paid at least the going rate of interest. Some credit unions, too, allocated a sum of money to scholarships, based on their earnings from these deposits. In fact, one of the consequences of the savings clubs was a growing awareness of educational issues, and many credit unions started scholarship programs in the early fifties, a tradition that became well-established in the provincial movement.

15. "Report of the School Savings Committee," Reports and Minutes, Sixteenth Annual Convention, B.C. Credit Union League, June 24-25, 1955, pp. 1-2.

The most divisive issue within the League, however, was the continuing debate over insurance; in fact, it would reach its most explosive stage during the mid-1950s. In a sense, the issue went far beyond insurance in that it was at heart a debate over how best to organize the credit union movement, provincially, nationally and internationally. As such, it brought into play all the political/regional tensions within the province and across the country – indeed, nearly all the issues that are basic to the Canadian experience. At the same time, within credit union/co-operative circles, it was central to a wide range of ideological and national debates that deeply divided credit unionists in the United States and Canada during the fifties and the following two decades.

Much of the controversy in British Columbia came to focus on Rod Glen, a credit union leader from Nanaimo. Glen had grown up in Ladysmith among mining families, although he was somewhat detached from them, since his father was paymaster for the coal company. Gregarious, aggressive, articulate, humorous and contentious, he was at the start of a distinguished career in the credit union movement. In 1951 he became president of the Nanaimo Credit Union and he led it to become – by most standards of measurement – one of the more successful credit unions in the province.

Glen also became one of the most effective "politicians" in the movement, able to sway conventions, organize coalitions, and create change. His network of allies and friends, built up in the early fifties, would remain largely intact for nearly 30 years. Ideologically, Glen was very much within the movement's communitarian tradition, in that he wanted the credit union to be a hub for all kinds of activities within local communities. In fact, under his leadership, Nanaimo would gain an international reputation for its innovative support of social and economic activities. Glen hoped other credit unions would follow suit.

He was almost immediately drawn into the insurance war as he became active in the early 1950s. Although the debate took place on many levels, perhaps the underlying issue was really a struggle over leadership in the CUNA movement. Between 1946 and 1955, Tom Doig was managing director of both the Credit Union National Association and CUNA Mutual Insurance Company. By the early fifties, controlling both organizations had become difficult and, as Doig's health declined, the two started to drift apart, particularly as CUNA Mutual became a stronger and more resourceful company, while CUNA engaged in some very difficult debates over its roles within the United States and Canada. When Doig finally retired in 1955, the difference erupted as each organization had its own preferred candidate to succeed him. Because of the structure in place at the time, the

A family affair

by Clarence Morin

Having several members of the same family active as officers of a credit union certainly is not unusual, but few cases can compare with the original roster at Ladner Fishermen's Credit Union (known today as Delta Credit Union).

It's a tenet of credit union philosophy that every credit union's membership has a common bond of association. The Ladner group met the condition in several ways — they were all fishermen, they belonged to the same union and the same co-operatives, and, of the 15 founding members and first officers, nine were related to one another.

Mike and Bill Vidulich were brothers. So were George and Homer Stevens, whose father was founder Nick Stevens. John Cosulich was the cousin of Ron Cosulich — who was also the step-brother of George and Homer Stevens. The Cosulichs and the Vidulichs were related by marriage (Ron Cosulich married Molly Vidulich), while Victor Gerrard was a foster brother of the Vidulichs. Only Eric Jensen, James William Read, Frank Dujmovich, Dominic Bussanich, Allen Townsend and Roy Anderson were not part of the "family" of officers.

Mike Vidulich, *below*, served as the credit union's president for 12 years and as a director for 39 years. Mary Nugent, the credit union's first full-time treasurer, served from 1959 to 1976. Mike and Mary came to know each other very well — and, eventually, they were married.

Association's Board of Directors had the final say and chose its own candidate, H.B. Yates.

Amid all this controversy over succession, the "communism" issue flourished. During the early 1950s, at the height of the Cold War, some prominent credit union leaders, notably Marion Gregory, CUNA's president in 1951-52, became involved with the anti-communist campaigns of the American government. Gregory would remain active in that cause for the rest of the decade.

His views were given strong reinforcement. In 1954, John Foster Dulles, the U.S. Secretary of State, addressed the CUNA convention, delivering a powerful speech attacking communists at home and abroad. He received strong messages of support from the CUNA leadership. At about the same time, Roy Bergengren wrote an article in *The Bridge*, CUNA's in-house publication, about credit unions as a way to combat communism, particularly in developing countries.[16] Both of these developments antagonized some of the leaders of the B.C. movement.

In October, 1954, Joe Corsbie, then president of the League, wrote a strong letter of complaint to CUNA's Canadian directors, objecting to the introduction of politics into the credit union movement by CUNA. He pointed out that the B.C. movement included people supporting a wide diversity of political viewpoints, including a few communists, and that political issues were avoided as much as possible because they could badly divide the provincial movement.[17]

Although he did not mention it in his letter, Corsbie was writing from rather bitter personal experience. The League's 1954 convention had been thrown into disarray when Prince Rupert Fishermen's Credit Union introduced a resolution calling for Canadian trade with mainland China.[18] A serious split had been avoided only by having the issue referred to the Board of Directors, which managed to shelve the matter indefinitely.[19]

Corsbie's letter was not taken lightly in the United States, perhaps because CUNA had had its own unannounced observer at the 1954 convention. The observer, so Glen later established, had reported back to CUNA that the B.C. League was dominated by radicals with communist sympathies.[20] A little later, during the summer of 1954, Willis Lonergan, a credit unionist from Longview, Washington, had asked to visit the League, and he sat in at one of the board meetings. Shortly thereafter, letters were exchanged between the CUNA officials in Canada and CUNA's head office confirming (from their perspective) that the B.C. movement was influenced by communists. In fact, for the next decade or more, a significant group of American credit union leaders (and some in the Kootenays)[21] would believe that the B.C.

16. Files in BCCCU Archives.

17. J. Corsbie to all National Directors, Canadian District of CUNA, October 26, 1954. Ibid.

18. Interview with Rod Glen by Miriam McTiernan, August 27, 1978, BCCCU Archives.

19. Ibid.

20. Ibid.

21. Interview with John Quail by Miriam McTiernan, January 26, 1978, BCCCU Archives.

movement was dominated by communists, among whom they included Rod Glen, at least for a while.

Glen came under suspicion because he was active, particularly during the 1950s, in the Co-operative Commonwealth Federation, even though within that party he was associated with the moderates who fought a long and acrimonious battle against communists. He was active in party affairs at the local level, served on constituency associations, assisted in election campaigns, and encouraged trade unionists to support the party. Within credit unions, many of his closest associates, such as Hilary Brown and May Campbell, were veterans of the social democratic movement.

Glen became personally embroiled in the communism issue in the spring of 1955 when he was preparing to attend his first CUNA meeting, to be held in St. Louis. A few weeks prior to his planned departure, he was called into his boss's office at the *Nanaimo Free Press*. There he was reprimanded because his boss had just been visited by the RCMP, who had enquired about Glen's political activities. The boss, who had different political views, was furious and said he would fire Glen, were it not for the union contract and the fact that Glen was the union's chief negotiator. In passing, the boss advised Glen to cancel his plans for attending the CUNA meeting because the U.S. government would not allow him to enter the country.

When an irate Glen returned home that evening, he found out that the RCMP had also interviewed his neighbours, "asking questions about us, who our friends were, did we have wild parties, who associated with us, what did they know about us...."[22] A few phone calls soon revealed that as many as 15 of the League's 18 directors and some League staff members had been investigated by the RCMP. The investigation, which had been conducted in a particularly clumsy way, created an uproar in the B.C. movement and led Glen to contact Colin Cameron, then the CCF Member of Parliament for Nanaimo. Cameron asked about the matter in the House of Commons, making the issue front-page news in the *Nanaimo Free Press*, and a matter of some significance for other B.C. newspapers as well.

Ultimately the issue died with more of a whimper than a bang. Colin Cameron quietly met with the Commissioner of the RCMP, convinced him of the silliness of the investigation – which Glen and others believed had been initiated by the FBI anyway – and received assurances that Glen could attend the CUNA convention. There he received a courteous welcome, even though he was known to be unsympathetic to the CUNA management of the day and in fact became immediately associated with efforts to change it.

In the years that followed, Glen relished telling the story about the RCMP investigation, and there is no doubt that it was an

22. Ibid.

unsettling event for him — as it was for many others. Nor is there any doubt that the investigation took place. But, in retrospect, the specific issue was also somewhat exaggerated. It was largely a manifestation of the bitter and somewhat unscrupulous politics to be found in the Canadian and American movements at the time and an inept performance by the Mounted Police. That it was an incident rather than a major issue is proven by the fact that Glen was quickly accepted by many in the American movement, and he rose to high elected office at unparalleled speed.

Nevertheless, during the 1950s and, to some extent in the 1960s, the communism issue dogged the international and Canadian movements. So, too, did the continuing squabble over who should manage CUNA and CUNA Mutual. As it turned out, Tom Doig was unacceptable to a significant block of credit unionists and the management issue did not die down after the 1955 convention. Indeed, it spread to nearly all the components of the American and Canadian movements. State and provincial leagues championed or opposed supporters of Doig; employees in Madison resigned because of the choice that had been made; annual meetings became times for bitter debates and constant political manoeuvering; elections to the boards of both CUNA and CUNA Mutual were hotly contested; and partisan politics — always a potentially disastrous factor within co-operative organizations — became a convenient vehicle for forming alliances. By 1957, the national and international structures of the North American credit union movement were in disarray.[23]

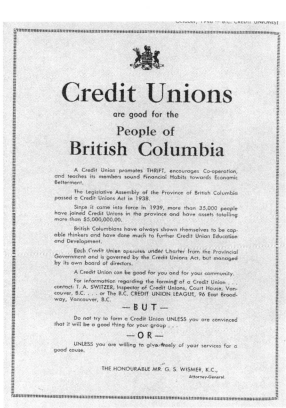

Various government ministers responsible for credit unions helped to promote their development over the years. One of the most committed advocates was Gordon Wismer, who served as Attorney-General in the Coalition Government from 1948 to 1952. This promotional piece was issued in his name.

In Canada, the national movement also had entered controversial days for its own reasons. During the late 1940s, credit union growth across the country had been impressive. By the end of the decade, the national movement had nearly one million members and assets of $250-million. In many communities, credit unions were becoming the financial institution of choice. In Quebec and Saskatchewan, as well as in B.C. communities like Dawson Creek, credit unions could boast the support of 40% of the population.[24] It was inevitable that such growth would encourage those who wanted to create a national financial nexus for the Canadian credit union/co-operative movement.

The dream, which had first surfaced in the mid-forties, gathered momentum at the decade's end, largely because of the enthusiasm of A.B. Macdonald, general secretary of the Co-operative Union of Canada, and several co-operative leaders in Saskatchewan and Nova Scotia. Co-operative Life Insurance, headquartered in Regina, opened

23. For a description of the struggles between CUNA and CUNA Mutual, see Moody & Fite, *The Credit Union Movement*, pp. 290-321.

24. *B.C. Credit Unionist*, February, 1949, p. 23.

Top rate security

by Clarence Morin

Credit unions have always boasted about their liberal lending policies and how a person's character was a key factor considered when granting loans, but few applied the theory as rigidly as Richmond Savings Credit Union when it granted its first loan.

With a few deposits on hand, the time came to earn some income. To get things moving and to see how loan granting worked, the president of the board of directors filed the first loan application. The credit committee, whose approval was required, looked it over very carefully and decided more security was needed. After much discussion at both the committee and board levels, it was decided the loan could be granted only if Father Patrick McEvoy, the parish priest and founder of the credit union, co-signed the president's application and accepted responsibility for payment if anything went wrong.

Father McEvoy agreed; there were no problems. The loan was repaid as scheduled.

Louis van der Gracht, who served as treasurer of the credit union for 32 years, said the credit union's officers learned many things from that first loan: loans could be granted with only a person's character as security, the president was an honest man, and credit union theories of saving and lending actually did work.

The credit union went on to become one of the largest in the province; by 1994 its assets were well over $1-billion.

offices in Alberta in 1947, in Ontario and Manitoba in 1948, in the Maritimes in 1949, and in British Columbia in 1950. The move into B.C. created immediate controversy because most of the co-operatives and several credit unions – led by Prince Rupert and other fishermen's credit unions – were drawn to the idea of a Canadian insurance company tied to the co-operative movement. They led a campaign, which was also supported by key leaders on the Prairies and in the Maritimes, to induce Co-op Life to offer insurance of loans and savings.

In 1951, the board of Co-op Life decided to enter the business, but instructed management not to promote it; rather, the board directed that the sales staff respond only to requests from credit unions. Given that commissions were involved – for both Co-op Life and CUNA Mutual personnel – those instructions could never be enforced with complete reliability and they were always open to controversy. For years the resultant competition between the two sales forces would contribute to the underlying tensions within the B.C. movement.

In addition to its involvement in the insurance issue, the League was also responsible for nearly all of the contacts with the provincial government – the only significant exception being relatively rare discussions between Central leaders and government officials concerning occasional changes to Central's by-laws. During the late 1940s and early 1950s, the League's relations with government were particularly fruitful since Gordon Wismer, the Attorney-General in the Coalition Government of 1948 to 1952, was very sympathetic to credit unions and, to a lesser degree, co-operatives generally. Wismer spoke frequently at annual meetings, was always receptive to delegations from the League, and spoke positively about credit unions at various public gatherings.[25]

Wismer was prompted in making these public pronouncements by the Inspector's Office. In 1948, Tom Switzer had replaced E.K. DeBeck as Inspector. Switzer was a committed credit unionist and shared with Jack Burns the distinction of having helped to start over 80 credit unions; Switzer, in fact, helped to start 100. He was a sensible, kind-hearted public servant who was preoccupied with the financial stability of credit unions, and particularly concerned about the training of elected leaders.

Switzer wrote a column for many years in the *Credit Unionist* about the practical issues confronting treasurers and loans committees. His advice – inevitably business-like and conservative – was always specific and probably very helpful to those who read it. Switzer also generally belonged to the school that preferred credit unions serving limited groups of members, especially within companies. Consequently, he was always concerned about the sometimes impractical enthusiasm and ambitious schemes that he found among some credit union leaders.

Credit unions issued a wide array of promotional literature during the 1950s.

25. For example, see text of a speech on credit unions that Wismer broadcast over radio station CJOR on November 1, 1948, *B.C. Credit Unionist*, November, 1948, pp. 16-17.

Meanwhile, credit unions around the province were undergoing significant change. Many of them were starting to emerge out of small cramped quarters in homes, beside mills or on side streets.

Several credit unions constructed large and impressive buildings, some of them on the main streets of towns or on the more well-travelled streets of Victoria and Vancouver. As the new buildings emerged, the credit unions took on more and more the appearances of banks – some of them even moved into vacated bank buildings. Teller cages replaced tables; filing cabinets replaced notebooks; safes were used instead of locked, portable boxes. An increasing number of credit unions were managed by salaried treasurers; full-time, trained tellers became common; and paperwork became a way of life.

This steady and sometimes spectacular growth did not go unnoticed in the wider community. In 1955, the *Vancouver Province* ran a series of four articles on the provincial credit union movement.[26] They were enthusiastic in their support, citing the fact that the province's credit unions had loaned over $100-million to their members:

> They [had] financed everything from teeth to taxis, furnaces to fumigators.
>
> Credit union money bought a fire engine for Roberts Creek, and a ferry for Hornby Island. It has helped finance at least 1000 homes (they've lost count) and 1500 fish boats.
>
> It has paid for honeymoons and divorces, and somebody said that every fifth baby in B.C. arrived on a credit union stork.[27]

The heart of the business carried out by credit unions in the early fifties was still the personal loan. Loans were restricted to "providential and productive purposes" by most credit committees, meaning that they were made for consolidating debts, for schooling, and for payment of medical expenses. Most were for a few hundred dollars and the basis of the collateral was often the reputation of the borrower. Typically, most borrowers were charged 1% on the remaining monthly balances of their loans, a convenient and reasonable interest rate most of the time.

The big change in the fifties, however, was the fairly widespread introduction of the mortgage loan. Although such loans had been made since at least 1943, they became increasingly important during the late 1940s when housing became plentiful and relatively inexpensive. By 1954, many credit unions were lending out about 25% of their members' deposits in the form of mortgage loans. Typically, they

This 1950 view of Stry Credit Union's office shows how credit unions had progressed in little more than a decade. Dick Monrufet, the elected president, is seen at left, along with Joe Chausse, the manager, and staff member Mrs Perkins.

26. *Vancouver Province*, December 11-15, 1955.

27. As quoted in the *B.C. Credit Unionist*, January, 1955, p. 5.

would lend up to 50% of the appraised value of the property, although in some instances, they loaned up to 66%.[28]

The demand for mortgage loans far exceeded the capacity of credit unions to meet members' needs. During the 1950s, as the province enjoyed relatively prosperous years and wage levels rose, the demand for housing became stronger, particularly in the Lower Mainland, Victoria and the new resource communities. Amid this boom, many credit union members could turn only to their families or their credit union to obtain the $2,000 to $3,000 loan needed to buy an average house – banks and trust companies were simply not interested in the needs of people with lower incomes. Credit unions, therefore, frequently met the needs of a particular kind of house-buyer: the purchasers of second-hand housing, probably for the most part young or modest wage-earners starting in the housing market.[29]

The increased demand for mortgage loans placed significant pressure on credit unions. Many of them could not meet their members' needs, even though many used the resources of B.C. Central. Even more importantly, many of them lacked the expertise to make good mortgage loans. Consequently, mortgage-lending meant that credit unions had to rely more and more on paid employees; volunteers could not be expected to master the requirements of mortgage lending without contributing more time than was reasonable. Moreover, the growing mortgage business meant that the Credit Union Act had to be revised repeatedly throughout the 1940s and 1950s to provide appropriate safeguards and procedures for credit union boards and committees wishing to serve member needs for mortgage loans.

Furthermore, the growth of mortgage lending particularly perturbed the Inspector; it reinforced his concerns about the lack of expertise among credit union directors. Much of the surviving correspondence from his office in that period, therefore, is concerned with instructing – sometimes chastising – certain leaders of local credit unions about their poor bookkeeping and, above all, bad lending practices. Mortgage loans were a central part of that problem because they were so different from the personal loans that had dominated credit union business until the end of the 1940s. Mortgages required careful documentation, the assessment of property and, on rare but important occasions, foreclosure – tasks that only a few credit unions could undertake effectively in the beginning.

In retrospect, this shift to mortgage lending was a crucial development in making credit unions more like banks in their daily operations and fundamental purposes. Mortgages would force credit unions to become more aggressive in attracting members' deposits, especially if they were also going to continue to provide personal loans. Their records would have to be carefully maintained over long periods, and

28. Ibid., April, 1954, p. 7, and July, 1954, p. 11.
29. Ibid., November, 1950, p. 2.

the liquidity of the credit union would have to be managed more closely. The advent of such loans, therefore, was one of the major steps in transforming credit unions from virtually volunteer operations to professionally-run organizations. It was a gradual process, affecting different credit unions at different rates, which began in the early 1950s.

Another problem that encouraged the employment of more professionally-trained people was loan delinquency. By the middle of the decade, delinquency in some credit unions had reached the entirely unacceptable level of 14% to 16% of the amounts loaned; in several it reached the 5% level, far above the 1% to 2% generally common and acceptable to credit unions. While a few of the credit unions in difficulty were in communities where severe general economic problems explained the delinquency, most were suffering because their leadership was very reluctant to put strong pressure on members. This reluctance was bad enough if it concerned relatively small personal loans; it could become very serious if large mortgage loans were involved.

Such problems, though, were the symptoms of success. The main point was that the movement was growing at unprecedented rates — when compared with either the Canadian or the American movements. In 1950 there were 182 credit unions; they had 52,805 members and total assets of nearly $13-million. By the end of 1957, 321 credit unions were in operation, with more than 161,000 members and $62-million in assets. There were 19 credit unions with assets exceeding $1-million by 1957, where there had been only one in 1950.[30] In 1957, too, Vancouver City Savings Credit Union opened a second branch, becoming the first B.C. credit union to do so.[31] Over all, growth was unprecedented, nearly 20% a year, straining the resources of the central organizations and involving significant numbers of inadequately trained leaders in the new local credit unions.

As the credit unions grew, so did their central organizations. By 1954, the growth in staff in the two provincial credit union organizations and in CU&C Health Services meant that another change in building was necessary. This time, the boards of the three organizations decided to construct their own building. It was erected on the same site — the corner of Broadway and Quebec — that had served as the centre of the provincial co-operative movement for more than a decade. In addition to the three provincial organizations, the building housed some nine credit unions. The ribbon was cut on September 18, 1954 by the Attorney-General, Robert Bonner, who took out a membership in Vancouver City Savings Credit Union the same day.

The credit union and co-operative building at Quebec Street and Broadway as it appeared in 1951. Expanded several times over the years, it housed the League, Central (until 1966), various co-operative organizations and up to nine credit unions.

30. All statistics are from the convention information package prepared for the Twentieth Annual Convention, B.C. Credit Union League, June 26-28, 1958, "Statistics – Credit Unions, Province of British Columbia," (last page), BCCCU Archives.

31. *B.C. Credit Unionist*, September, 1957, p. 9.

A key function of the League was to sell supplies to its member credit unions.

32. See W. Polnar, "Attitudes of League Directors Towards Stabilization Plans and a Government Program of Share Insurance," BCCCU Archives.

33. See "Draft Outline for Presentation and Discussion of Provincial Reserve Fund", "Document D", Proceedings of the Eighteenth Annual Convention , B.C. Credit Union League, BCCCU Archives.

Thus, when delegates gathered at the University of British Columbia in June, 1957, for that year's conventions, they were proud of what was being accomplished, but worried about the possible consequences of growing too fast. The problems were many. There were growing differences in the ways in which many credit unions operated. In about 40 credit unions, as much of the day-to-day work as possible was carried out by full-time general managers and staff, even though the existing legislation envisioned most of the work being done by volunteers. In perhaps another 75, part-time secretaries or managers did much of the work, and in the remainder the work was carried out almost entirely by volunteers, one of whom would receive a modest honorarium.

There were also concerns about how well records were kept. The documentation for loans was steadily improving in the larger credit unions, though the records for mortgages still caused the Inspector concern. In many small credit unions, however, particularly outside the main cities, annual audits were either inadequately carried out or not conducted at all.

These managerial difficulties were the source of growing concern. Each year a handful of credit unions encountered serious difficulties; in some instances, those with the more serious problems were liquidated by the Inspector's Office or absorbed by other credit unions. In no known instance, though, did any member lose funds deposited in a credit union that was dissolved or absorbed.

Serious credit union operating problems were frequent enough that the leadership of the provincial movement feared that a really serious situation might develop and, during 1956 and 1957, League directors frequently discussed the possibility of creating a reserve fund that might be used to help credit unions temporarily in financial difficulty.

They were dealing with a problem that was common enough in the credit unions of North America. In the United States, several Leagues were considering similar possibilities at the same time.[32] During the 1930s, the American government had introduced the Federal Reserve system to stabilize banks, especially through the introduction of federal deposit insurance. This approach imposed measures of "stringent controls" over participating banks. In the mid-1950s, the federal government indicated its intention to place federally-incorporated credit unions in the reserve system, a move that would severely limit the capacity of those credit unions to control their own policies. Anticipating a similar move by state governments, a number of state leagues, most notably Michigan, created their own reserve or stabilization systems.[33]

In Canada, the first league to investigate creation of a reserve fund was Saskatchewan. In 1952, the Saskatchewan movement was confronted by a serious problem when two large credit unions encountered financial difficulties because of misappropriations. The movement reacted quickly and reviewed the reserve systems already established in Quebec and those being developed in the United States. In 1953, the Saskatchewan movement created the Mutual Aid Fund, which would become a model for the rest of English Canada.

The Saskatchewan approach was of immediate interest to the leaders in British Columbia. During 1955-56, members of the League and Central boards discussed creating a fund in British Columbia and reviewed all the literature they could gather from other jurisdictions. It was thoroughly described and discussed at the 1956 League convention, a reflection of how important the matter had come to be.

All of these discussions about security, delinquency and stability were simply indications that credit unions were more and more a part of the conventional marketplace. Increasingly, credit unions were no longer just associations of friends; they had to find ways to protect themselves from the risks endemic to any financial institution serving a diverse clientele.

Given this growth, the League and the chapters were hard pressed to meet the training needs of the hundreds of new directors elected each year. Many of them, particularly in the new credit unions, were not sufficiently prepared for the tasks they had to undertake, especially when they were expected to do most of the work in taking deposits and making loans. In short, the movement was reaching the limits of volunteerism, and needed to rethink how it should be structured to respond to the demands being placed upon it.

Increasingly, too, government officials were worried. On a simplistic level, they were becoming impatient with the apparently continuous need to revise the Credit Union Act. In fact, the Attorney-General, Robert Bonner, mentioned the probable need for a systematic review of credit unions needs and a wholesale revision of the Act during a meeting with Farley Dickinson, the League's president, early in 1957. His suggestion quickly bore fruit. On a more serious level, government officials were increasingly concerned about the potential liability in the event that the now rather large credit union system encountered severe difficulties. These were issues that similarly concerned many credit union leaders.

There were, therefore, many things to discuss when Farley Dickinson opened the League convention in the University's Brock Hall at noon on Thursday, June 13, 1957. The setting was appropriate for what would be one of the more important and thoughtful meetings in the B.C. movement's history. Over the years, B.C. credit unions had received strong support from the University and from a few faculty members in particular.

In the more recent years, John Friesen of the Extension Department had played an especially significant role as a speaker and facilitator. Friesen brought to the B.C. movement a commitment to adult education, a commitment originally honed within the remarkably dynamic rural co-operative movement among Mennonite people in southern Manitoba during the late 1930s and the 1940s. He would continue to have a significant impact on the central provincial organizations and several credit unions, particularly Vancouver City Savings, until he departed for India to work for the Rockefeller Foundation in the 1970s.

To a very significant degree, the close collaboration with adult education was an important feature of credit union development from 1945 to about 1960. The collaboration was natural since the two movements had been associated for generations. In the case of British Columbia, and primarily through UBC, adult education provided a powerful network and a means to reach a steadily larger group of people. As well as helping to contact individuals through study club techniques, it also offered a positive, empowering approach to individuals and groups. Indeed, adult education, like the co-operativism from which it originated in part, took an optimistic view of what people could do for themselves, and it had an abiding faith in the potential of individual human beings. When its influence waned during the 1970s, the credit union movement would lose one of the most effective ways it had to reach a growing group of people within the province.

Another individual imbued with the techniques of adult education was Harold Chapman, Principal of the Co-operative Institute (later Western Co-operative College); indeed, he was the main facilitator for the 1957 convention. Like Friesen, perhaps even more so, Chapman was devoted to the group discussion method, the essential process preferred by adult educators of the period. This approach, which encouraged discussion on the floor by delegates sitting around tables, was an attempt to make the large co-operative gathering an effective way to empower members and to reach for new ideas. It was a reaction to the tendency, already evident in too many co-operatives and credit unions, to make meetings merely ratifications of decisions that could not be changed and for manipulating support for projects favoured by whatever group happened to have power. It was an approach that worked particularly well at the 1957 League convention, as it did at many other conventions in years to come.

There were four main issues that confronted the delegates who assembled in Brock Hall. One was a proposal to create a provincial reserve fund to assist credit unions in difficulty. During the winter of 1956-57, the League's board, impressed by what it had heard and read about the experiments in Saskatchewan and the United States, had appointed a committee under the direction of Bob McMaster to consider how a stabilization fund could be created in British Columbia. That committee brought a recommendation to create a reserve fund to the convention, where it became the subject of an intense but valuable debate.

The committee recommended that the board of the proposed reserve fund be appointed by the Lieutenant-Governor but be dominated by individuals selected by the credit unions. Further, it recommended that most of the reserves be deposited in B.C. Central Credit Union to be invested conservatively within the movement. The delegates accepted these general principles readily enough, but there was much debate over details of organization and account-ability. An extensive list of suggestions was generated from the discussion groups organized by Harold Chapman, and that list was referred to the League's board for further consid-eration. During the coming year, events would force the board's hurried attention to those suggestions.

The second issue was the need to gain a more detached and sophisticated view of what was happening among British Columbia's credit unions. The simple fact was that the movement was growing too fast. In 1956 alone, the number of members had increased by nearly 15,000 – from 121,000 to 136,000; assets had increased by $10-million – from $40.5-million to $50.85-million, making it the fourth year in a row that had seen assets increase by more than 20%.[34] Ten credit unions, not including B.C. Central, had more than $1-million in assets; two of them – Prince Rupert and Lake View – had more than $2-million.[35] Between seven and ten credit unions were being created each year, an increasing number of them with community bonds.

Such growth raised "in the minds of thoughtful persons, both inside and outside the Credit Union Movement, the question as to whether the foundations upon which the Movement [were] built [were] sound enough and broad enough to stand the strain of such rapid expansion."[36] One indication of the pressures was the frequency with which the League and Central requested revisions to the Credit Union Act. Revisions – mostly dealing with the powers of credit unions and Central to undertake different kinds of businesses – had been requested and granted in 1951, 1954, 1955 and early in 1957. Two other requests in 1957 – to allow funds from insurance companies to be deposited in Central and to allow credit unions to receive govern-ment funds for agricultural purposes – were turned down.[37] Both of these requests were made in part because the rapidly expanding move-ment perpetually needed more capital than Central could provide. In

In addition to receiving pins, "founders" were also recognized by a citation and a card.

34. Statistics – Credit Unions, Province of British Columbia, 1957 Convention booklet, unpaged, BCCCU Archives.

35. Ibid.

36. "B.C. Credit Union League Presentation at Workshop Sessions Re Survey," Document E, Ibid.

37. Ibid.

fact, Central was nearly always at the limit of its $2-million in loans from one of the major banks.

The government rejected these requests at least partly because the Attorney-General, Robert Bonner, wanted to be assured that the movement was developing prudently. It was a suggestion that many within the movement welcomed because there was growing concern about whether the accumulated funds of the movement, now much larger than anyone had anticipated a few years earlier, were being invested appropriately.

Moreover, the sheer size of the movement and, in particular, the size of many credit unions, made it increasingly difficult for directors to maintain the same kind of involvement as originally intended. For example, under the Act as it existed in 1957, a director could not "endorse an application [for a loan] unless he is satisfied that the applicant is industrious and of good character." One wonders how this was possible in credit unions with over 2,000 members. Moreover, credit committees had to inquire carefully into the "character and financial condition" of each loan applicant, an immense burden in credit unions where scores of loans might be made in any given month. Presidents were also under increasing pressure: they normally attended all meetings, they had to sign all cheques, and they were typically involved in most of the daily business. As a result, it was becoming increasingly difficult to find individuals with the time and dedication for a position that was unpaid. Perhaps the limits of volunteerism, at least in large credit unions, had finally been reached.

The problem was that the movement had grown at such a rapid yet uneven rate that even the management and directors of the two central organizations had only an impressionistic understanding of how the local credit unions functioned. There was a need to comprehend fully how well credit unions were dealing with delinquent loans; how they were interpreting the legislation; how they were deciding to distribute dividends; and how well they were being audited. The League's board decided, in the spring of 1957, that the only way to answer these questions – and to understand what reforms to the provincial structures were necessary – was to commission a survey that would study the operating procedures used by credit unions in British Columbia. It brought that suggestion to the convention.

The debate on the survey was intense. Some credit unions were suspicious of an attempt to use a survey as a way to concentrate power within Central and, especially, the League. There were concerns that it might lead to higher dues for membership in Central, already an issue because of the growing expectations the League was called upon to meet. A few believed that the suggestion from the government really cloaked an attempt by the Attorney-General and the Inspector to increase their control over the movement. Others feared embarrassment over the results and a few were concerned that the outcome would be used to the benefit of the larger credit unions. After all the debate, however, the delegates voted up to $5,000 for the survey, leaving open how it might be conducted.

The third issue that dominated the 1957 convention was the deepening crisis over insurance and British Columbia's relationship with CUNA in the United States. The struggle continued between the two factions in the management of CUNA, creating intensely competitive battles for positions on the boards of CUNA and CUNA Mutual. The more difficult tensions, however, were caused by the continuing desire to create a distinctly Canadian co-operative financial system. Naturally enough, more and more Canadians wanted to have their own national organization, which would be clearly independent of the American movement. Many, too, wanted to develop a strong insurance program and, given the pressures on Central for capital, also wanted the insurance companies to invest in the provincial credit union movement.

The 1957 CUNA meetings, held in Omaha in May, had been particularly acrimonious because of the re-emergence of the passionate debate over communism. The issue surfaced twice, first when an invited guest speaker, Jerry Voorhis of the Co-operative League of the United States, was called upon to speak. He was abruptly, if briefly, prevented from speaking when CUNA delegates from Kentucky requested that he not be allowed to speak because of his alleged communist sympathies. Partly, this charge was a carry-over from the 1948 Congressional elections when Voorhis's promising political career was cut short in a particularly bitter, smearing campaign waged against him by a youthful Richard Nixon. Partly, too, it was a consequence of the fact that there were some co-operatives within the Co-operative League that did indeed have long-standing associations with Marxist groups in Minnesota and Michigan.

This unfortunate incident, exacerbated by the continuing McCarthyite passions of the time, carried over into the elections, and they were particularly important for the B.C. movement. Because of the intense feelings in recent years, the elections were fought much like any political election, replete with buttons, campaign "headquarters" and platforms, and hosted parties. As in political elections, rumours and innuendo became the stock-in-trade. The old rumour that the board of the B.C. League included some communists was used against

B.C. candidates, especially Rod Glen. It was an issue that would remain alive for a few more years, to the discredit of some of the leaders of CUNA, and with significant ramifications for the B.C. movement.

The last issue was more pleasant. Since its inception, the provincial movement had always been concerned about youth. It was one of the ways in which a "movement culture" had been consistently manifested. The underlying rationale was that credit unionism was not just concerned with helping members today; it also aimed to build a series of integrated organizations that could help to build a better world in the future. But for that to happen, the movement had to foster growing bands of informed youth willing and prepared to take over from the existing leadership.

The Credit Union Building at 96 East Broadway, long a focal point of the provincial movement, is seen here in its final form as a three-storey structure.

The concern for youth was demonstrated in two ways. First, the delegates discussed the schools program at great length and supported increased emphasis on it, at both the local and provincial levels. Second, they enthusiastically endorsed the creation of a foundation to provide education and research for the credit union movement. Unable to use the name credit union in the title, they called it Westcu, an abbreviation of "Western Canadian Credit Union."

With the creation of a foundation, a proposal for a reserve fund, and the decision to undertake a systematic survey of the movement, British Columbia's credit unions emerged from the 1957 convention as a stronger movement, aggressively looking forward. There were tensions, some of them growing, and dealing with growth and change would not be easy, but there could be no doubt that there was a determination to do so.

*We live today in a world which is changing far more rapidly than any of us realize.
The social habits of people are changing; their ways of life are changing; their desires
and needs are changing. New products, new forms of entertainment, more leisure time,
the impact of automation – all these are having an effect upon our lives now and will have
an even greater effect on our future. And as a result the world of finance is changing too.
This is the world in which credit unions have operated; the question we face is
whether we can continue to operate in this type of world. We must ask ourselves
whether we really want to stay in existence, and, if we want to continue,
we must ask ourselves to what extent we want to change and in what way
we propose to make changes.*

Rod Glen,
March, 1965 [1]

1. From Glen's speech to the annual convention of the Quebec Credit Union League, March 6, 1965. A typescript is in the author's files.

*T*HE 1950S WERE GOOD YEARS FOR MOST BRITISH COLUMBIANS. The province expanded as it had rarely done before in its history. Most of the expansion came from growth in the primary industries – forestry, mining, fishing, agriculture – and most of the jobs that were created provided good incomes. Only a few of the agricultural industries languished somewhat as the province's farmers, especially those in the fruit industry, found the competition from other producers difficult.

All the other key industries, particularly forestry and mining, boomed. The demands of the Korean War helped stimulate the growth, but the main trend was that the province prospered through supplying raw materials for the general North American economic boom. It was what one historian called "the great clambake", a period when all the optimism of the North American boosters seemed justified, a time when it seemed that the Great American dream was becoming a reality.

Evidence of the boom could be found nearly everywhere in the province. New lumber mills appeared each year, and old ones were operating at full capacity. The revolution in the woods brought on by the power saw increased production beyond the dreams of those who had worked for generations with axes and cross-cuts. In the mills, the increasing popularity of plywood for construction made a new industry possible, even necessary.

Lumbering communities flourished on Vancouver Island, along the Northline, and in the interior, as new mills were created and new harvesting areas were opened. Kitimat, an instant city with all the southern conveniences, was opened in 1953 for the smelting of aluminum. It was a remarkable megaproject, even for an age of megaprojects, but it was just one manifestation of the boom in mining and smelting. Further east along the Northline and in the Kootenays, the mining industry delivered more of the province's wealth than ever before and promised to be even more bountiful.

Amid all this growth, improvements in transportation started to break down some of the traditional barriers. The Social Credit government, elected in 1952, invested considerable funds in highways and adroitly took advantage of (and credit for) federal government funding for building the Trans-Canada highway in British Columbia. Consequently, roads fanned out from the Lower Mainland, incorporating gleaming new bridges crossing what had been impassable rivers. Air transportation similarly compressed distances, as Trans-Canada Airlines expanded its western operations. A new large regional carrier emerged – Pacific Western, created through the amalgamation of three small provincial lines, Central Pacific Columbia Airways, Kamloops Air Service and Skeena Air Transport. It would soon fly to nearly every major centre in the province.

All told, for most British Columbians, the province was a privileged place, and credit unions were a part of the remarkable expansion on which prosperity was largely based. In fact, they even exceeded the frantic growth they had known in the mid-1950s. The number of credit unions in operation increased from 318 in 1958 to 328 in 1961; thereafter, the impetus behind organizing credit unions lost momentum, and the number had declined to 304 by 1965. Nearly all of the credit unions that disappeared were either amalgamated with, or absorbed by, other credit unions. It was the beginning of a consolidating trend that continues to the present day.

By the 1960s credit unions had moved on to Main Street. In the above photo, members of the board of Trail Credit Union, Ray Mulvihil, Keith Ruckstuhl and Albert Hokl present George Fletcher, the Mayor of Trail, with his membership.

Growth in membership and assets, however, remained impressive. In some ways, it was even intimidating. Each year between 15,000 and 20,000 people joined credit unions, so that the total membership increased from 180,000 to 256,000 between 1958 and 1965. In the same period, assets more than doubled, from $79-million to nearly $175-million.[2]

The challenge of regulation becomes evident very quickly when one considers what this growth meant for local credit unions and their provincial organizations. Many of the prospering credit unions served unionized workers in towns dependent on primary resources. For example, Trail Credit Union had only 1,000 members, but more than $6.6-million in assets by 1965, making it one of the largest in the province; Alberni had $5-million, Kimberley $2-million, and Lake Cowichan $1.5-million. In the context of the time – when $6,000 was a good annual income – these were significant sums.[3]

By the mid-sixties about half of the roughly 300 active credit unions operated with closed bonds. Between 25 and 30 of these were based on religious or ethnic associations, or both; all the rest were organized by employee groups. Some of the employment-based credit unions, especially those organized by public servants, were deeply involved in the activities of Central and the League. Many of the others, however, that were organized in mills, store chains and factories, tended to be relatively disinterested in the provincial organizations and jealously protective of their independence.

Moreover, closed-bond credit unions generally saw their obligations as being limited to benefiting their own members. Their main

2. Statistics are from the Annual Reports of the B.C. Credit Union League.

3. "B.C. Credit Union Statistics," 27th Annual Report, B.C. Credit Union League, 1966, unpaged.

The Loans Committee of the Trail Credit Union in 1950. *Left to right:* George Webb, Dave Home, John Duttorpe, Vic Ferguson, Albert Scott and Bill Blair. For their membership, for their town, they were an important group whose decisions determined whether families could purchase homes, send children to post-secondary education, or go on special holidays.

4. For example, see interview with Michael J. Rogers by Schroeder and McTiernan, April 29, 1977, BCCCU Archives.

concerns had little to do with the general credit union picture in the province. Instead, the focus was on how their credit unions related to the employer. Did they have space for an office? Could they arrange for an individual to have time off, when necessary, to look after credit union affairs? Could they secure automatic payroll deposits or deductions?

Many closed-bond credit unions, therefore, resisted what they thought of as outside "interference," whether it came from the Inspector's Office, the League or Central. In the debate over creating a reserve fund at the 1957 convention, some were opposed or lukewarm to the idea because they feared it would mean more regulation.[4] Numerically, closed-bond credit unions could be very significant at League, Central and chapter meetings, and, in some instances, they "voted with their feet." Among the 25 to 30 credit unions in the province that did not belong to the central organizations in the mid-1950s, half or more were closed-bond. They reflected a tendency toward a different institutional culture than one would generally find within community credit unions.

Another obvious trend between 1958 and 1965 was the way in which credit unions – some closed-bond but especially the community-based organizations – participated in the "suburbanization" of the province. The province shared in – and benefited from – the great North American social revolution made possible by the automobile, inexpensive housing construction, and the widespread distribution of social services, like schools and hospitals. British Columbia was part of the social revolution that placed families in new neighbourhoods and drew fathers (and about 30% of mothers) away to their daily work in factories, offices, mills and mines. It was a way of life that had its antecedents in the 1920s but reached its culmination after World War Two. It was a way of life credit unions helped to build in British Columbia.

Credit unions participated primarily by helping to finance the purchase of cars and housing. At a local level, the most important innovator in the development of mortgage lending was Vancouver City Savings, or VanCity as it was coming to style itself. From its roots in the central Vancouver area, it became arguably the first credit union to define its "community" as a city rather than a neighbourhood. By 1960, more than 70% of its loans were in mortgages; it had opened two branches (and would open a third in 1962), and it was continually searching for funds with which to meet the increasing needs of its members.

VanCity's growth was assisted by the Inspector's Office and the League, both of which encouraged small credit unions in difficulty to accept absorption by VanCity.[5] For other Vancouver area credit unions, this continual expansion – especially the opening of branches – often seemed like dangerous encroachment; for VanCity (or City Savings, as it rather argumentatively advertised itself briefly in the early sixties) it was just natural development.

Other credit unions were also experiencing growing pressures for mortgage loans in the late 1950s. By 1960, in fact, a survey indicated that credit unions with assets exceeding $500,000 were investing about 20% to 25% of their loan portfolios in mortgages. They were by far the most active in this kind of lending, accounting for about 50% of all credit union mortgage loans in the province.[6] While some of these credit unions were based on community bonds in the booming Lower Mainland – credit unions like Richmond, Surrey and North Shore – several were in the prospering small cities and towns around the province.

Mortgage lending was a significant and controversial step in part because it challenged the traditional credit union idea (as it had been developed in the United States) that the same rate of interest should be charged on all loans, usually 1% per month on the reducing balance. Many credit unions, but especially the larger ones, changed this simple approach by moving to split rates on different portions of loans.[7] In fact, the practices seemed to vary considerably, causing anxiety and disagreement among those deeply schooled in the American approach or concerned about maintaining a simple, easily understood, relationship between depositors and borrowers.[8]

The growth of credit unions outside of the main cities of Vancouver and Victoria was another major trend of the period. In fact, they played comparatively much greater roles in the economic and social life of their communities than did even the larger credit unions in Vancouver and Victoria. By 1965, there were 29 credit unions outside of Vancouver with assets exceeding $1-million. In towns like Duncan, Nanaimo, Courtenay, Campbell River, Dawson Creek, Prince Rupert, Kamloops, Kelowna, Osoyoos, Powell River and Trail, credit unions were important public institutions. They reflected community ambitions, brought increasing status to their elected officials, and contributed significantly to their local economies.

During the 1960s, local credit unions around the province were organized into 13 chapters. One of these – the Pacific Chapter – consisted of 90 of the smaller closed-bond credit unions in the Vancouver area. There were four other chapters in the Vancouver/Fraser Valley area, three on Vancouver Island, one along the Northline, two in the Okanagan, and two in the Kootenays. While they varied somewhat in the projects they undertook and the type of communities they

Credit unions provided opportunities for their members, directors, and staff to enjoy themselves.
Top: Young people had their own table at this annual meeting.
Middle: Adults celebrate at an Edelweiss Credit Union function.
Bottom: Credit union representatives gather at a Kootenay Chapter education meeting.

5. Quail interview.

6. Tables 6 & 7, Survey Report, Credit Unions, Province of British Columbia, November, 1960, p. 31.

7. Ibid., pp. 11-12.

8. Quail interview.

tended to represent, all were active, and all had the responsibility of monitoring the activities of the League and Central.

Indeed, chapters served several valuable purposes at this time, when they were arguably at the height of their importance. Many of them held monthly meetings; a few met even more frequently. Much of the formal and informal training of the volunteer leadership took place at these gatherings. It was there that many directors and committee members first grasped the meaning of delinquency and liquidity; it was there that they compared notes on how to grant loans and prepare better monthly reports; it was there that they first grappled with the nature of a board member's responsibilities.

Chapters also created networks for social activities. They sponsored bowling leagues, organized picnics, supported youth projects, and ran dances. Particularly outside Vancouver and Victoria, chapter meetings were important events for many credit union enthusiasts. Attending meant travelling to nearby towns for weekend gatherings. Staying overnight meant renewing acquaintances, organizing dinners, providing entertainment, and forming new friendships. Perhaps even more so than the annual conventions, the chapters contributed to the social dimensions of the provincial movement in the 1940s and 1950s.

But what did it mean to operate a credit union in the early 1960s? How did the changing nature of the province affect the roles credit unions could play? How were credit unions being changed by technology? What role would volunteers play as credit unions changed? What should be the responsibilities of their managers? How would credit union opinion-makers define the role of credit unions in a society that was changing around them? All of these questions came very much to the fore during the early- and mid-1960s. A series of reports from that period helps to explain, at least in part, how they were answered, directly or indirectly.

The first report was the Survey commissioned by the 1957 convention. The convention had expected that the report would be conducted by the federal Department of Agriculture, partly for cost reasons and partly because the department had been gathering statistics on credit unions since the 1920s. The League's board, however, ultimately reconsidered that option on the urging of the provincial government, which wanted a more independent study. Ultimately, the League asked several local credit union leaders to undertake it.

The committee was chaired by Bob McMaster, the lawyer for both the League and Central. At the time, McMaster was far more than a hired barrister: he was a committed credit unionist who contributed far more over the years than his fees ever covered. Much of the research was carried out by Fred Graham, then and for many years the external auditor for the League and Central. Like McMaster, his interest was as much philosophical and personal as it was professional. In the late fifties, their commitment was demonstrated by the work they did in helping to prepare the Survey Report, which was not completed until the spring of 1960. The second report was prepared by Gilles Mercure on behalf of the Royal Commission on Banking and Finance. It made errors in interpreting the movement west of Quebec – most particularly by assuming it was a clone of the American movement – but it made several important observations on the challenges confronting the movement generally.[9] The third was actually a series of reports on operating ratios prepared by CUNA International (as the Credit Union National Association was renamed in 1964). The fourth report, written by two university economists, Russell Robinson and Gerald Johnson, provided an economic appraisal of the province's credit unions.[10]

Most of these reports were commissioned because of a growing concern over how credit unions should be safely controlled. There was a deepening concern among credit unionists and within government that the movement was not being regulated properly – either by its leaders or by the Inspector's Office. Finding the best way to regulate the growth and diversity of the province's credit unions became arguably the dominant theme of the early 1960s.

In the most obvious sense, regulation meant the ways in which the provincial government inspected and controlled credit unions. Defining how the government would undertake that task was not easy for either credit union leaders or government officials. For credit unions, it meant accepting a degree of government intervention that an increasingly independent leadership was loath to endure. For government, it meant establishing what was necessary – within an always limited budget – to maintain public confidence in the institutions.

Regulation also meant the ways in which credit unions controlled their own development. It meant ensuring that elected leaders were able to play their stewardship role effectively. It meant developing audit systems as they became necessary. It meant providing secretary-treasurers with training and equipment so they could keep track of their business. In total, it meant learning self-regulation, the most difficult form of regulation to learn – and to practice.

Part of the regulation problem was revealed in one of the common incidental findings of the various reports published in the early sixties. All of them demonstrated that British Columbia did not have a homogeneous movement. Instead, there were several types of credit unions in operation, for different reasons and for different kinds of members.

One set of distinctions was really a function of size. An important break-point occurred in those days when credit unions reached the plateau of $200,000 to $250,000 in assets. Almost inevitably, that

9. Gilles Mercure, "Credit Unions and Caisses Populaires," *Working Paper Prepared for the Royal Commission on Banking and Finance* (Ottawa, 1962).

10. T. Russell Robinson and G. Gerald Johnson, "An Economic Appraisal of Credit Unions in British Columbia," unpublished paper, World Council of Credit Unions Archives, Madison, Wis., "B.C. Credit Unions pre-1980" File.

size of credit union – there were 113 of them in 1965 – meant that a paid secretary-treasurer (as managers were still called) had to be employed. As credit unions approached $400,000 to $500,000 in assets, they generally hired full-time managers and started to employ tellers.[11] As assets reached $1-million, middle management groups started to appear, either to run branches or particular functions, such as lending. All of these changes meant that larger credit unions were beginning to cope with a different set of problems than those confronting smaller, traditional credit unions. By the early sixties, their different needs and priorities were becoming obvious.[12]

Some of the differences were apparent when the Credit Union Act was revised in 1961. With the revisions, managers could be given the power to grant automatic loans on a member's signature or the member could pledge bonds as security. In credit unions with more than $1-million in assets, the credit committee could be appointed rather than elected, and a credit officer, reporting to the manager, could exercise considerable discretion. Credit unions were also given the alternative of appointing an accountant as auditor instead of electing a supervisory committee. Many credit unions took advantage of these possibilities quickly, in the process probably becoming more efficient but also less reliant on volunteers.[13]

The growing and varying importance of professional managers created another set of divisions within the provincial movement. Managers started to meet as a group on a formal basis in 1963 and their meetings quickly became important events, especially among some of the larger Vancouver credit unions. Informal networks of managers also became obvious factors in the deliberations of the League and Central. In fact, Central's board was increasingly made up of managers, and the same was true for the League's board. Inevitably, their impact was to encourage the more exclusive consideration of economic matters rather than social issues.

Although the increasing importance of managers raised some concerns about their possible domination of the movement, these concerns do not seem to have run very deeply, at least in the early sixties. Partly, this reflected the fact that many of the managers themselves had started out as elected directors. Indeed, one of the benefits of the early reliance on credit and supervisory committees was that many elected officials became very knowledgeable about the business. A few of them, including such prominent leaders as Rod Glen, Dick

Mike Driscoll, treasurer of Rossland Credit Union in 1953, represents a typical male treasurer of the period using the latest technology.

11. Based on the results recorded in the Survey, p. 5.

12. See "Supplementary Report of the National Directors to the B.C. Credit Union League, 1961", "Document N-1", Convention Book, B.C. Credit Union League, 1961.

13. "Statement re Credit Unions in British Columbia, Submitted to the Royal Commission on Banking and Finance by George T. McCulloch, Acting Chief Inspector of Credit Unions for British Columbia, May 14, 1962," BCCCU Archives.

The make-up of the board of Surrey Credit Union in the early 1950s, with its mixture of experience, youth and the sexes,was probably typical of credit unions of the period.

Monrufet and "Rip" Robinson, chose to manage credit unions when the opportunities came their way.

Despite the growing importance of professional managers, most credit unions still relied extensively on the contributions of volunteers. In a later age, when apathy or temporary volunteering are more common, it is surprising to realize how much volunteers contributed in those times. Board meetings were typically held at least monthly. If there were complex issues to deal with, the meetings could last five or six hours; often there was more than one meeting a month. Credit committees could meet very frequently – four or five times a month in credit unions with more than $100,000 in assets.[14] Supervisory committees tended to meet five or six times a year, executive committees at least once a month, usually more frequently. In addition, many directors contributed weekends to chapter meetings or training sessions, not to mention the week-long annual conventions – and all of this for no pay.

The good intentions of the volunteers, however, did not diminish the concerns of those responsible within government or the League about the effectiveness of credit union management. In 1958, the well-respected Tom Switzer retired as Inspector and he was movingly recognized for his contributions at the League convention that year. He was replaced by Milt Culbert, who was not as well received by the

14. Survey, p. 15.

115

movement during the three years in which he was Chief Inspector, as he immediately called himself. To some extent, the difficult relationships that developed between him and the credit union leadership helped to bring the regulation issue to the fore.

In the view of many credit unionists, Culbert was erratic and too often ill; he also was accused of giving advice that was conflicting or that did not square with the Act.[15] Culbert was also opposed, or was at least unsympathetic, to credit unions making mortgage loans. He disliked the tendency to move to differential interest rates that mortgages required, and he feared having large loans to a few members. This opposition soon embroiled him in controversies, especially with the larger and more aggressive credit unions.

Some of the officials in the Inspector's Office – individuals like George McCulloch and, later, Pat Grant – did have the movement's respect; unfortunately, they did not have the mandate or the resources to carry out an effective inspection service. Indeed, because of the immensity of their tasks – and the sheer impossibility of physically inspecting more than 300 credit unions – the Office became known for its cursory work. Moreover, in those days, the Inspector's Office, partly in recognition of the impossibility of its mandate, became primarily concerned with ensuring that the Act was being followed, and not in carrying out an audit in any satisfactory sense.

To some extent, the League also had responsibility for ensuring that credit unions were operating efficiently and honestly. In 1957, it began to organize its training programs more systematically so that they could be taken around the province. In that year, Jac Schroeder was hired to prepare and deliver educational programs particularly for directors. Like John Friesen, Schroeder came from the dynamic adult education movement in southern Manitoba. He had been employed by the Southern Manitoba Federation of Co-operatives for some years. In the early fifties, he and his family, along with some other Mennonite families from southern Manitoba, were involved in the development of a co-operative farm near Vanderhoof. Although the farm had been very successful, it had broken up when two of its key members left for better-paying jobs.

Schroeder was an ardent advocate of education as the basis for the development of credit unions – indeed, of any co-operatives. He was very adept at using slides, films and workshops, and he was a talented artist with a flair for presentation. Among training officers and academics associated with credit unions in Western Canada and the United States, he soon became well-known for his work in B.C.

In 1958, Schroeder was joined in the Education Department by John Quail, the first qualified accountant hired by the League. A former member of the British Marines and a rather blunt individual

15. Quail interview.

116

with strong opinions, Quail would have a significant impact on the provincial movement during the eight years he was employed in the department. Among his first tasks for the League was to work at the annual convention, held that year in Victoria. (Quail later ruefully recalled that he performed his first job as a fieldman at that convention: he cleaned up after an incontinent horse that had been brought on to the convention floor by "Big Jim" Herriot, a delegate from Vancouver Police Credit Union, during a tense moment.)[16]

Quail's main contribution, however, was to improve significantly the level of accounting practice throughout the provincial movement. In this task, he concentrated equally on the secretary-treasurers and the supervisory committees. He wrote several booklets and advisory publications for them on such topics as delinquency, the nature of credit union securities, bookkeeping machines, auditing procedures, and the calculation of interest rates. The booklet on interest rates became something of a classic, was featured on several radio programs, including the CBC, and contributed subsequently to truth-in-lending legislation in both Canada and the United States.

In the 1960s, Quail also sought to introduce increased standardization into the daily operations of credit unions. He reached an understanding with all the suppliers of posting machines in the province, whereby they agreed not to "over-sell" credit unions wishing to enter into machine accounting.[17] This was a major issue in the 1960s for credit unions with more than $100,000 in assets. The problem — as with later technological innovations — was that every secretary-treasurer was an "authority," but not all invested wisely. In the early sixties, a few invested what would be the anticipated surpluses for several years in machines that were too sophisticated for their needs. Quail's negotiated agreement with suppliers undoubtedly saved local credit unions considerable money.

The greatest impact made by Quail and Schroeder in British Columbia, however, came through the many training tours they made individually and together around the province. Normally, they spent between 15 and 20 weekends a year away from home, and most days on the road involved, Quail later claimed, between 14 and 18 hours of work.[18] Because of the difficulty in gaining full attendance at training sessions during the summer, they organized most of their trips in the winter months, not always the best time to travel, particularly in the North and the Kootenays.

During his visits to credit unions throughout the province, Quail would review their books of account — as long as he was given permission to do so. In some instances, he never succeeded in gaining access to the books. For example, there was the case of one credit union that was "run" by a chiropodist, who also ran a chicken farm; and as Quail

16. Ibid.

17. See correspondence with National Cash Register Company, BCCCU Archives.

18. J. Francis Quail to R.A. Monrufet, December 11, 1964, BCCCU Archives.

recalled, "he was secretary of the hospital and I think he was on the town council and on top of all this he ran the credit union. I never did get him to show me the books."[19] He also encountered other obstacles, such as the treasurer who never used an adding machine and calculated all transactions in his head – correctly, it would appear.

Quail, however, quickly became very adept at the rapid evaluation of credit unions. In fact, he could prepare a succinct analysis by studying annual statements while waiting his turn to speak at annual meetings. He would compare the operating results with provincial and national credit union averages, and he would evaluate borrowing patterns through comparisons with studies prepared by the Dominion Bureau of Statistics (the forerunner of Statistics Canada).

Quail also devised a system using "synoptics" that would allow treasurers and supervisory committees to keep a running record of receipts and disbursements. He became so well-known for his capacity to evaluate credit unions quickly and for his synoptics that he was invited to other Canadian provinces and to Madison to train other field representatives from throughout North America.

Quail could also be brutal. He later recalled the technique he commonly employed at annual meetings. He would

> …stand up and blast everybody for not doing very well…. I went up and I threw down the Statistics Canada report…I threw down their annual statement and said "well, I don't know, you call yourself a credit union. I'm shocked," I said. "You've got a good manager, you've got a good board, I said it must be you people. You've got a 4% dividend, you're not supporting the credit union. Look at what you're doing; this is what you are doing; this is what the indebtedness is"; and so on and so forth; and gradually softened the line and then started introducing a few jokes. They'd finish up laughing their heads off, except when I'd get a Baptist minister in the audience and he'd complain about my telling dirty jokes….[20]

Between 1958 and 1966, Quail, Schroeder and the other fieldmen identified several unsatisfactory practices. They unearthed about 15 instances in which treasurers took funds from their credit unions and were found out before they could repay what they had taken.[21] In two instances, the amounts were significant and led to court cases. They also found a rather lax attitude toward cheques returned for insufficient funds. In several instances, rather gentle boards individually paid the amounts owing rather than continuing to harass the member or allow the matter to come to annual meetings – or, even more embarrassingly, to the attention of the Inspector's Office.

The most important problem they found, though, was that too many members of supervisory committees and boards did not have the knowledge and skills needed to monitor the activities of the treasurer.

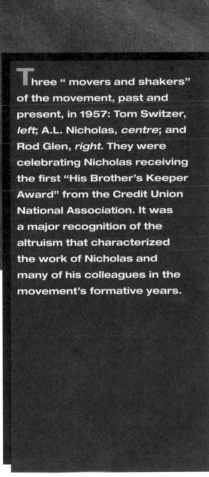

Three " movers and shakers" of the movement, past and present, in 1957: Tom Switzer, *left*; A.L. Nicholas, *centre*; and Rod Glen, *right*. They were celebrating Nicholas receiving the first "His Brother's Keeper Award" from the Credit Union National Association. It was a major recognition of the altruism that characterized the work of Nicholas and many of his colleagues in the movement's formative years.

19. Ibid.
20. Ibid.
21. Ibid.

To help volunteers undertake their supervisory tasks properly, Quail organized a special workshop on fraud. At first, he whimsically called the workshop "How to embezzle money from your credit union," as an amusing way to attract elected leaders. He was successful in that he had groups of 100 or more in various parts of the province attend the workshop. His somewhat unamused superiors, however, were shocked by the title of the workshop – he soon changed it to the more prosaic "Preventing Fraud." (The irony of this presentation did not become apparent until 1975, when Quail was convicted of fraud for illegal activities he carried out at Stry Credit Union.)

This workshop and others conducted by the field representatives in the late fifties and sixties provided immense benefits to credit unions and indirectly to the province. Through their efforts, some 3,000 to 4,000 British Columbians were introduced to accounting and general business practice and to the operation of organizations. It is difficult to think of a comparable adult education activity – in the days before community colleges – with a similar economic and social impact across the entire province. In that period, and for many years thereafter, the credit union movement contributed to the economic and social growth of the province by teaching elementary economics and organizational theory to many people. Those skills would be transferred to many other enterprises.

Such efforts, of course, did have some immediate impact. The training session offered by the League attracted scores, often hundreds, of elected leaders. In his reports, Quail proudly commented on the improvements he saw when he returned to credit unions even a few months after offering one of his training sessions.[22] Unfortunately, events were moving too quickly to rely exclusively on the gradualist, educational approach. The main event occurred in an unlikely place, Britannia Beach, a small mining community located on the coast some 30 kilometres north of Vancouver.

The Britannia mine had opened shortly after the turn of the century, and for about 50 years it had sustained a prosperous community. Mining families lived in company housing along the beach and up the hill toward the mine. Year after year, copper, lead and zinc were produced – in fact, for several years Britannia was the largest copper mine in the province. Like so many mining towns that achieve a high level of stability, Britannia Beach boasted a well-developed sense of community, shaped by a strong working-class culture and encouraged by a generally benevolent employer.

In almost every respect, it was a company town. Everyone in the community depended directly or indirectly on wages earned in the mine. The company managed the only store, ran the swimming pool, cared for the tennis courts, provided the church building, and operated

22. See Quail's reports on some of his trips to various regions in "Office Memoranda, 1965-70," BCCCU Archives. Unfortunately, only a few of the reports survive.

the hospital. In 1955, the company had helped the townspeople to organize a credit union. It provided the credit union with space and, if necessary, assistance "when it came to handling the financial problems of its member-owners."[23] This tradition of benevolence was in sharp contrast to the sudden way in which the company closed the mine, the town's only source of livelihood.

Predictably, the credit union was under siege the day the mine closed. Many of the 334 members wanted their deposits out immediately, fearing they would not get them if a rush developed.

Others wanted their loan payments suspended until they could find other employment. The credit union had more than $80,000 loaned to members, from a total asset base of $109,000 (not counting the savings of some 158 children in a Schools Savings Club).[24] It could have been a disaster, not only for the members of the credit union but for the provincial movement.

Fortunately, the secretary-treasurer, Else Conway, was a resourceful and trusted individual. She immediately contacted the Inspector's Office and the League. The League quickly called on member credit unions to invest in the shares of Britannia; 30 of them did so, and more than $11,000 was raised. The League also created a trust fund, which raised another $7,000.[25] With this infusion of funds, the credit union was able to meet the immediate demand for withdrawals and survive the pressure of the first few months. Rather remarkably, nearly all of the loans were repaid by the members, even though many of them were in dire straits and forced to move. The books of the credit union were closed in the autumn of 1961, and no-one had lost any money.

The Britannia failure galvanized the provincial movement. It dramatically demonstrated the need to press forward in the creation of a stabilization fund. The 1957 convention had authorized the League's board to proceed in organizing such a fund, and the Britannia situation clearly showed the urgency. Shortly after the crisis broke, the League's board submitted a plan for a reserve fund to the B.C. government.

The proposed fund, based on the discussions at the 1957 convention, was to be used to assist credit unions that had encountered difficulty not of their own making. Significantly, it was not to be used to help credit unions that had problems because of errors, incompetence or fraud. In part, this was because the relatively weak inspection and supervisory/auditing systems made the potential risk too wide open. Nevertheless, there was strong opposition to the proposed fund from some credit unions, particularly in the New Westminster area and the Kootenays. For that reason, Robert Bonner, the Attorney-General, insisted that the fund would only be

23. Jean Pattison, "Britannia Waives the Rules," *B.C. Credit Unionist*, July-August, 1961, p. 8.

24. Ibid.

25. Ibid., pp. 8-9.

implemented when it had gained the support of 85% of the province's credit unions, representing at least 85% of the movement's assets. That degree of support was achieved in July, 1958.

Another difficult issue, which would not be resolved until literally the last moment, was the composition of the fund's Board of Directors. The League believed that three members of the five-person board should be designated by the credit union movement, since all of the funds were coming from the movement. From the Attorney-General's perspective, it was he who was recommending the board to the Lieutenant-Governor-in-Council (actually the Legislature), and therefore he had a responsibility to ensure the board was independent. It was a difficult issue that ultimately became a matter of personalities and politics. It would not be resolved until the summer of 1959, when the Minister, despite literally last-minute pressure from League representatives in a room adjoining the Legislature, insisted on making the appointments he preferred.

The newly-formed Credit Union Reserve Board (CURB), although intended to help credit unions unavoidably in difficulty, could not escape involvement in the inspection issue swirling around within the B.C. movement. By 1962, the obviously unsatisfactory regulation of credit unions had become an alarming problem. In November, the Reserve Board received a report indicating that more than 20 credit unions, "including some large ones," were facing serious delinquency problems.[26]

As the Reserve Board reviewed the situation, it was critical of the League to some extent, but it reserved most of its criticisms for the government.[27] George McCulloch had become Acting Inspector of Credit Unions in 1960, and he had remained in that rather uncertain appointment ever since. More seriously, there were only two inspectors to serve more than 300 credit unions, an obvious impossibility that brought into question the common credit union boast that they were regularly inspected by the provincial government.

Most credit union leaders, but not all, believed that such haphazard inspections were potentially disastrous. Most wanted an efficient and dependable inspection service and began to demand it publicly. Consequently, in November, 1962, when the Reserve Board's report became known, a joint committee of the League and Central undertook a study to see how better inspections could be achieved. After reviewing the system used in Quebec and considering whether the Reserve Board should be placed in charge of inspections, the committee decided that it was best to leave the task with the Inspector's Office. It resolved, however, that the inspection system needed to be significantly improved, and it made a series of recommendations as to how this could be done.[28] It called for the hiring of more and better qualified

Women were actively involved in credit unions from the beginning of the B.C. movement. In this photograph, six women in a study group review literature provided by the B.C. Credit Union League.

26. "Minutes of the Meeting of the Committee Appointed by the Credit Union Reserve Board at its Meeting of November 6th, 1962, Held on Wednesday, November 14th, 1962," BCCCU Archives.

27. Ibid.

28. "Memorandum to the Honourable the Attorney General re. Various Matters relating to Inspection and Proposed Prescribed Rules to the Credit Unions Act," BCCCU Archives.

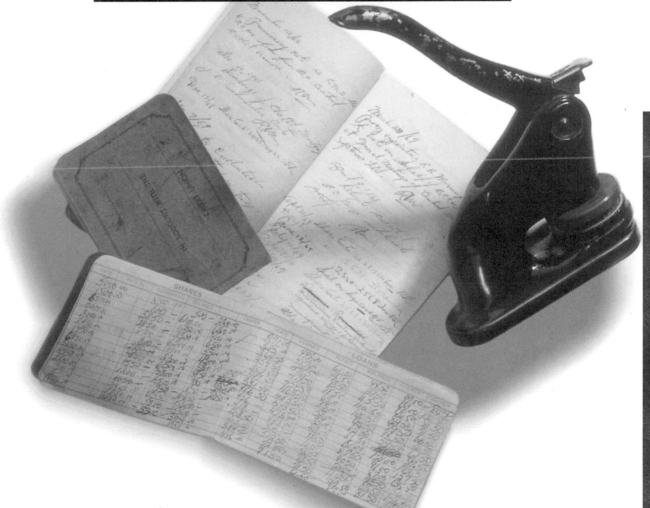

inspectors, and it recommended that the department be financed equally by the provincial government and the movement.[29]

The committee further proposed that representatives of the League and Central should meet with the Attorney-General, indicate their unhappiness with the existing service, and request that the department be revitalized.[30] The two boards responded positively and gained the support of representatives of more than 200 credit unions attending a special meeting in March, 1963.[31] At about the same time, the Attorney-General had his own report prepared.

There followed a battle of reports and a protracted series of negotiations with Attorney-General Robert Bonner and his staff over how inspections should be carried out and funded. The funding issue became particularly acrimonious and was not resolved until February, 1964, when representatives of the movement reluctantly agreed to a proposal that meant credit unions would be responsible for about 60% of the department's costs. At about the same time, George McCulloch was finally made Chief Inspector, and more inspectors were hired.[32]

This initiative is important because it demonstrated the increasing maturity of the provincial movement. The leaders of the League and Central recognized that they had a public responsibility to ensure that local credit unions were operating prudently and honestly. They recognized that there was a legitimate role for government in this process. They were willing to pay even more than what they thought was a fair share of the expenses.

The issue – and the debate over the appointments to the Credit Union Reserve Board – is also significant because of what it suggests about the importance of relations with the provincial government. The regulation issue had immense potential for adversarial relations with government, and that potential was to some extent realized in the 1960s. Partly, it was a question of personalities, since relations with Robert Bonner were not as cordial as they had been with Gordon Wismer, the previous minister.

But the problems went deeper than mere personalities. The point was that the movement had reached a point where it was no longer a minor concern for government. The relationship between government and credit union leaders, therefore, was becoming more formal and more serious. With some 250,000 British Columbians having more than $275-million on deposit in credit unions, this was entirely appropriate.

The drawn-out discussions over regulatory reform also exacerbated political tensions within the provincial movement. As the discussions became heated, intense debates broke out among the League's directors and among the province's credit unions. The League was rather inexperienced in carrying out long and complex discussions with

29. "Outline for Discussion with the Attorney General Re Inspection," BCCCU Archives.

30. "Joint Committee of League and B.C. Central re Credit Union Inspection Services - Nov. 14, 1962", BCCCU Archives.

31. Report of Proceedings, Special General Meeting, March, 1963, for the purpose of "consulting and receiving instruction from members of the League with respect to Inspection Service," BCCCU Archives.

32. Quail interview.

government; it had difficulty maintaining consensus; and it was ill-prepared to make the kinds of decisions needed in an expeditious manner. Some directors were alienated, notably Reg Robinson of South Burnaby Credit Union, who subsequently resigned from the board.[33]

Among credit unions, there were many causes for disagreement. One factor, certainly, was resentment by many leaders over the advocacy of enhanced inspection. More and longer inspections would be costly and inconvenient, and raised the spectre of increased centralized control in the minds of many credit union leaders. During the same period, the League's dues were rising regularly, creating resentments that were further nourished by the prospect of increased costs for inspection.

For others, especially some rumoured to have contact with Robert Bonner, the issue had political ramifications. Political associations became significant because many leaders of the League were known to be supporters of the CCF and Liberal parties. In the heat of the discussions about regulation, some of them made disparaging comments about the government. Credit unions led by individuals closely tied to the governing Social Credit party naturally resented these comments, and the resultant acrimony helps explain the withdrawal of several credit unions in the mid-1960s.[34] It was an unfortunate development in a period when political turmoil was already at an unacceptable level.

The other key issue that continued to stir the political pot was the relationship with CUNA and CUNA Mutual. The communism issue of the 1950s had receded from the public debates, although it survived in rumour and innuendo, particularly whenever there were discussions about creating a strong, independent national organization for Canadian credit unions.

By the early 1960s, the CUNA organizations in Canada were employing over 40 people from their office in Hamilton. The manager was Gordon Smith, a tough, feisty, ambitious credit union leader. Smith apparently was one of those who believed that radicals, possibly even communists, were powerful within the League, in one instance citing editorials on credit unions in the *Tribune*, the Communist Party of Canada's newspaper, as evidence of their influence.[35]

The reality was that there was no direct communist influence in the sixties, just as there had been none in the 1950s. No one on the League's board was a Marxist, and the only significant groupings of communists within the movement were in some of the credit unions organized among fishing people. The fishing unions, until the 1980s, were strongholds for the Communist Party, but there is no indication that credit unions were ever significant issues in their deliberations and strategies. As in so many countries, and in keeping with what became

33. Reg Robinson to the Board of Directors, December 28, 1962, BCCCU Archives.

34. Most of the withdrawals occurred in the spring of 1964, when the discussions over inspection were at their most acrimonious. The credit unions that withdrew, some at least partly because of "politics", were: Westminster, Marpole, Grandview, Warfield, Elco, South Burnaby, Edgewater, and Kamloops. In addition, there were usually about a dozen credit unions, nearly all closed-bond, that were not members of the League in the 1960s. Files in BCCCU Archives.

35. See correspondence between Smith and H.B. Yates, BCCCU Archives.

orthodox Marxism, co-operative organizations were, at most, of only passing interest.

The much more important issue was how Canadian credit unions could best organize themselves. Canadian credit unions, including most of those in British Columbia, continued to use the services of CUNA Mutual. Indeed, the savings and loans insurance program offered through the American company was one of the reasons why credit unions became so important: it was often the only insurance members possessed.

There was, however, growing Canadian competition for the insurance business within credit unions. The caisse populaire movement developed its own insurance company to offer the same services, and Co-operative Life was always seeking to expand its share of the business. The Canadian companies also offered to deposit funds in provincial centrals and leagues, which the American company could not do, or perhaps did not want to do. B.C. Central, particularly intrigued by this possibility – given the continual demand for more deposits – lobbied hard in the early sixties for legislative changes to make it possible for insurance companies to deposit in a central credit union. Central was very disappointed when the credit union insurers did not take significant advantage of this opportunity.

 CUNA Supply Co-operative also had significant business with Canadian credit unions, including those in British Columbia. However, this business came under scrutiny as the leagues grew. The leagues themselves could purchase or print supplies for member credit unions, meaning that there was always a question about what should be produced locally and what should be purchased through Madison.

In addition, there was the issue of national structure. The Canadian Co-operative Credit Society had been created in 1953, perhaps prematurely, since there was relatively little need for a national financial intermediary. There was, however, a need for a forum for national discussion, and for lobbying as circumstances required. Until the later 1950s, these purposes had been met through a Canadian Section of CUNA, the successor of the Canadian Federation of Credit Unions. It met in Canada at least once a year and at the CUNA meetings wherever they were held. As the management debates within CUNA escalated in the fifties and continued in the sixties, the issue of whether there should be a more independent Canadian organization became pressing. The Canadian views on the issue varied regionally, with the leadership from Nova Scotia and Manitoba being satisfied with the existing situation, and the B.C. leaders preferring an independent organization.

In 1957 and 1958, the issue of a distinctly Canadian organization was debated extensively. The matter was complicated because the caisse populaire movement was not interested and there were issues about how a Canadian organization would relate to the CUNA staff operating from Hamilton. Gordon Smith was the only person who still worked for both CUNA and CUNA Mutual after the separation of the two organizations in 1955. He was reluctant to divide his staff and therefore lobbied, with the support of some Canadian directors, to keep the two organizations united in Canada.

Smith did not succeed. In 1958, the Canadian movement, much influenced by Farley Dickinson of British Columbia, voted to create its own national organization, the National Association of Canadian Credit Unions (NACCU). At the end of the debate, the Manitoba, Ontario and Alberta centrals did not immediately join, meaning that the organization was rather ineffectual in organizing or speaking for the national movement until 1962.

In that year, however, the need for a national organization became evident when the federal government announced the formation of a Royal Committee on Taxation, to be chaired by K.L. Carter, a Toronto tax lawyer. NACCU assumed responsibility for working with the caisse populaire movement to prepare a brief on behalf of the two movements. The research team responsible for preparing the brief included Bob McMaster of British Columbia and Walter Francis, a Saskatoon lawyer also well-known for his understanding of credit union and co-operative law.

There was great urgency in preparing the credit union position on taxation because of the activities of the Equitable Income Tax Foundation. Incorporated in 1962, the foundation was primarily, perhaps exclusively, concerned about the taxation position of co-operative organizations. Supported by the Retail Merchants Association, whose members were beginning to feel the competition from co-operative stores, and by the private grain trade, the foundation conducted a continuous (often strident) campaign against the tax treatment of co-operatives by the federal government.

The heart of the taxation issue was whether or not surpluses or profits in co-operatives should be taxable. Since 1917, co-operatives had waged a generally successful campaign over how surpluses or profits would be treated for taxation purposes by the federal government. Initially, co-operatives successfully argued that surpluses were the result of members trading together, and the surpluses should not be taxed because they were like rebates for good performance. To tax them would be the same as taxing a discount given to customers by chain stores. However, following the McDougall Royal Commission in 1944, the federal government had decided to tax co-operatives but at a reduced rate, based on the capital they employed.

Until the 1960s, the federal government gave credit unions the same treatment as co-operatives generally, following the McDougall

Commission: in other words, it did not tax the surpluses. By 1962, however, complaints from banking circles, echoed by the Equitable Income Tax Foundation, compelled the federal government (which probably needed little persuasion anyway) to reconsider the matter. It became, in fact, an important issue for the Carter Commission, which funded two independent studies of the matter.

Aware of the struggle that was forthcoming, credit unions and caisses populaires prepared a large brief, which was presented in all regions in altered forms. Rod Glen, who was NACCU's president in 1963, was very active in preparing and presenting both the national and B.C. briefs. Along with McMaster and Francis, he was instrumental in developing a brief that emphasized the voluntary, self-help role of credit unions, even though, as a movement, credit unions were no longer small and essentially rural.

They were only partly successful in making their case. When the Carter Commission finally reported, in 1967, it recommended that some form of the surpluses of co-operative organizations, including credit unions, should be taxed. However, in other respects, the Commission was very impressed with what credit unions and caisses populaires had accomplished in a virtually unrecognized way. The submissions put forward by NACCU and the presentations made at several sessions of the Commission had made an impact.

One of the features that impressed the Carter Commission and the reporters covering the sessions was the way in which credit unions could be vehicles for economic and social development. It was a theme that found echoes in other quarters during the sixties, a decade when co-operative methods were widely supported as tools for social and economic reform.

For over a decade, in fact, the United Nations had been promoting the viability of co-operatives. For about the same period, the Roman Catholic Church in many parts of the world had resumed its active promotion of them, an activity that could be traced back to the turn of the century. In Canada, in the mid-fifties, many co-operative leaders embraced co-operatives as a tool for international development. In 1959, St. Francis Xavier University opened the Coady Institute in Antigonish to serve overseas students interested in community development through co-operatives. In Ottawa, the leaders of the Co-operative Union of Canada (CUC), especially its president, Ralph Staples, advocated the development of co-operatives through the Colombo Plan, the country's first serious experimentation with international assistance in Asia. They also started the CUC's "Co-operatives Everywhere" program to promote co-operatives among Canada's aboriginal people, especially the Inuit.

Credit unions played an increasingly significant role within this co-operative renaissance, internationally and within Canada. Promoting the development of credit unions outside of the United States and Canada, however, was not entirely new. In the 1940s, CUNA had started its international assistance program with initiatives in Jamaica and British Honduras (now Belize). In the next decade, Father Marion Ganey of Nova Scotia began his work in Fiji, from which much of the Asian credit union movement would spring. In 1954, one year before his death, Roy Bergengren made an emotional and successful appeal for the creation of an "overseas" program.

In the early 1960s, several leaders within CUNA became particularly committed to encouraging the development of credit unions in other countries. They organized special sessions on development issues at the annual conventions, and these gatherings were enthusiastically reported on at League conventions. At the B.C. League's 1959 and 1960 conventions, the CUNA sessions were successfully replicated in panels on "World Extension." The leaders in this initiative were Hilary Brown and May Campbell. In 1962, they organized a committee for international credit union development; it focused primarily on organizing a credit union for "foreign" students at the University of British Columbia, an unsuccessful experiment that lasted for four years. It also attempted to raise funds for overseas projects, but with limited success.

The committee also took responsibility for welcoming visitors from other countries; such visits had begun in the 1950s but became much more frequent in the 1960s. Most of the visitors came from Pacific Rim countries and, in the early 1960s, a particularly close association with credit union leaders in Australia emerged. Leaders from the state of New South Wales visited British Columbia in 1963 and 1964 to study the League's training programs and to better understand the province's community-bond credit unions.[36] It was an association that would grow through meetings of delegates from the two movements at CUNA conventions and through trips to Australia by B.C. leaders, notably Rod Glen.

In fact, by the mid-sixties, Glen was a prominent leader within CUNA. It was a crucial period in the history of that organization, as it began a long and difficult process of reorganization. Between 1976 and 1978, Glen co-chaired the Planning Committee of CUNA, which had been charged with reconsidering the organization's goals and structures in light of the internationalization of the movement. In co-chairing this committee, Glen came to several conclusions based on what he had observed in British Columbia and what he was beginning to understand about credit unions in the rest of the world. The report of the Planning Committee in 1965 was particularly significant in showing

36. See correspondence between Dick Monrufet and Stan Arneil, BCCCU Archives.

his thinking and for providing an important perspective on what was happening in British Columbia.

The main change noted in that report was the shift away from the promotion of thrift as the underlying rationale for the credit union movement. The teaching of thrift had been a major objective for credit unions as they had emerged in North America, including British Columbia. Indeed, the promotion of thrift was still particularly important within many closed-bond credit unions, in British Columbia as well as elsewhere, and that is why they had adhered for so long to the idea of lending only for "providential" purposes. It also helps to explain why they had such difficulty with the idea of variable rates and the allocation of large sums of money to a few members through mortgage loans. Thus the report was remarkable because it argued, before an audience essentially made up of representatives of closed-bond credit unions, for a greater and more sophisticated emphasis on lending, especially long-term lending.[37]

Glen brought these views back to British Columbia. Consequently he began to argue, along with others, for the expansion of credit unions into term deposits and pension funds as soon as they could legally do so. He even advocated that credit unions, preferably through their central organizations, should borrow from other financial institutions to meet the needs of their members, if necessary — an idea that was regarded as heresy by more traditional credit unionists.

In a more general way, Glen, like a few others within the B.C. movement, was beginning to see credit unions as full-service financial co-operatives capable of meeting, or helping to organize to meet, all the financial needs of a modern society. Many of these insights he gained as a result of his international experience; he was not the first — nor would he be the last — to sharpen his understanding of the Canadian and B.C. movements by travelling abroad.

Basic to any reconsideration of credit unions — at least as they were evolving in prosperous industrialized societies — was an understanding of what was happening to their members. It is surprising how few of the surviving records tell us very much about the members of credit unions. There can be little doubt, though, that the relationship with members was starting to change in the 1960s.

In small, particularly closed-bond, credit unions, workplace relationships to some extent ensured that loans were extended for "providential" purposes on the basis of "character", though even these operations were forced to become more "business-like": to lend on the basis of security defined by statistics.

In community-bond credit unions, too, it was not difficult to find heart-warming stories of how they were able to help individual members. When the briefs to the Carter Commission were being

Annual meetings were noted for their levity and their earnest discussions. For many, too, they were moving occasions considering important work on behalf of the common people. Jean Haynes caught this more serious purpose in one of the several poems *(opposite page)* she wrote as the theme for the 1959 Convention.

37. Proceedings, 31st Annual Meeting, Board of Directors and Members of CUNA International, Inc., May 14 and 15, 1965, San Francisco, WOCCU Archives.

prepared, the B.C. League requested local credit unions to submit examples of how they had gone out of their way to help members. The file that survives is more than an inch thick. There are stories of helping widows, making it possible for young people to complete university, assisting families in debt through counselling, providing retirement planning, aiding groups in the community, and, in exceptional circumstances, forgiving loans.

As Grow the Roots, So Spread the Branches

Man, who was born to labor, finds his way
Rugged, and blocked with obstacles too many
To enumerate; builds out of stone and clay
Monuments to commemorate his passage.

Man, in a span so brief his shadow falls
Before him on the path he walks,
Pauses to aid a stumbling brother,
To steady faltering steps — then moves on.

No one has measured, or can set a limit on
Man's humanity or inhumanity to man —
But like a torch filling the dark with light,
Shine deeds of kindness, brightening empty space.

We are custodians of the human race,
Pledged to give surety to those who need it —
Our credit unions — built not for one but all,
Lighting the darkness, shine like candles.

Each for the other — sharing equally with all.
Each a brother's keeper — brothers woven together
To one another by thread invisible, service
For each other, not for one, and not for porfit.

No thought of race, or creed, or color can mar
The slow expanding web of service carried
Across the world, bringing hope to the hopeless,
Light to the darkness of other lands.

This we believe. All men are brothers,
And brothers' keepers. We know
We have a debt to pay — a debt we owe to those
Who grew the tree that shelters us,
Whose branches strong now cover all the earth.
All the people sharing this strength of ours —
The Credit Union Tree.

Jean C. Haynes

There is little evidence, though, that credit unions were meeting the needs of the very poor on a systematic basis. Rather, their natural constituency seems to have been self-employed workers and public servants, along with fishing, farming and mining families. In the cities, groups of factory workers were strong supporters. Partly, that was explained by the continuing importance of closed-bond credit unions, which, almost always by definition, would not include the very poor. Partly, it was explained by the "image" projected by credit unions – associated, as it often was, with the working classes, and especially the employed working classes.

Such efforts as there were to reach out to the poorest in society – notably through church-based credit unions and in two cases involving Native groups – were unsuccessful. There was, of course, an irony in this regard, since the provincial movement was generally if not overwhelmingly supportive of "overseas" and northern efforts – most of them successful – to promote credit unions among the poor. It was nevertheless an issue that would not sit easily in the minds and souls of the B.C. movement's most idealistic members.

More and more, the business of credit unions was associated with either the purchase of houses or the meeting of consumer needs. In very direct, concrete ways, credit unions were part of a consumer revolution in Canada that began in the late 1940s. At its core was a shift from perceiving credit as an evil acceptable only in emergencies to regarding credit as a way to meet real or imagined consumer needs based on rising levels of expectations. It was a revolution that changed common attitudes from the "Depression generation," on which so much of the original credit union perspective had been based (in B.C. and elsewhere), to the risk-taking generation that would assume power in the 1960s and 1970s.

In short, credit unions were changing because the population mix in post-war Canada was changing. The so-called "baby boom" was in its ascendancy, and Canada had one of the fastest growing populations among industrialized countries. Credit unions benefited from this change, and there is some evidence that credit unions and caisses populaires were successful in attracting more than their share of the "young married" and "young families" to their membership in the 1960s and the 1970s. The banks were slow to react to this social revolution partly because, under the Bank Act, they could not charge more than 6% interest on mortgage loans. This meant that finance companies, consumer loan companies and credit unions/caisses populaires had a golden opportunity. They rose to the occasion: in 1948, these three types of financial institution accounted for 23% of all consumer loans; by 1964, despite an aggressive pursuit of that business by the banks a year earlier, they accounted for 44%. Credit unions had their share of this new business, accounting for 12% to 15% of all consumer loans across the country and in British Columbia.[38] In the marketplace, their competition was most frequently finance companies, whose interest rates tended to be higher than those of credit unions.

The credit unions fared well in their competition with the finance companies whenever they effectively explained their service commitment, low costs, and social purposes to prospective members. In fact, probably the single greatest social benefit they offered in the 1960s was the opportunity for many Canadians to halve the interest rates they paid on loans – from the 24% charged by most finance companies to the 12% or less that credit unions charged. That kind of saving was of immense importance to many lower-income Canadians.

By 1965, however, the slumbering banks were arousing themselves. In 1963, the Bank Act had been revised to allow banks to become more involved in consumer loans and mortgages for "ordinary Canadians." Within a year, banks were moving aggressively in both areas, taking direct aim at credit unions and mortgage companies. Reacting to that competition would be much more difficult for credit unions, though far from impossible. It would be the marketplace challenge of the future – indeed, it continues to the present day and shows no sign of diminishing.

Reacting to the new realities, however, would require even greater change within credit unions. For example, since the early 1940s, the movement had grown by opening new credit unions in new locations. By the mid-1960s, this was becoming difficult. Credit unions had been developed in most B.C. communities. There were some possibilities for organizing more closed-bond credit unions, but even this possibility was not as easily pursued as before. The reality was that the map was largely filled, demonstrated by the fact that growth in membership in credit unions was starting to slow down. If credit unions were to continue to expand, it would have to come primarily through growing larger, through appealing to new constituencies.

The challenge, therefore, was to decide how credit unions could expand on a local level, an issue fraught with turmoil since it would lead – indeed, was already starting to lead – to acrimonious competition among credit unions. It would also lead inevitably to continual change in the way that credit unions related to their members. And it would mean reconsidering how to allocate the resources that had been accumulated on a provincial basis. How should the movement structure and support its provincial organizations so they could meet needs efficiently yet within the social mandate of the movement? It was an issue that would dominate the last half of the sixties – and in a sense it would never be fully resolved.

38. Robinson and Johnson, "An Economic Appraisal of Credit Unions in British Columbia," pp. 6-7.

Uniting
1966-1970

> ...the credit unions of British Columbia will not long survive as some 223 separate, autonomous institutions, each one going its own way. Like it or not, the meaning of the "communications revolution" is that survival and growth lie in our ability to inter-relate, to co-operate, to act together and to build together, and to become part of our own "system." The focal point of the "system" is, and must be, B.C. Central Credit Union. And it is upon B.C. Central Credit Union that rests the major responsibility for the preservation and prosperity of our credit unions.

Board of Directors,
B.C. Central Credit Union[1]

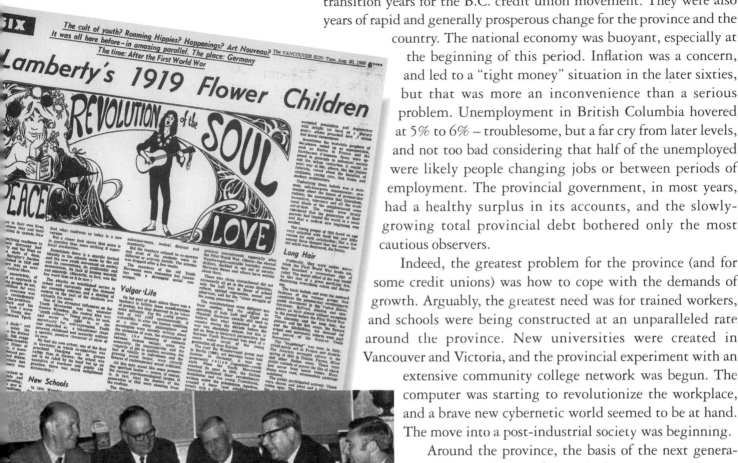

THE YEARS BETWEEN 1966 AND 1970 WERE IMPORTANT transition years for the B.C. credit union movement. They were also years of rapid and generally prosperous change for the province and the country. The national economy was buoyant, especially at the beginning of this period. Inflation was a concern, and led to a "tight money" situation in the later sixties, but that was more an inconvenience than a serious problem. Unemployment in British Columbia hovered at 5% to 6% – troublesome, but a far cry from later levels, and not too bad considering that half of the unemployed were likely people changing jobs or between periods of employment. The provincial government, in most years, had a healthy surplus in its accounts, and the slowly-growing total provincial debt bothered only the most cautious observers.

Indeed, the greatest problem for the province (and for some credit unions) was how to cope with the demands of growth. Arguably, the greatest need was for trained workers, and schools were being constructed at an unparalleled rate around the province. New universities were created in Vancouver and Victoria, and the provincial experiment with an extensive community college network was begun. The computer was starting to revolutionize the workplace, and a brave new cybernetic world seemed to be at hand. The move into a post-industrial society was beginning.

Around the province, the basis of the next generation's prosperity was being laid. Negotiations were completed and construction begun on the hydro-electric development of the Columbia and Peace rivers. The pulp and paper industry grew at rapid rates, the logging industry prospered, and the fishing industry enjoyed good years, although it was plagued by continuous labour disputes. British Columbia's trading potential with Japan was starting to be appreciated, even realized, with the development of joint ventures in the forest industries, the opening of the northern mining frontier, and the controversial construction of Roberts Bank. They were booming, tumultuous and confident years – characteristics that applied equally to the B.C. credit union movement.

In 1966, the province's credit unions numbered 287; they had some 276,000 members and $207-million in assets. By 1970, the number of credit unions had declined to 223, but they had more than 354,000 members – a 28% rise – and $346-million in assets – an increase of 67%.[2] The decline in the number of credit unions occurred because of the amalgamation of many smaller credit unions and the

1. "Credit Unions and the Future," Annual Report, B.C. Central Credit Union, 1970, p. 18.

2. Statistics based on Annual Report, B.C. Central Credit Union, 1973, p. 5.

absorption by larger credit unions of smaller units, especially in Vancouver, Prince Rupert, the Fraser Valley and Victoria.

This sudden and rapid decline in the number of credit unions was important on several levels. Perhaps above all, it represented a shift away from the original "American" model of relying as much as possible upon closed bonds, be they related to workplace, ethnicity or religion. In B.C., that model had served many credit unions well and would continue to do so for decades, particularly for certain employee groups and ethnic groups.

But, almost as a consequence of their structure, closed-bond credit unions could not respond effectively to the needs of large numbers of people. In fact, with mortgage lending becoming so important, many of them could not attract the deposits to meet the needs of their members. They had to turn increasingly to Central. Through syndication, Central accumulated funds from the deposit-strong credit unions for distribution to other credit unions, where they would be used for mortgage lending.

Many closed-bond credit unions also had difficulty generating the income to purchase the new technology required to offer the range of services that were increasingly in demand. In the changing society of the late 1960s, closed-bond credit unions would still have their place, but they no longer would be a driving force in the expansion of the movement.

The decline in the number of credit unions also represented a recognition by many of the provincial leaders that they had created far more credit unions than could be reasonably managed. It was simply impossible to provide the training for directors and management needed to operate more than 300 credit unions. This fact was recognized by all three provincial institutions – the League, Central and the Credit Union Reserve Board. In fact, all three encouraged rationalization of credit unions despite the "political" turmoil that sometimes ensued. There was a growing consensus within the provincial leadership that the future belonged to fewer, better-operated organizations: growth of successful credit unions was preferred to uncontrolled growth through new entities.

On the other hand, there were many reasons why well-operated community credit unions could expand easily. One key to their growth and change was their willingness to have flexible interest rates for both deposits and loans, especially mortgage loans. Another was the desire to attract more members, especially those wishing to build or purchase homes – a desire that made them particularly responsive to their neighbours.

For example, because many credit unions served people in agriculture and logging, they were sensitive to the needs of members wishing to have access to their accounts on Saturday – their day off from work, when many "went to town." Consequently, many credit unions were open for business on Saturday and closed on Mondays – an important benefit for members and one which clearly differentiated credit unions from banks. Another example was open-ended mortgages, first offered by Vancouver City Savings in 1960. Being able to pay off a mortgage as fast as one wished could mean immense savings for a family. By their very nature, community credit unions in the sixties and seventies were very close to their members. Inevitably they benefited from that relationship – whenever they chose to cultivate it.

Throughout the years, credit unions made a special effort to support local youth sports teams, such as this peewee team sponsored by Kootenay Savings Credit Union in the late 1960s.

That does not mean that all community-bond credit unions moved easily or quickly into full-time participation in the marketplace. Doing so, in fact, usually required a lot of soul searching, as significant change always does in any co-operative. Expansion meant opening branches, more depersonalized service, more control for managers, and less influence for directors. Above all, reacting to the needs of members meant that community-based credit unions had to enter the marketplace aggressively in order to gain the funds to make loans, especially mortgage loans. Consequently, the focus was increasingly drawn outward; for a while, at least, it would not be as inward, concentrating on a known membership base, as before.

And credit unions had a golden opportunity. While banks and other financial institutions were starting to discuss making mortgage loans to the general population, in fact they rarely did so, especially in the small communities and even in many of the growing suburbs. Indeed, housing was becoming a serious national problem and it was particularly acute in parts of British Columbia.

Most of the housing in which credit unions invested consisted of single-family homes, but a few credit unions became interested in co-operative housing. In fact, one of the first continuing co-op housing projects was begun by Abbotsford Credit Union in 1969, largely through the efforts of Glen Haddrell, then the assistant general manager of the credit union. Subsequently, he went on to become one of the founders of the national co-op housing movement.

If credit unions were going to meet the more general, rapidly-growing borrowing needs of most of their members, however, they would ultimately have to change significantly. At first, they had the advantage. In the mid-1960s, they were probably the most efficient financial organizations in British Columbia, perhaps in Canada.[3] They paid their employees relatively low salaries, especially for the responsibilities they shouldered, and they generally had lower overhead charges to pay.

This was a temporary advantage, however, which would soon be lost as they grew larger and, ultimately, as other financial institutions became more involved in mortgage lending.

The challenge of change was exacerbated by the fact that the world of family finance was changing rapidly. "Involuntary savings", in the form of pension plans, health insurance and disability insurance, reduced disposable income but provided long-term security for individuals and families. This change – sometimes called the "riskless society" in the 1960s – became obvious across many employee groups and professions. It encouraged individuals and families to borrow money to meet expanding consumer needs and wishes. With the absolutely necessary requirements being provided for automatically, why not borrow for a second car, a cottage and better kitchen appliances? For a steadily growing number of Canadians, consumerism was becoming a way of life. Credit unions played their role in encouraging that social revolution.

In the late 1960s, Westcoast Savings Credit Union was in the forefront of technological change. *Above*, Rodger Lutz, May Campbell (one of the most prominent elected leaders in the movement at the time), Ron Dumont, a fellow director, and branch manager Ted Wright examine a new Burroughs machine.

The revolution tended, often in dramatic ways, to create differences among the generations generally and in credit unions specifically. People who had grown up in the 1930s were particularly hesitant to borrow money. They did so only for emergencies or for the major expenditures of a lifetime – a house, cars, possibly education. That reluctance to borrow was not so obvious among those who matured in the sixties.

The opening of job opportunities all across the province encouraged mobility, and mobility meant expenditures and, often, debt. On the other hand, it also meant income levels previously unknown in many families – income levels that made paying off debt relatively easy. Credit also became more readily available through department store credit cards and the forerunners of Visa and MasterCard. For an increasing number of Canadians, the issue became not how to avoid debt, but how to manage it.

This change quickly affected the lending practices of credit unions, nearly all of which moved away from insisting that loans should be made only for providential purposes. For example, many credit unions offered "accommodation loans," temporary loans of $10 to $50, loans that could tide individuals and families over to the next payday. In an earlier age, credit unions would probably have stressed thrift and been less willing to accommodate bad management of personal finances, as it would often have been construed. The heavy hand of the Great Depression was beginning to loosen its grip.

3. Robinson and Johnson, "An Economic Appraisal of Credit Unions in British Columbia," pp. 38-40.

Indeed, a new generation of leaders began to emerge in the later 1960s, a group of individuals who would significantly change the movement at that time and in the succeeding decades. One of these was George May. He was a dynamic, resourceful and determined leader who came into the movement from Richmond Savings Credit Union. In Richmond, he had gained prominence in local politics, and he had established a broad range of business and political contacts across the Greater Vancouver area. Once elected to the board of Richmond Savings, he quickly embarked on a career as an elected official in the League. By 1968, he was its president. In many ways, he would dominate the provincial movement from the late 1960s to 1978.

Another new leader was Geoff Hook, who had started his career in 1950 as an accountant at B.C. Co-op Wholesale. He had responsibility for the accounting and latterly management agreements of some 20 consumer co-operatives scattered around the province. In that position, he met frequently with Rip Robinson and for many years he served on the board of Vancouver City Savings Credit Union. In 1965, after Robinson had retired, he became Central's general manager. He was a strong, conservative, organized and dedicated credit unionist who brought modern management techniques to Central, then to the Credit Union Reserve Board and ultimately to VanCity. He would have a major impact on the movement in the succeeding 25 years.

Two of the new "movers and shakers" of the period: *Above*, George May; *Right*, Peter Podovinikoff.

There were others. Aj Gill, for example, came from a New Westminster family that had successfully operated an innovative, national transportation firm – not an easy task amid the provincial and national regulations of the day. Perhaps because of that background, Gill tended to think regionally, pragmatically and flexibly. Above all, he was entrepreneurial. Trained in commerce at UBC, he had a strong predilection for professionalism and a corresponding suspicion of the "amateurism" on which many credit unions were based. Clearly, he believed that the credit union movement offered immense possibilities for the accumulation of capital resources, resources that could be employed in numerous ways around the rapidly-growing province.

Gill started his credit union career in the early 1960s with Lake View Credit Union in Dawson Creek, where managerial problems had created a negative situation. His assistant at Lake View was Rodger Lutz, who would go on to manage Westcoast Savings Credit Union in

Victoria. During the 1970s, the two of them often found themselves on opposite sides on several issues, especially the growth of Central. Gill was elected to the League's board in 1966, and he soon became one of its most active members. Articulate and bright, he seemed, for some, to represent the kind of leader the movement required.

Another newcomer was Peter Podovinikoff from Grand Forks. An ebullient, articulate and idealistic credit unionist, he had grown up in a Doukhobour family with a strong commitment to co-operative activities. After attending business college in Vancouver, he gained employment in the local co-op store, an experience that helped make him an advocate of co-operatives throughout his career. In 1961, he was hired by the local credit union in Grand Forks and soon became its manager.

Within the credit union, Podovinikoff was involved in trying to bring together the deeply divided factions of the Grand Forks community. The activities of the Freedomite sect in the area had divided the Doukhobour community, which, in turn, had been somewhat estranged from other groups in the town. The credit union, whose first member and president was a Japanese-Canadian, became an important agency for coping with the community's turmoil and for bringing people together. Podovinikoff was deeply involved in that process, and he learned the arts of listening and conciliation well – arts that would be among his greatest gifts when the difficulties of the late 1970s emerged in the credit union movement.

Podovinikoff was elected to the League's board in 1966, and he quickly established himself as one of its dominant figures. His support for the co-operative enterprises associated with Central was strong, and by the end of the decade he was becoming well-known in co-operative circles across the country. In 1976, he became manager of Delta Credit Union, which he promptly propelled into a period of rapid growth. Podovinikoff was a successful credit union manager, one of the few in the sixties to earn his accountancy degree. In the process he became known as an advocate of "growing" credit unions, a commitment that placed him among the leaders of the emerging consensus within the movement.

May, Hook, Gill and Podovinikoff joined with a wave of newcomers to make a significant impact on the movement's provincial organizations as the 1960s came to an end. But not all the innovators were young. Some of the older leaders were coming to believe that a drastic change in the provincial credit union system was necessary. Stan Stonier and A.H. Moxon, both of whom had served as elected officials of the League for many years, were proponents of change. On Central's board, Wes Darling and John Lucas were sympathetic to change. But perhaps the most convinced advocate for reformation among directors of the provincial organizations was Rod Glen.

By nature, Glen was a restless, continuously "driven" individual. No matter what had been accomplished, he would always aspire to do more. Glen was also typical of the reformism of the 1960s. He was deeply influenced by liberal reformism in the United States, epitomized for him by Jerry Voorhis, Ralph Nader and Hubert Humphrey, all of whom he knew to varying degrees. By the late 1960s, Glen believed that North American society was at an important crossroads. All of the unprecedented economic power that had been accumulated in North America since World War Two would either be harnessed in the general interest or it would be increasingly controlled by a few.

For Glen, the co-operative movement was one of the best ways to democratize economic power, but he was interested not only in local influence; he was also committed to amassing power at provincial, national and international levels. He reflected some of his long-term commitment, combativeness and optimism in an article he wrote for an American credit union magazine in 1968.

> There will be few times of tranquility for us. There will be no relief from harassment and no haven from problems. Our movement is now truly a part of mankind, perhaps relatively small in its size and present impact, but growing in importance. To keep it so is our goal....[4]

All of these individuals were significantly different from each other. They were characterized, however, by a commitment to greater efficiency, a more integrated movement, and an increased level of professionalism. In that sense, they reflected the emerging generation of leaders that was starting to appear in local credit unions. Individuals like Don Bentley at VanCity, Rodger Lutz (ultimately at Westcoast Savings), Del Taylor at Abbotsford and then Fraser Valley, and Louis van der Gracht at Richmond Savings were all starting to "grow" their credit unions in the late sixties. Similar leaders could be found among managers outside of the larger cities. Among these leaders were Helmut Krueger at Kootenay Savings, Bud Berner at Alberni, Vince DeVries at Victoria Public, Bernie Proft at East Chilliwack, Harry Down at Saanich Peninsula, and Georgie Blackie at Vernon. Many of the new managers came from finance companies, which were then beginning a rapid decline because of increasing competition from the banks. From this background, they brought with them stronger lending skills and knowledge, thereby helping to confront delinquency problems in many credit unions.[5]

One of the movement's most creative leaders was Don Bentley, who became VanCity's manager in 1955. A native of Saskatchewan, he was trained as an accountant, and had previously been employed with the fishing co-operatives. Bentley was financially conservative, but very innovative, and he had a strong commitment to the welfare of the

Don Bentley, widely regarded by his peers as among the most innovative and effective managers of the period, was the individual arguably most responsible for the rapid early expansion of Vancouver City Savings Credit Union.

4. Rod Glen, "Knowledge is the key to power," *Credit Union Magazine*, June, 1968, p. 4.

5. Interview with Barry Forbes, Chief Executive Officer, Westminster Savings Credit Union, September 8, 1995.

credit union membership. He spearheaded VanCity's expansionist endeavours, and by 1970 the credit union had 13 branches. Under his leadership, VanCity pioneered several savings plans for its members. Bentley had an active, imaginative and diverse Board of Directors to work with. VanCity's commitment to growth would become a powerful model for other credit unions in the 1970s: it became the principal example of what a strong community credit union could do.

Such promoters of change were buttressed by a series of reports on the B.C. movement in the mid-1960s. The first report was triggered by the withdrawal of 12 credit unions from the League between 1961 and 1964. At the League's 1964 convention, which was quite acrimonious, delegates instructed the board to examine the reasons for their departure. The board hired Dr. Cyril Belshaw, a UBC sociologist, to undertake the study. He reported in June, 1965.[6]

To a large extent, the departures were explained by animosities aroused by the CUNA Mutual insurance issue. In 1961, the League's board had declared that it was acceptable for Co-op Life to write loan protection and savings life insurance business in the province, as long as it did not actively solicit the business. In response, CUNA Mutual said that it would accept business from credit unions not affiliated with the League, contrary to its usual practice. That decision, in turn, made it easier for credit unions to withdraw – and some did. Belshaw pleaded for a business-like approach to these issues and a transcending of the personality conflicts that had contributed significantly to them.

Belshaw pleaded similarly for a business-like approach to the relationship with co-operatives, an increasingly divisive issue. He called for a reformation of the electoral process, so that League directors would more systematically represent the different regions and the different types of credit unions. He called for more effective annual meetings. He warned that the directors in many credit unions were increasingly being dominated by managers. He questioned why credit unions were not doing more to help the underprivileged in Canadian society. He suggested that credit unions had to have more powers, but recommended that the movement work with government to improve the inspection process, before gaining those powers. He called for an independent analysis to see how credit unions might better organize themselves to compete in a rapidly-changing environment. At the same time, he recognized that there were differences in size, scope and purpose among credit unions in British Columbia, and he pleaded for tolerance of those differences – rather than assuming that the ways pursued by one's own credit union were necessarily the only or the best ways for organizations to operate.

It was a controversial and hard-hitting report that criticized the League's board of being too "cliquish" and self-perpetuating, while

6. "Credit Unions in British Columbia," Report of Dr. Cyril S. Belshaw, June, 1965, BCCCU Archives.

accusing the League's critics of being too harsh and parochial. It was so controversial that it received rather short discussion at the 1965 convention. It was not ignored, however, because it had put the spotlight on the need for the provincial movement to think seriously about how it should be best organized, what its priorities should be, and how it could best prepare for increased competition. These challenges were continuously remembered as the decade unfolded.

The second report was prepared in 1966 by Stevenson & Kellogg, a management consultant firm. It too was a major catalyst for change in the B.C. movement. It called for "one voice for all credit unions" in the province, a single voice that would have a special responsibility to expand communications vertically and horizontally. It would work to secure modern promotional techniques and would strive to provide improved financial services. It would be built on regional bases of strength that would seek to reduce competition among credit unions and expand their capacity to work together.[7] In short, it called for the amalgamation of the League and Central into a single entity that would be the "hub" for the provincial movement.

Because of legal complexities in converting the League into a financial body, the report recommended that Central become the umbrella organization. It also proposed a revised structure for the new organization: there would be six regions, each with a regional committee elected by the constituent credit unions. The electoral system, following the pattern established in recent changes to the Co-operative Associations Act, would be proportional, based on the number of members in each credit union.

The third report was prepared by Aj Gill. In 1967, he chaired a committee for the League's board that looked into the problems facing local credit unions.[8] His report called for increased standardization, especially among the larger credit unions. He believed, as did many within the movement, that credit unions were losing some of their potential effectiveness because they did not provide a common front to the public. Signs were different, products could vary, and policies were not the same. Moreover, a member could not move easily from one credit union to another. If credit unions were going to build on each others' strengths and create maximum efficiency on behalf of their members, they would have to work more closely together.

Gill, having inherited a difficult situation at Lake View and having talked with a number of managers throughout the system, was also concerned about the increasingly intimidating challenges confronting managers. He believed that managers were being called on to undertake too many different kinds of activities, particularly since so many of them were inadequately prepared. He was accurate in that assessment because almost all of the managers of the period were individuals

7. Stevenson & Kellogg Report and files, BCCCU Archives.

8. Gill Committee Report and files, BCCCU Archives.

who had learned on the job. Typically, they were individuals who had been attracted to the position, many of them having initially served on boards of directors, without first understanding the complexities of managing financial institutions. In a very real sense the management of credit unions was inevitably changing, forcing managers to focus less on the details of the credit union's operations and more on how to select and motivate people around them. It was a process that several did not survive.

Gill's strongest point, though, was that the movement was fragmented, lacking a strong central focus and a clear identity. He was also very critical of the way in which the provincial system reached conclusions, and he was scornful of the political process that it used. His solution to such problems was the creation of a single credit union for British Columbia, an idea that had been mooted about the province since at least 1960. The proposed new entity would be based on local advisory committees that would replace boards and be responsible for selecting representatives to regional committees. In turn, the regional committees would elect directors to a single central board for the provincial system.

Gill believed that such an organization could lead government to reduce its inspection activities significantly, along with the associated inconvenience and expense. Most importantly, though, it would offer the kind of consistency and professionalism he believed to be missing in the existing provincial system. It was, needless to say, a controversial vision that sparked considerable debate, although it ultimately gained some support, especially among managers of a few large credit unions. The report, however, also antagonized many credit union leaders, who felt that Gill had underestimated the importance of local communities, as well as the value of ensuring that member diversity was adequately represented. It nevertheless was a vision that did not die, even though its original supporters were few in number.

The drive for change, though, did not surface simply because a series of reports were written. One strong impetus came from the activities of the Credit Union Reserve Board, which was managed between 1965 and 1970 by Rip Robinson. Every year, the Reserve Board, along with the Inspector's Office and to some extent the League, became aware of credit unions that were suffering from different kinds of problems.

In a few instances, the root of the problems was dishonesty, and in other cases it was the economic decline of single-resource communities. Most often, however, the problems were the result of inadequately trained managers and boards. In any given year, between 20 and 30 credit unions were in some difficulty and needed some form of assistance. This was a situation that naturally perturbed many leaders, even though many of the problems were easily resolved.

The sense of urgency to make changes was also encouraged by the way in which the Canadian banking industry was beginning to change. In the first place, there were now more banks. In 1966, the province had created its own bank, the Bank of British Columbia, which appealed to regional pride in much the same way as did credit unions; for many credit unionists, it posed a potential threat to their future. The Bank of Western Canada made its appearance, and there were rumours that the Province of Alberta would soon create its own banks.

Even more ominously, the established banks were reconsidering their own situation, and were gradually paying attention to small depositors and borrowers, people they had previously ignored. In 1967, the Bank Act was amended, liberalizing restrictions on the ability of banks to offer competitive interest rates. Soon, for the first time in Canada, there was some apparent competition on rates, competition that would become very intense within a few years.

There were even signs that banks were starting to think about how they could become "friendly" institutions rather than the cold, impersonal businesses they had seemed to be for so many Canadians. Bank architecture began to change, plastic replaced mock Grecian pillars, teller lines became less formidable, walls were painted in colours other than bone white. Local branches began to sponsor baseball teams, and the use of alluring advertising – depicting red convertibles and exotic holiday locations – became common.

All of these changes indicated that the banks and trust companies, given more freedom by the new legislation, were beginning to change: they were offering more kinds of accounts, longer opening hours, and easier credit. By the later sixties, although credit union membership and assets were continuing to grow in British Columbia, other financial institutions were growing more rapidly. This increasing competition, plus the fact that the number of credit unions was declining rapidly, meant the future was more uncertain, the present more difficult.

One aspect of the increased competition from banks across the country was the emergence of the Canada Deposit Insurance Corporation. Recommended by the Porter Commission in its 1964 Report, the CDIC was an attempt to provide a stable base for banking and to protect depositors from bank failures. In 1967, the federal government announced plans to develop a fund for such a corporation, which would insure deposits up to a maximum of $20,000. It represented a potential problem for credit unions since, as provincially-incorporated institutions, they would not be able to join. In the competition for deposits, the credit unions could be at a disadvantage if they did not have a similar guarantee.

During 1967 and 1968, therefore, representatives of the League, Central and the Credit Union Reserve Board met together and with representatives of the Attorney-General's department. By early 1968, they had prepared a proposal to create a provincial guarantee fund. The fund would guarantee all deposits to 100%, a considerable advantage over the CDIC guarantee – and an indication that credit unions were competing more than before for larger depositors.

Protecting the security of the fund meant that credit unions would have to increase their annual contributions to CURB, but there was relatively little opposition among credit unions to doing so. Somewhat more controversial was the corollary that the movement would have to accept more careful monitoring. In the first place, that meant the Inspector's Office would have to have more powers of inspection and supervision. Second, CURB would be given a stronger role to play, an issue for some since its board was controlled by the provincial government, not the movement. This changed relationship with government, within the context of a greater emphasis on accountability, meant that credit unions were facing greater scrutiny and more regulation. The reins were getting tighter.[9]

Credit unions were beginning to change rapidly in the 1960s, creating issues and uncertainties for managers and directors alike. By 1970, the approximately 220 credit unions in the province employed about 600 people, with women accounting for two-thirds of this work force.[10] The vast majority of credit unions employed two or three people; only a few employed more than five or six. In many credit unions, staff still performed their duties manually, using only an adding machine. As the sixties drew to a close, a growing number purchased posting machines, but they were still in a distinct minority until the 1970s, when almost all – certainly all that were open regularly – purchased these machines or even newer technology. In the process, the credit union workplace began to change rapidly.

If one could turn back the clock and walk into a typical credit union in the early 1960s, one would probably see a relatively small lobby, two or three teller cages, a desk or two behind them, a row of books at the back of the room in which member records were kept, a safe (perhaps the most imposing feature of the room), and probably an office for the secretary-treasurer. The tellers would invariably be women, since in those days custom decreed that it was not "man's work." In fact, credit unions were very much influenced by women in their formative periods. Most of the women were tellers – as they were then called – and tellers were central to the operation of the credit union in ways that would be less influential as the organizations grew larger. In the first place, a woman enjoyed considerable status as a teller in the 1960s and early 1970s. The work was challenging, it was

1. Outline Process Chart

Subject: Accounting – *Manual method*

1. Business transacted — teller
2. Docts. arr. in a/c # seq — teller
3. Transactions taped — teller
4. Transactions posted to c/d sheets — teller
5. c/d sheets taped/balance — head teller
6. c/d sheets posted to subsid., ledger — machine operator
7. c/d sheets posted to synoptic — accountant

2. Relationship Chart

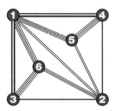

1. Members
2. Manager
3. Loan Officer
4. Accountant
5. Tellers
6. Secretary

Closeness

Reason

3. Relationship Diagram

9. For a fuller account of these discussions, see Mike Youds and Pixie McGeachie, *A History of the Credit Union Deposit Insurance Corporation of British Columbia* (Vancouver: Credit Union Deposit Insurance Corporation of British Columbia, 1985), pp. 28-30

10. Convention Proceedings, 1970, B.C. Central Credit Union, Appendix "F", p. 3.

Reflecting a more analytical approach to management, business processes and staff-member relationships are depicted in charts, *upper left*.

Left and above, typical teller lines and tellers in the later 1960s.

"responsible," and it commanded respect. Tellers would be well known in the community, especially in communities where credit unions had strong and extensive bonds of association. Almost invariably, too, they would know more about financial matters than the people they served, particularly before banking became so influenced by advertising and competition over rates and services – a growing characteristic from the 1970s onward.

Nor was the work of tellers as routine as it would become. Normally, they started work at 9 AM and probably spent the first hour sorting cancelled cheques and preparing for the opening. At ten o'clock, the door would be opened, often to a line-up of people who had shopped or picked up the mail after dropping their children off at school. Lunch-time could also be busy, as could the closing time – which was usually at 5 PM, two hours later than the banks. After closing, the tellers had to check the balances, with the rule generally being that no one went home until everyone "balanced."[11]

Perhaps more importantly, tellers in the 1960s and 1970s worked on a variety of tasks. There was a limited range of deposit and borrowing accounts to be maintained and understood; interest rates did not vary by more than fractions of one percentage point during a year, so there was little difficulty in keeping "on top of the job." An ambitious teller, therefore, could master the savings, share and endowment accounts easily, and then, if she wished, go on to learn about lending. In fact, as credit unions grew, a lot of the lending was done by women who learned the business in the intertwined activities of the late 1960s and early 1970s. This integration of duties was one of the ways credit unions differed from the banks, especially the increasingly common large bank branches, where separation of duties became the norm, limitation of responsibility the rule.

The relatively significant role that women played in the 1960s may also have made a difference in lending practice. By reputation, at least, women were more inclined to lend to other women, a practice that was most uncommon in banks. Indeed, in 1960, VanCity became the first financial institution in the province, perhaps in the country, that would lend to a woman in her own name – a practice apparently replicated throughout the movement. Female loans officers may also have been more willing still to take into account the character of borrowers, and they may have been less inclined to rely on statistical summaries as the chief way to evaluate a potential borrower.[12]

Moreover, the opportunity to learn lending meant that a significant number of women went on to higher positions as credit unions grew. Some became controllers, a crucial position when credit unions began to expand. Others, perhaps as many as 40, became secretary-treasurers

11. This description is based on the following interviews by the author: Marion Holmes, Delta Credit Union, September 10, 1994; Teresa Freeborn, B.C. Central Credit Union, September 9, 1994.

12. Holmes interview.

in the late 1960s. And, in many growing credit unions, numerous women became loans officers after beginning their careers on the "teller line"; in those days, one would search far and wide within the banks to find women in the same position.

This picture of a typical credit union began to change during the late 1960s, at least for those that started to grow rapidly. In large part, the change was shaped by technology and in most instances it was led by men. In particular, all of the very aggressive community credit unions were managed by men, a tendency that meant the 30 to 40 female managers were in charge of slower growing organizations.

One of the common ways the more dynamic credit unions pushed forward was through the adoption of new and better machines. The typical early credit union, described above, was a labour-intensive organization. Account records were kept by hand, and the emphasis was on avoiding human error. The main tasks were to make sure that member deposits and withdrawals were recorded accurately and that interest credits and charges were calculated correctly. In short, it was the kind of business that new technologies could transform almost overnight.

During the later 1950s and the 1960s, many credit unions relied on a range of posting machines, but these only made final daily and monthly calculations easier to establish; they did not significantly change the way in which the business was done. Nevertheless, without posting machines, it was difficult for a credit union to grow beyond $4-million in assets or to serve more than a few hundred members. That was true even though the new machines still required a great deal of manual entry, especially at certain times of the month. Nor did they allow for frequent, reliable calculation of member interest – payments or credits – or easily furnished statements on demand. That is why the computer seemed tailor-made for the banking business to those who took note of the new devices as they emerged.

Much of the early interest in computers within the B.C. co-operative movement was focused, with good reason, within CU&C Health Services. A crucial part of that company's business was to maintain its members' health-care records. Consequently, as computers became more common in the province during the 1960s, CU&C began to experiment with them. In 1964, it started to provide data processing services for five credit unions. These developments were viewed with interest by some credit union managers, notably Don Bentley of VanCity and Louis van der Gracht of Richmond Savings. Some of the League's leaders were also interested in the possibilities of using CU&C's computer, but the task of organizing the diverse interests and degrees of enthusiasm was overwhelming.

Encouraged by the computer's potential, B.C. Central – along with VanCity, B.C. Co-op Wholesale, CU&C, Gulf & Fraser Fishermen's

Credit Union and Prince Rupert Fishermen's Credit Union – organized Central Data Systems (CDS) in 1967. Don Bentley was one of the driving forces behind its creation. His interest was triggered by his desire to create a fairer and more accurate way to pay and to charge interest. In 1967, under his leadership, VanCity introduced Plan 24, a daily interest savings account. It was probably the first such account in North America. More importantly, it was a very significant benefit for depositors who previously had been paid interest on the minimum monthly or even minimum six-monthly balance. For that reason, Plan 24 garnered remarkable publicity for VanCity and, as it was adopted by most credit unions during the 1970s, for the movement as a whole.

Indeed, in the view of some, Plan 24 was one of the main reasons that credit unions prospered over the next decade. It was a very clear illustration that they were different, and it demonstrated the value of diversity and decentralization. It also had the inestimable advantage of being obviously more honest. And, on the other side of the business, it had the very significant benefit of helping greatly in attracting deposits and in overcoming the "tight money" problem of the period.

The advent of the computer was viewed, however, as a mixed blessing. The League's board mused on the computer's impact in its final report to the membership in 1969:

> The sudden growth of technology has created philosophical problems of the first magnitude. Old customs have crumbled, the relationships between members and credit unions, between management and members of credit unions, have been and are changing rapidly.
>
> Technology has the wider effect of changing the physical environment in which we operate and we must adjust ourselves to the changed surroundings. The movement's dilemma arises from the ever-widening disparity in terms of accomplishment and of magnitude of consequences between the physical inventions and the movement's social adaptation to the new conditions which the inventions create.[13]

All of these changes in credit unions at the local level reinforced the drive for change at the provincial level. By 1968, a significant proportion of the leadership was convinced that the Stevenson & Kellogg Report was correct in recommending amalgamation of the League and Central. A joint League-Central committee had started to work on the issues associated with amalgamation in 1966, shortly after the report had been received. As it proceeded through its work, the committee was able to introduce some of its recommendations, notably a regional structure and an advisory council based on that structure, both in 1967. Its work, however, was very complicated and controversial. By

13. "Directors' Report to the 1969 Convention of the B.C. Credit Union League," Annual Report '69, B.C. Credit Union League, p. 16.

1968, meetings were being held virtually every week, at nights, on weekends, whenever it was necessary and possible.

The driving forces behind the push toward amalgamation were in the League, and Rod Glen was the most important of those individuals. Glen had a vision that a combined League and Central would create an organization of immense power. He saw the amalgamation as an opportunity to build a focal point for a cohesive co-operative movement that could profoundly influence the future of British Columbia.

For Glen and others, the League was handicapped by the fact that it had to rely on dues to fund all its activities. An institution with a wide range of business activities operating at the provincial level could become a significant bank; it could also be a powerful instrument for reform, able to marshal the social power in co-operatives and, thereby, to tackle many of the emerging and pressing social issues of the day. For others within the League, notably George May, the interest was more in the possibilities of the power that the provincial credit union assets could create, but to some extent they shared Glen's vision as well.

As the committee's work progressed, many of the credit unions that had left the League returned to membership. The area that had always been least inclined to support the League had been the East Kootenays. In part, its reluctance to participate had been a consequence of the insurance debates that had been waged since the 1950s. CUNA and CUNA Mutual representatives, notably Jack Burns, Bob McLaughlin and George Sterling, had strong supporters in the area. The tension became so great that members of the League's field staff would not even visit some of the East Kootenay credit unions.

Dissatisfaction with Central and, especially, the League was often put forward most vociferously by East Kootenay credit union leaders. One of these was Ace Bailey of Trail Credit Union, an intimidating man who had been a hockey star with the Toronto Maple Leafs. He believed that very little good could come from Vancouver and seemed to be convinced that the League was being run by communists. Thus when Trail and Rossland, another strong critic of the League, rejoined in the late 1960s, it marked the beginning of the end of the long-standing insurance debate within the B.C. movement.

When credit unions delegates met in a special meeting in Penticton in June, 1969, to consider a recommendation for amalgamation, only six credit unions were not members of the League. In retrospect, the meeting was remarkably quiet, given the turmoil of the recent years. There were questions about the proposed dues schedule, the value of shares, types of shares, liquidity management, and terms for directors. The only issue that seemed to create controversy was the size of the Board of Directors, hardly a fundamental issue. There was no serious questioning of the desirability of amalgamation, and the two

During the later 1960s, work within credit unions began to change, largely because of new machines and procedures, especially with the arrival of posting machines.

14. Annual Report, B.C. Central Credit Union, 1966, p. 3.

boards were instructed to finalize the proposed amalgamation agreement. Somewhat begrudgingly for some, one suspects, but almost universally it seems, the movement had come to believe that a single organization would secure a better future.

But what was the nature of the two organizations that the movement's leadership had voted to bring together? Most obviously, by the late 1960s, they were significantly different from each other. The Central was a cautiously-managed, disciplined organization, circumspectly involved in a few activities. Its board was led through much of the period by Ian Strang, John Lucas, Geoff Hook and Wes Darling. All four were strong, dedicated credit unionists, and well-respected throughout the movement. Neither Strang nor Lucas was initially in favour of amalgamation. Like Geoff Hook, they tended to think it was preferable to keep the "business" side of the movement separate from the "philosophical" or trade association organization.

Wes Darling was somewhat more sympathetic, and his support was important. He was then the manager of Vancouver Federal Employees Credit Union, and one of six managers on Central's board. He had a long history of involvement in the movement, beginning in the late 1930s when he and his father had been associated with the Common Good Co-operative. He had been involved in numerous Central and League activities ever since. Darling would play an important, conciliatory role in the merger discussions as they took place.

In general, Central was in a strong financial position during the late 1960s. Virtually all credit unions belonged to it, as did more than 90 co-operatives. Nearly all of the credit unions and many of the co-operatives did business with the organization. By 1966, B.C. Central Credit Union had built up nearly $35-million in assets – in a movement that had more than $205-million.[14] By 1969, its assets had topped $53-million, compared with $335-million for the movement.

There were two managerial changes at Central in the mid-1960s. In 1965, Rip Robinson had retired, and was replaced briefly by Ray Ferry. Robinson had made a major contribution to the B.C. movement in his years as manager. He was efficient and cautious, and these qualities contributed to the financial success the organization achieved. In many ways, however, his most important contribution was derived from his diplomatic skills and popularity. He was a tireless traveller who spent much of his time in the field, working with credit union secretary-treasurers and building support for Central. In fact, his constant travelling no doubt contributed to the two heart attacks that led him to retire.

Late in 1965, Geoff Hook became Central's chief executive officer (as the manager's position then became known). While similar to Robinson in his fiscally conservative approach to management, Hook belonged to a new generation of managers. He was well-informed about modern money management and about analyses of credit unions. Under his direction, Central became a more professional organization, with more continuous advisory communications with credit unions. Hook was also more concerned about strategic issues concerning rates and investments.

Soon after becoming CEO, Hook moved Central's operations to 510 West Hastings Street in downtown Vancouver. At the time, Central was becoming a steadily larger organization. One of its most important activities was cheque-clearing, work that was done largely by hand. In 1965, Central purchased its first machines for sorting cheques.

The annual meetings of Central were invariably polite and business-like. They were also brief, seldom lasting for more than half a day. In contrast, the League's annual conventions lasted three days and the delegates never quite said all they wanted to say. The issues were frequently broad, the demands for action carried the League into all kinds of activities, and the debates were remembered with relish (at least by some) even 30 years later. The individuals most prominent in the League – Rod Glen, George May, Aj Gill, Peter Podovinikoff – were all forceful, articulate and passionate. In their different ways they were struggling to prod the movement to take advantage of the golden future they believed it could have.

During the late sixties, the League undertook a variety of new activities and expanded on some of the old ones. In 1968, because of increasing demands for advisory services, the League appointed a regional district representative in the Okanagan. This project was the first attempt at co-ordinating regional credit union activities so they could be integrated and consistent.[15] In the same year, the League started a Collection Department to assist local credit unions in an area where they seemed to have considerable difficulty.[16]

To help local credit unions even further, the League began an extensive program of organized assistance. It employed a field staff of four people who undertook between five and ten operational analyses each year. These analyses examined management procedures, employee training, technological requirements and business efficiency on a fee-for-service basis. The staff also advised on the construction of new buildings, the opening of branches and the purchase of equipment. Finally, they conducted training programs, particularly for staff in smaller credit unions. Much of this training was conducted in collaboration with Western Co-op College, sometimes in British Columbia, but often at the college's new premises in Saskatoon.

The Supplies Department of the League (and, after 1970, Central) provided a wide range of supplies for member credit unions. It is significant that, by the later 1960s, the department had to remind large as well as small credit unions that it could meet all their needs.

15. Convention Proceedings, 1970, B.C. Central Credit Union, pp. 9-10.
16. Ibid., p. 8.

Credit unions in the Victoria area grew rapidly in the 1950s and 1960s. In 1958, when travelling to the Island was still inconvenient, Central had opened an office in Victoria. It was managed by Frank Humphrey, a tall, affable fieldman who left a significant mark on the Island's credit unions.

Credit unionists take a break from a 1961 training seminar at the UBC Department of Extension. The department's connection with credit unions and co-operatives dates back to the earliest days of the B.C. movement in the 1930s.

One of the common concerns perplexing the leadership of the League and Central in the later sixties was the lack of a clear image for credit unions in British Columbia. In 1968, the League hired Professor Frederick Webster of the University of British Columbia to prepare, distribute and interpret a questionnaire on how the public viewed the movement. The most obvious conclusion was that people had a blurred and inconsistent vision of credit unions – including many of those who were members. This particular finding reinforced a growing conviction among the League's directors that it was necessary to develop a provincial – and even a national – approach to advertising. That year, the League started a provincial advertising program, funded by dues. It was concerned essentially with "image" rather than "products"; it focused on particular events, such as the Apollo moon shot, and it was increasingly devoted to television advertising.

From the beginning and as always, the expenditure on advertising created some controversy. There are few activities in which more people believe they are experts and are therefore inclined to be critical. Some credit unions will always prefer to promote only their own activities. Some will always want more accountability in how the advertising decisions are made. At least some, in any given campaign, will dislike whatever advertisements are produced. Nevertheless, once begun, the advertising campaign was generally well received, and it was a concrete reaction to the growing problem of identity.

During this period, the League, along with Central and the Credit Union Reserve Board, increasingly supported the process to amalgamate credit unions. It therefore assisted credit unions considering this alternative, by providing advice and preparing reports. By the end of the decade, with this encouragement, between 15 and 20 credit unions each year were amalgamating or, more commonly, were being absorbed by larger credit unions. VanCity and Westcoast Savings in Victoria were particularly active in absorbing or purchasing credit unions – indeed, it was one of the chief explanations for why they grew so quickly in this period. The main reason so many smaller credit unions were

153

The End of an Era

On March 31, 1970, the British Columbia Credit Union League ceased to exist as a separate entity. Today its work is carried on under the name of the Credit Union Services Department of the BC Central Credit Union.

The move is part of a trend that has been taking place for a number of years not only locally and provincially but nationally and internationally. Today, the corporate structure of the world wide credit union movement is completely different to that of a few years ago.

Merging of the operations of the League with those of BC Central Credit Union concludes two years of studies, discussions, meetings and resolutions passed at general and special conventions of the two organizations.

Late last year the administrative offices of the League were moved to the same office building as BC Central Credit Union in downtown Vancouver. Next step in the development of the two organizaions into one will be the appointment of a general manager. At the present time work is underway and the selection is expected to be announced shortly.

For the average credit union member these moves will have little significance. For the credit unions' officers and staff, especially the managers, the merging of the League with BC Central Credit Union will mean a more effective provincial organization and the elimination of duplication of services in some areas of operations.

BC Central Credit Union came into being on May 25, 1944. Since that time its assets have increased from a modest $44,000 to more than $50 million.

BC Central Credit Union began as a credit union for credit unions — a place where local credit unions could deposit surplus funds or borrow extra money when required to better serve their own individual members.

Today the operations of BC Central Credit Union are much more than that of a central financial facility. It still accepts deposits from its member organizations, makes loans to them, provides clearing facilities for cheques and other negotiable items. In recent years it established a mortgage service to provide long term loans for housing; organized a retirement savings plan for individual members of credit unions; operates a computer facility to meet the needs of its member organizations for modern data processing. And now it includes all of the services formerly supplied by the BC Credit Union League — field service, promotion and development, insurance, printing and supplies, mailing, loan collections, legislation, etc.

BC Central Credit Union today is a truly full service organization for the credit unions of British Columbia.

Enterprise, April 1970

As the 1970s dawned, as the League and Central merged, the movement was in a dynamic phase. Early in the seventies, Central and some credit unions started sponsoring co-operative housing as depicted on the cover of *Enterprise, right. Above,* a booth at a late sixties convention provided information on the diverse services provided by the League.

Rod Glen *(second from the right)* joins colleagues from across Canada considering the reconstruction of the national movement.

ENTERPRISE

A MAGAZINE FOR CREDIT UNION MEMBERS · VOL. 28, NO. 9, OCTOBER 1968

OPERATION HOMEOWNER

B.C. delegates attend a meeting of CUNA International in Detroit. Jim Hewitt, *far left*, served as a fieldman for the League and went on to manage successfully in the Okanagan, before being elected to the B.C. Legislature and serving as a cabinet minister in the Social Credit government. Beside him, *left to right*, are Stan Stonier, Peter Podovinikoff and George May.

17. *B.C. Credit Unionist*, June, 1966, p. 10.

disappearing was their inability to meet the demands of members for increased services and funds; in a few instances, it was because of mismanagement.

The League and Central were engaged in different activities, had different internal cultures, and related in different ways to the provincial movement. They would not easily be brought together to form a cohesive whole, and the internal political issues would not be easily resolved. Nevertheless, their amalgamation – on March 31, 1970 – was a forward step, and it marked an important change in the provincial movement.

In the same years, the national and international movements were going through similar changes, and British Columbia's leaders, especially Rod Glen, played very significant roles in those changes. In particular, in the late 1960s, Glen started to make his major contribution to the international movement. In 1965, he helped in the restructuring of CUNA into CUNA International, a first step in recognizing the growing influence of credit unions outside the United States. Under this change, the movements in the United States and Canada would hold separate annual forums, as did District 12, which in the new system included representatives from credit unions in all other countries.

In 1966, Glen became president of CUNA International, the first non-American to achieve that rank. His election, by the largest majority in the history of CUNA to that point,[17] was partly a tribute to his work at several CUNA meetings. It was also an acknowledgement of the need to ensure that the CUNA organization adequately reflected the ideas and aspirations of credit unionists outside the United States. In particular, it represented a recognition of the role that B.C. credit unions had played in CUNA ever since the B.C. League had become the first non-American member in 1940.

In another sense, Glen represented a strong determination to restructure and revitalize the international movement. He was a leading figure in the formation of ICU Service Corporation, an attempt to provide systematic examinations of how local credit unions functioned and how services could best be provided for them. In his activities within this organization, Glen gained insights into the problems and challenges confronting credit unions, including some large and sophisticated organizations in the United States. He brought these insights back to Canada, and they influenced the way in which the provincial movement developed during the 1970s.

Glen also played an increasingly important role in assisting in the development of credit unions in the Caribbean, Latin America and Australia. Although these activities were occasionally criticized by some B.C. credit unionists, they became an important part of his life. Glen was one of the first B.C. leaders to recognize the global responsibilities and long-term possibilities of the international movement. He welcomed many international leaders to his home in Nanaimo, encouraged donations for international development through the Westcu Foundation, and encouraged international visitors to attend the annual conventions in B.C.

Perhaps Glen's greatest contribution to the international movement, however, occurred in 1968 and 1969 when he, along with others, carried out the restructuring of CUNA International. The new organization was a major step in recognizing that credit unions had spread beyond the United States and had taken on the needs, aspirations and convictions of people in other lands. The new organization, named the World Council of Credit Unions, would be governed by a 15-person board drawn from the various national movements.[18] It would hold major congresses every three years, and it would become in time a genuinely international organization.

These changes within the international movement coincided with similar changes in the English-Canadian movement. In 1958, the directors of the Canadian District of CUNA voted to incorporate as the National Association of Canadian Credit Unions (NACCU). It thus became a strictly Canadian entity, representing the credit union leagues in Canada that were associated with CUNA. It was nevertheless largely a forum for meeting and a place where Canadian credit union leaders could organize in preparation for meetings of CUNA, and therefore it was unfortunate that some Canadian credit union organizations were not affiliated. Thus, in 1966, NACCU's by-laws were changed to make it possible for all types of credit unions in the country to join, an important preliminary to forging a truly national organization. Glen and others hoped that it would be merely the first step in creating an integrated, aggressive national system.

At the same time, the Canadian Co-operative Credit Society, which served as a national clearing-house and lobbying organization, remained small and insufficiently used. Glen was among a small group in the late 1960s who believed it would be beneficial to unite the two organizations and begin a truly national effort on behalf of credit unions. This initiative was not unlike those in British Columbia that led to the amalgamation of the League and Central.

18. Moody and Fite, *The Credit Union Movement*, p. 349.

Indeed, the reasons were much the same: there was a need to utilize resources fully; there were many projects to be undertaken; there was a need for more professionalism; and there were advantages in having a clearly powerful central organization. These good reasons, however, were not in themselves sufficient to overcome quickly the localism and provincialism within the English-Canadian movement – but they would bear some fruit in the following decade.

And so, when the delegates to Central's 1970 convention gathered in Vernon in late June, some three months after the amalgamation, they were facing a decidedly different future for the provincial credit union movement. The previous five years had witnessed long, often intense debate over the future of the movement. The divisions that had appeared were understandable and significant. In many ways, they were related to the fundamental issue of what made credit unions distinctive. The essential rationale for the provincial credit union movement was changing.

Between the late 1930s and the early 1960s, a powerful underlying dynamic in B.C. credit unions had been the "emancipation" of ordinary people. This perspective had focused largely on people of limited means. It had sought, initially as much through education as good financial services, to liberate people from the effects of low incomes, inadequate financial services, and bad financial management. For some, too, the accumulation of money co-operatively was a prelude to other and broader co-operative endeavours. It was a powerful vision on which the idealistic efforts of many were based.

That vision could certainly still be found in the late sixties, most obviously in Rod Glen and his closest allies, but it was beginning to fade. The decline came partly because the co-operative roots were not as strong in B.C. as they were elsewhere, such as Saskatchewan and parts of the other Prairie provinces, but it was also connected to the rapid growth of community credit unions. For them, the pressures to become more diversified, more efficient, more market-oriented organizations were overpowering. The desire to enter into new services, to become more efficient banking organizations, to play different roles in the community, to achieve higher levels of professionalism – these were the determining imperatives.

The question left unanswered was whether these forces would mean the homogenization of credit unions into just another banking institution, or whether they could be harnessed within a different, perhaps even more relevant, co-operative vision. The question would not be answered quickly.

WORLD AWARD

to *British Columbia Credit Union League*

In recognition and appreciation of the generous voluntary contributions of our credit union members to support the self-help efforts of less-developed countries through the world extension programs of CUNA International, Inc.

PRESIDENT, CUNA INTERNATIONAL, INC.

MANAGING DIRECTOR, CUNA INTERNATIONAL, INC.

June 24, 1970
DATE

1. *Enterprise*, July-August, 1979, p. 14.

We have the dichotomy of some credit unions being virtually unchanged since the nineteen forties. Others, where socio-economic conditions permit, and where directors and management have become leaders in innovation, technological utilization and development of new members' services, are hardly recognizable as being credit unions in the traditional image of the forties. Today, if we take the two extremes in credit unions, we find that they have only the name and the basic organizational structure in common. The way things are moving, before long the extremes will probably have only the name "credit union" in common, for even the organizational structure is being changed to meet the demands of the movement.

Peter Heyming,
President, B.C. Central Credit Union[1]

BY 1970, BRITISH COLUMBIA'S credit unionists had made a fundamental choice. In the way English-Canadians often come to such decisions, they had done so without much direct or significant debate. The decision was about how large their credit unions should be. The answer was that credit unions should grow to whatever size their business activities warranted. Thus, when the issue was finally raised directly in the mid-1970s, it was too late for serious discussion.

This was not the only decision that could have been made. In Quebec, where the bonds of the Roman Catholic parish had been important in the early evolution of caisses populaires, there was a considerable uniformity in underlying philosophy and, consequently, a natural limitation on the size the caisses would achieve. After World War Two, the Quebec movement consciously decided over a period of years to limit the size of local caisses and to concentrate new and more expensive activities in regional organizations or in the central organization at Lévis. In other words, much of the responsibility for change lay in the upper levels of the federated structures.

In the United States, the strong preference for closed-bond credit unions had also tended to keep most credit unions smaller. That tendency was imported into Ontario and helped to create a movement significantly different from other movements in English Canada. In British Columbia, where any serious debate over limiting size would have deeply divided the movement, size became a consequence of entrepreneurship, almost by default.

The significance of that largely unconsidered decision became increasingly clear during the 1970s. In British Columbia, the first eight years of the decade were not without their economic difficulties, but from the perspective of the economically more uncertain 1990s, they appear as something of a golden age, the blossoming of the last frontier.

The decade even seemed to spawn a new kind of western entrepreneur. It was the age of Nelson Skalbania and other dynamic developers. It was a time when the Vancouver Stock Exchange entered one of its great boom periods. Above all, it was a period of extensive urban development, particularly in Vancouver and Victoria. To some extent, credit unions were caught up in that escalating economy, largely profiting from it, but also paying a heavy price, in several instances and respects. Powerful entrepreneurial instincts were particularly evident in local credit unions. The impact of new management approaches brought by some of the new managers in the later sixties had a decisive impact in the 1970s. If a person had expansionist instincts and took pride in "building," it was a wonderful, even heady, time to be involved in British Columbia's credit unions — as a director and particularly as a manager.

That was especially true if one compared credit unions with banks. One of the main ways in which credit unions differed functionally from banks and trust companies was that loan approvals could be gained rapidly and conveniently. All it took was to convene a meeting of the credit committee and, in most credit unions, members of those committees were prepared to meet frequently. Loan limits were also flexible from credit union to credit union, subject only to the watchful eye of the regulators and the policies adopted by a credit union's board. The only really significant restriction was the capacity of a credit union to attract deposits.

The drive for more member deposits led inevitably to branching. Aside from the main offices of each credit union, there were only 20 branches throughout the province in 1970. Eight years later, there were 128, most of them operated by a small number of credit unions in the major metropolitan areas. VanCity alone had 17, but Richmond Savings was also heavily engaged in a major expansion program, to be followed quickly by Surrey, Westcoast Savings and Saanich Peninsula Savings.

Most expansionist credit unions adopted a policy of opening a new branch when they believed they had attracted most of the potential members in a given area. In some instances, when faced with a shortage of deposits, they opened branches where they believed deposits could be attracted. In a few cases, when they had surplus deposits, they opened where there was a demand for mortgages.

When building branches, credit unions were usually responding to member requests, although occasionally some growth-oriented credit union leaders could hear a multitude when only a few had spoken. It is nevertheless true that the rapidly improving transportation systems, along with significantly different housing costs in adjoining communities, meant that an increasing number of members chose to live in one community and work in another. Inevitably, some of them asked for a credit union branch close to where they worked and another near where they lived. Such requests were often made and frequently answered.

The opening of branches created tensions in several areas of the province, but notably in Vancouver, the Fraser Valley and Victoria. From the later sixties onwards, there was scarcely a general meeting of Central that did not reflect the resentment and apprehension many smaller credit unions felt over having their "territory invaded" by larger credit unions. It was also a political issue because aggrieved leaders of the threatened credit unions carried their complaints to regional and provincial meetings, to the Inspector, and sometimes even to the Attorney-General.[2]

The issue was a particularly difficult one for the Inspector.[3] Under the Credit Union Act, credit unions were restricted by their common bonds to specific geographic areas, and often the geographic areas were very limited. He therefore had to restrict closed-bond credit unions severely and impede the larger community credit unions beyond their patience; put simply, it was an approach that was impossible to enforce.

For example, the fact that it was limited to the City of Vancouver proper meant that VanCity could not expand into many of the most rapidly growing areas of the metropolis. In fact, VanCity was specifically denied this possibility by the Inspector of Credit Unions in 1971, a ruling it challenged in 1972 when it opened a branch in North Burnaby. Doing so precipitated a long-standing controversy between the credit union and the government, and among credit unions. That controversy slowed VanCity's growth somewhat, forcing it for a few years to concentrate on the approximately 400,000 people who lived in Vancouver proper. For a while, it did not follow its members who were fleeing downtown to join the over one-million people who lived in the suburbs outside the municipality of Vancouver.

But, even as it sought to expand within the city, VanCity ran into some 15 other credit unions whose geographic bonds were the same or were confined to specific neighbourhoods in that city. Thus, almost inevitably, when VanCity opened a branch, it could be perceived as "invading" another credit union's territory. And, indeed, in some instances, VanCity opened branches that were uncomfortably close to other credit unions, although it resisted placing branches beside other credit unions, or at the same intersection.

Across the straits in Victoria, several areas had no credit unions. The two more entrepreneurial community credit unions – Westcoast Savings and Saanich Peninsula – were soon competing intensely to be first into the under-served areas. Their struggle and the resulting

2. Interview with Geoff Hook, September 24, 1994.
3. Ibid.

tensions, personalized in the rivalries between the two managers, Rodger Lutz and Harry Down, would last until the late 1980s. Competition also emerged during the seventies in the Fraser Valley, involving Richmond Savings, Surrey, Delta and Fraser Valley credit unions. The situation would not disappear quickly, nor be resolved easily.

By 1975, the pressure to change the common bond provision of the Credit Union Act had gained momentum, and the Act was amended. Under the revisions of that year, a community credit union could admit anyone "who, in the opinion of the directors, may be conveniently served by the credit union." It was an approach that sparked considerable heated debates at subsequent annual meetings of B.C. Central. In 1977, Central appointed a committee, chaired by Ben Voth of East Chilliwack Credit Union, to see if there was some way to resolve the issue in a co-operative fashion.

The committee received comments from around the province, and it became clear that, while branching was an issue primarily for the metropolitan credit unions, it nevertheless was tending to dominate the movement's deliberations. The committee therefore proposed an arbitration process to resolve disputes. It is significant that this rather reasonable approach did not gain support. It demonstrates the degree of self-sufficiency and prideful independence that credit unions had achieved; it also shows the power of the entrepreneurial imperative. The result was that the animosities and dissatisfaction continued, particularly in Greater Vancouver and Greater Victoria. It would long remain as an undercurrent in the provincial movement.

As the larger credit unions expanded through branching and became increasingly sophisticated, their management changed. Much of this change came about through the increasing use of computers. It was the computer that made possible the creation of a range of deposit accounts. It was the computer that facilitated the management of large groupings of assets. It was the computer that made more sophisticated investment strategies possible.

By 1970, most credit unions were on the "Burroughs system." This meant that, each day, the tellers in each participating credit union key-punched a record of the day's transactions on to white add-punch tapes. These tapes were sent to Central Data Systems, where they were entered into a computer. The results were then returned to the credit union, usually the next day.

But, on balance, it is the changes among people within credit unions that explain the major differences that occurred in the period. Boards, particularly in larger credit unions, clearly started to change. For example, board members increasingly came from professions that previously had not been well represented. Accountants, contractors, realtors, trade union officers, lawyers and salespeople joined the teachers, public servants, farmers, fishing people and woodworkers who had previously dominated boards of directors.

One result was that the number of women on boards seems to have declined, although no complete figures are available. In all likelihood, though, this did indeed occur, because boards were increasingly looking for people with business experience. Only a small minority of the relatively few women in that period with such experience would have had the time to devote to credit unions as volunteers.

Another consequence of the shift was that many credit union boards in the towns and cities became more influenced by the perspectives and ideologies of business people, professionals and small business operators. Inevitably, these people brought with them stronger management skills than the rank and file of earlier directors had possessed. They also tended to think of credit unions as another form of business, not as a distinctive type of enterprise, and their conceptions of community were at odds with the general communitarian traditions of the movement in its earlier days. In general, too, they were more conservative in their politics, meaning that the left-wing tone of the earlier credit union gatherings and policies gradually declined.[4]

Among general managers of large credit unions (or chief executive officers as they increasingly preferred to call themselves), the nature of management changed significantly. The opening of multiple branches obviously made delegation of authority necessary and created another level in the managerial hierarchy. Growing and more complicated asset bases meant that more credit unions hired professional accountants. Computers meant hiring experts to run them, and they changed the nature of decision-making: numbers and trend analyses became more important than tradition or "gut instinct." At the same time, the need to attract more deposits meant hiring first advertising and then marketing experts. As staffs grew larger, personnel experts were needed. In brief, the staff of credit unions became more professional, more segmented, and more narrowly-focused.[5]

The increasing need for more highly trained and technologically sophisticated managers tended to encourage the almost universal appointment of males to senior administrative posts in local credit unions. The executive "teams" of the early seventies were almost invariably made up of men, some of them graduates of the business schools and the marketing and accountancy programs that were then largely male preserves. In branches, though, female managers continued to be much more common than in banks, and in at least 20 of the smaller credit unions the secretary-treasurers were female. The immediate impact of the technological changes and the increased business preoccupations of credit unions, though, was to increase the number of powerful men within the provincial movement.

A measure of the change within credit unions by the 1970s was the fact that many of them now employed executive secretaries to assist managers and boards of directors. *Above,* Ole Turnbull from Western Co-operative College is seated among a group of executive secretaries from B.C. credit unions. The College, from the early 1960s to the early 1980s, provided training for numerous elected leaders, managers and staff from the province's credit unions.

4. Interview with Peter Podovinikoff, September 17, 1994.

5. Philip Moore, "Towards 2000 – With Participation," paper published by B.C. Central Credit Union, probably in 1975. Archives of Greater Vancouver Community Credit Union.

This steady accretion of professionals meant that managers of large credit unions became generalists, trouble-shooters, motivators, and key decision-makers.[6] It also meant that the "culture" of credit unions changed dramatically. More planning and better communication and information systems were needed – all of which cost money. The workplace became more regulated, often more impersonal. To set objectives, measure performance and reward employees appropriately, many credit unions moved to management-by-objective systems, a distinct shift from the informal relations that had previously characterized credit unions.

At the same time, the role of tellers began to change. By 1978, over 30 B.C. credit unions employed more than 40 people each. Some, like VanCity, Surrey, Westcoast Savings and Richmond Savings, had staffs numbering in the hundreds. Most of those employees were female tellers. Some of them made long-term careers in credit unions, but many worked for short periods or on a part-time basis. Increasingly, much of their work was done by machine, not by hand as in the past. Increasingly, too, more and more of their time was devoted to meeting members. As memberships grew, some of the pleasures of informality could be lost and there was increasing pressure to learn about a growing number of steadily more complicated "financial products." In short, the job was becoming increasingly specialized and routinized; the days of easy movement between deposit-taking and lending activities were starting to disappear, in the larger credit unions at least.

Tellers also became more tied to their work-stations. Previously, with so much work to be done by hand, tellers divided their time between the front counter and desks. Now, with a greater reliance on technology, they spent nearly all their time at counter work-stations. In that respect, their work became similar to a supermarket clerk's job. They seldom escaped the pressures of meeting the public, and the range of skills they required declined. Some of the tellers had difficulty in making this transformation, and their discomfort contributed to the unionization drives that occurred in some credit unions in the 1970s.

By 1972, there was a serious shortage of trained tellers for the system. Central and the larger credit unions began to offer specialized training programs geared particularly to familiarization with the emerging technological changes. In 1974, Jac Schroeder, on behalf of Central, prepared an extensive program for tellers, one that was widely used over the succeeding decade.

Given the issues that inevitably arise as staffs increase and the workplace changes, there was a growing need for personnel policies and advice. The larger credit unions hired personnel managers; in fact, one of the first ways in which those credit unions began to work together

6. Interviews with Peter Podovinikoff, Marion Holmes and Geoff Hook, September 1994.

independently of Central was in the exchange of information on personnel policies.

In some 15 credit unions, staff joined unions, most of them in credit unions serving trade unionists or in Vancouver Island communities with long trade union histories. These successful attempts at unionization were encouraged in part by memberships and boards who, on principle, believed it was appropriate for employees to organize unions. Partly, too, they were the result of growing pressures on tellers and loans officers from the increasing complexity of their jobs. In particular, much of the dissatisfaction came from female tellers finding it difficult to work in more structured and specialized environments.

The campaign to organize these credit unions was comparatively orderly and uncontroversial.[7] Similarly, in the succeeding years, the negotiations between the credit unions and the unions were resolved smoothly and amicably. The major exceptions were a strike in Nanaimo in 1975 and another at Fraser Valley in 1982/83. The Nanaimo strike became somewhat emotional because it was a trendsetter and because it was so painful for Rod Glen, a long-time trade union leader. Once the strike was resolved, though, the credit union reverted quickly to its normal harmonious employer-employee relationships. As with most other unionized credit unions, Nanaimo over the years has reached agreements with its employees with little controversy.

All of these changes meant a different relationship between boards of directors and the hired management. In smaller credit unions, directors had and continued to have a relatively clear and active role. Very few decisions were made without board involvement – in many instances, this even included the hiring of people reporting to the secretary-treasurer. Certainly, all lending activities were reviewed closely by the board or a committee of the board.

As credit unions became larger, direct board involvement inevitably declined. There were too many decisions that could not wait for board approval; many directors felt unqualified to make essentially technical decisions; and the number and nature of loan applications were too extensive to be approved by volunteers. In a growing number of instances, moreover, directors lacked the experience and understanding to make sound decisions about the rapidly-growing credit unions for which they were responsible. Some boards were hard pressed to monitor management, to evaluate performance, and to make prudent decisions. It was a widening gap that would create problems, particularly in the next decade.

At the same time, managers were forced to make considerable changes. Perhaps above all, they had to learn how to delegate. Having "grown up" within their credit unions, some of them found it difficult to let others assume responsibility. Moreover, they had to learn new skills and

7. "Labour Relations Involvement," August 15, 1975, BCCCU Board Minutes.

165

activities, especially as loans became larger and more diverse and the range of deposit accounts grew wider. At the same time, they had to learn how to use the new technologies effectively, which was not an easy task for many people in their forties and fifties. There could be stress and failure amid the boom that credit unions experienced in the 1970s.

Invariably, these changes also meant that many within the larger credit unions began to view members differently. One of the first changes was that credit unions discovered advertising. There had been some advertising before, in newspapers and on the radio, but many credit unions began to use advertising continuously and systematically in the seventies. It was effective. Undoubtedly, the rapid increase in membership and assets during the 1970s was partly related to the higher profile credit unions assumed.

But the advertising tended to be about specific products, to promote a deposit rate, to encourage personal loans, and, above all, to push mortgages. In other words, advertising often had the effect of narrowing the relationship with members to a particular set of services. Rarely did credit unions promote themselves as distinct organizations; rarely were all the "products and services" organized into a coherent whole. It is, therefore, not surprising that the movement woke up at the end of the decade with thousands of members who really did not know what they had joined.

During the mid-seventies, some credit unions and Central moved beyond advertising into marketing. The difference was simply that they analyzed more completely their memberships and the nature of their communities. The earliest provincial experiment with marketing began in 1972 when Robert Wyckham, a member of the faculty of Simon Fraser University, prepared a report for Central on "Marketing Credit Unions in British Columbia." The report revealed that credit unions had little formal, documentable understanding of their members and that the movement was ill-organized to undertake marketing activities. He called for an integrated system-wide approach, emphasizing clear product definition, reasonable objectives, and effective measuring of results.[8] For more than a decade, Wyckham promoted this approach to marketing as he became one of the most trusted advisors within the provincial movement.

By 1974, the first widely-used approach to marketing had evolved, and was described as follows:

1. the need to ascertain present and potential member needs.
2. delineate your market area based upon what segment of those needs you feel your credit union can fulfill.

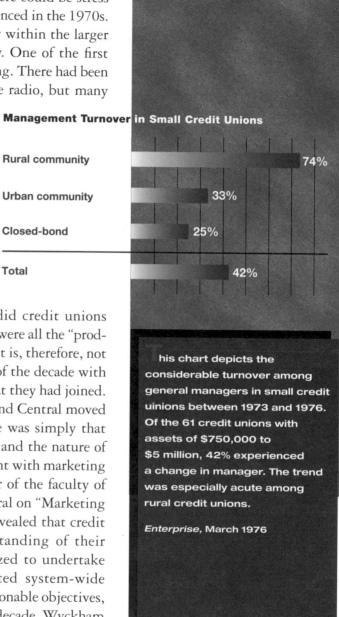

Management Turnover in Small Credit Unions

Rural community — 74%

Urban community — 33%

Closed-bond — 25%

Total — 42%

his chart depicts the considerable turnover among general managers in small credit unions between 1973 and 1976. Of the 61 credit unions with assets of $750,000 to $5 million, 42% experienced a change in manager. The trend was especially acute among rural credit unions.

Enterprise, March 1976

8. Robert G. Wyckham, "Marketing Credit Unions in British Columbia," May 19, 1972.

3. implement services to meet those needs.

4. obtain feedback from your members as to your success in meeting those needs.

5. re-evaluate your approach based upon the results of number four.[9]

This approach, which quickly became more sophisticated, was widely applied by Central staff advising credit unions; it also was applied within Central itself. As it developed, it encouraged credit unions to think of members as groups, as segments of the population differentiated by age, income, saving patterns and credit needs. The challenge then became to encourage mixtures of groups that would complement each other's needs. It was potentially a new way to conceptualize a credit union and improve services to members. It could also, if abused, become manipulative and exploitative.

The emergence of new kinds of accounts and services also changed the way in which members were connected to their credit union. In the early years there was only one kind of account – the share account, which did not earn a specific interest rate but could receive dividends at the end of the fiscal year. In other words, ownership, investment and patronage were completely integrated. As chequing became commonplace, chequing accounts were created and they usually earned a very low interest rate, if any. By the late sixties, savings accounts were added, and they earned a competitive interest rate; rates were calculated either on a minimum daily balance, as in Plan 24 accounts, or on minimum monthly balances in credit unions that could not offer Plan 24 because they lacked the computer to do so. As mortgage lending became important, credit unions sought long-term deposits from their members in order to manage their mortgage lending effectively. These deposits earned various rates of interest and were taken for differing terms, therefore requiring more sophisticated planning and monitoring.

This growing list of accounts diversified the relationships with members. At the same time, some of the general assumptions of the mainstream banking industry came to dominate credit unions. In the competition for term deposits and savings accounts, share accounts were de-emphasized; many credit unions even stopped paying dividends on them when financial pressures increased, meaning that those accounts remained unchanged and largely unnoticed. In many credit unions, too, life insurance on loans and savings, once a clear indication of difference, was cut back or eliminated, largely because it was not sufficiently remunerative.

In retrospect, these were significant changes within credit unions because they devalued some of the obvious benefits of member-ownership – and one of the structural ways in which credit unions were different from other financial institutions. It would not be until the 1990s that some credit union leaders would start to rethink how share

9. Philip Moore (then an employee of B.C. Central Credit Union) to Rod Glen, September 26, 1974. Archives of Greater Vancouver Community Credit Union.

167

accounts and distinctive forms of co-operative ownership could be important elements in reinvigorating the relationship with members.

Even more importantly, credit unions in the seventies began to compete with other financial institutions primarily on the basis of rates and service. This emphasis, of course, was in large part inevitable, given that they were functioning in the same marketplace. What many did not do, though, was to devote enough time and resources to training, marketing and surplus (or profit) distribution to ensure that members could easily understand the structural and philosophical differences of credit unions.

Nevertheless, there were some obvious ways in which credit unions continued to be different from their competitors in daily operations. Probably the most striking for most members was the hours of opening. Most credit unions were open until 5 PM, a radical concept for banks that for years had been open just from 10 AM to 3 PM. Many were open on Saturdays (and closed on Mondays), a remarkable practice in the financial industry of the time.

Credit unions had unusual opening hours in order to serve members working on shifts; some, in fact, were open in the evenings. In a few instances, as with Vancouver Federal Employees, collectors went to the workplace on paydays to cash cheques and conduct other business. As the decade progressed, moreover, more credit unions, especially closed-bond operations, successfully negotiated for employers to deposit pay-cheques automatically into member accounts. This practice was, of course, very beneficial for the credit union and, for the most part, convenient for the members. It did, however, create marital tensions for some members because it meant wives for the first time learned exactly what their husbands earned.

Credit unions were also different in their practices and policies regarding mortgages. Most could approve mortgages in a matter of hours; this was in sharp contrast to many of the banks, in which mortgages were approved centrally and through a bureaucracy. Credit unions, therefore, became particularly popular with some real estate salespeople, who naturally wanted to close deals as quickly as possible. Even more importantly, most credit unions offered mortgages that could be paid off at the member's pleasure. This meant that members could save large amounts of money by paying down mortgages quickly; they could also change housing more easily as family size changed or better jobs became available. It was a significant benefit that helped thousands of British Columbians build better lives for themselves.

These innovations were all manifestations of the remarkable entrepreneurial spirit evident within the province's credit unions in the 1970s. Where did this entrepreneurship come from? It would be misleading to assume that it was just a spill-over from the general entrepreneurial spirit evident in the province. Although it did not happen entirely in isolation, it was not just a replica of private enterprise unleashed. To some extent, it was a natural manifestation of co-operativism, which is always expansionist when functioning properly. Good co-operatives have their roots in member needs. When well organized and effectively led, they always respond to the evolving needs of their members; they always have a tendency to grow.

Thus it should not be surprising that one of the foremost entrepreneurs of the period was Rod Glen, who epitomized the "co-operative entrepreneur" in many respects. Glen adopted the classic co-operative approach of considering members in a total perspective. He saw his credit union not just as being in the "banking" business; in essence, it was in the member development business. Thus it was not illogical for him to marshal the resources of his credit union, especially its social power, behind a consumer co-op, a travel agency, a recreation facility, an insurance agency and a printing business.

So powerful was his dream, so charismatic his personality, that he and his associates sparked the formation of a chain of "direct charge" co-operatives, largely through credit union memberships on Vancouver Island. Glen and others in Nanaimo were convinced that there was a need to create an efficient consumer co-operative to meet the needs of people on lower incomes and to prevent exploitation by the agri-food industries. The "direct charge" or "service fee" co-operatives they formed collected the costs of operating the store in regular, usually weekly, membership fees, and then sold food and consumer goods at close to cost price. The stores were functional and simple; no money was "wasted" on advertising, and the board was directly accountable to the membership for how the store operated, including the quality and variety of goods. It was a revolutionary approach to consumption that rather sadly was not grasped by enough people in conventional consumer co-operatives, nor by enough credit union leaders, to enable it to reach its full potential.

By the end of middle seventies, then, there was a significant if diverse group of entrepreneurs in B.C. credit unions, especially in credit unions with more then $30-million in assets. They led "management teams" with highly specialized training and well-segregated duties. They had become determined to enter resolutely into the general banking community, to confront the banks and trust companies largely on their own terms. Some of them dreamed of "building" their credit unions as agents for social change through co-operatives and other forms of social activism.

While the differences were of degree, this approach contrasted with that to be found more commonly among smaller credit unions. By 1978, there were 118 credit unions with assets of less than

$10-million, divided about equally between closed-bond and community credit unions. In most, one-person managements supported by two or three tellers were the norm. In many instances, they depended on a few people, sometimes on just one person, for their momentum.[10] As these spark-plugs lost their fire, retired or died, they were not always replaced. In the Vancouver area alone, 44 small credit unions were liquidated or merged between 1970 and 1975.[11]

One of the most common problems confronting small credit unions was the increasing cost of management. The day of the essentially volunteer secretary-treasurer was coming to an end, and it was becoming increasingly difficult to find capable part-time secretary-treasurers. Many small credit unions were able to pay only low salaries, and this contrasted with the good pay given management and staff in larger credit unions – where the salaries paid in the banking industry were becoming the norm. In other words, professionalization was exacting its price.

This did not mean that small- and medium-sized credit unions were unimportant, either for the movement or, above all, for their members. Despite all the mergers and liquidations, about 55% of the 167 credit unions in 1978 were still based on closed bonds; five closed-bond credit unions were among the largest 25 credit unions in the province, although none of them was among the largest 10.[12] On the other hand, of the 118 credit unions with assets of less than $10-million in 1978 – by then thought to be small – about half were closed-bond. They tended to be growing relatively slowly at that point, by about 10% a year, in contrast to the 20-40% growth generally achieved by community credit unions, large and small.

The difference in growth was most dramatic in Vancouver. Between 1968 and 1973, the eight largest credit unions grew by a staggering 518%; in contrast, the 14 largest closed-bond credit unions grew by 180%. The same large credit unions had assets of $357-million in 1973 compared to $107-million for the closed-bond credit unions; by 1977, the largest credit unions had just over $1-billion in assets, while the closed-bonds had $210-million.[13]

Few of the closed-bond credit unions, though, were declining in assets, indicating that they were meeting the needs of important, if restricted, groups of members. The question was whether they could keep on meeting those needs. The same question was confronting the smaller community credit unions. Most were located in small towns, though, where limited competition and perhaps (for a while) member demand meant that they did not have to offer a wide range of services. In fact, partly because they were encountering low development costs, many of them were among the most profitable credit unions in the province.

10. Interview with Geoff Hook, September 24, 1994.

11. "Small Credit Union Service Centre," February 12, 1976, BCCCU Board Minutes.

12. *Enterprise*, May-June, 1979, p. 22.

13. Submission to the Common Bond Review Committee by Greater Vancouver Catholic Credit Union, 1977, BCCCU Archives.

No change

Minor change

Changes ?

Implement plan at start of operational period

Minor adjustments

Major plan change

Means

Ends

Resources

Control

Implement

The planning function

Assess plan for its usefulness in directing operations

Collect information about operations under present plan

lanning the future of your credit union..."
Enterprise magazine, October/November 1972.

14. Philip Moore, "Report on Small Credit Unions," undated (possibly 1974), Archives of Greater Vancouver Community Credit Union.

Within the larger cities, smaller credit unions were disappearing or amalgamating because neighbourhoods were changing. As younger people in the larger cities matured in the 1970s, they tended to move out of such communities as Mount Pleasant in Vancouver or James Bay in Victoria. If they stayed near home, they moved to the cheaper houses and more modern schools in the suburbs. Newcomers, often retired, from other parts of Canada, or immigrants, then largely from Europe, moved into the older neighbourhoods. Community bonds consequently changed, accompanied by a decline in the associational networks on which many small credit unions had been based. Communities were not what they once had been.

Smaller credit unions, like their larger brethren, were also confronting a changing marketplace. By the early 1970s, the increased competition allowed by the 1967 Bank Act was having a significant impact. A study conducted at that time clearly demonstrated that members, even in the small credit unions with strong associational bonds, were demanding new services, the same kinds of services they could generally receive from a bank. In particular, credit unions had to offer chequing, a variety of savings accounts, and, increasingly, retirement savings plans. On the other side of the ledger, credit unions had to have money available for loans, especially mortgages. Unless they could offer all or most of these services, they would only grow slowly, if not languish.[14]

In the long run, this meant that smaller credit unions, both open- and closed-bond, would have to struggle to keep pace with the essential changes in the banking industry. Many of them also sought, often with considerable success, to compete and hold members by their emphasis on personalized service, their support for social activities, and, in some instances, their commitment to cultural programs and languages. For many members, who did not welcome technological change, plastic counters, fern plants and ritualized greetings, those qualities were reason enough to be loyal.

Nevertheless, in the larger credit union picture, the major trend was unparalleled growth. In 1970, the credit union leadership was justifiably proud of the fact that the assets of the provincial movement were $346-million. That figure would soon be dwarfed. By 1974, total provincial assets had grown to $1-billion; by 1978, they were nearing $4-billion. Membership nearly tripled between 1970 and 1978, from 350,000 to more than 900,000. As a percentage of the provincial population, those membership figures meant that, while 18% of the population were members in 1970, approximately 35% had joined by 1978. Average share and deposit balances per member had increased from just under $1,000 in 1970 to nearly $3,800 in 1978. This figure indicated increasing support and confidence; it also suggested that there was considerable room for further growth. The average size of a credit union had grown in the same years from $1.35-million to $23-million.[15] In many parts of the province, credit unions had entered the mainstream; they had become an important part of the provincial economy. Entrepreneurship, whether imitative or co-operative, had found its own rewards.

Nor was entrepreneurship reserved for the local credit unions; it was duplicated, perhaps even exceeded, by B.C. Central. Indeed, George May was arguably the most entrepreneurial and visionary of the movement's leaders in that period. There is no doubt that he dreamed of creating a credit union movement that would be a determining force in the economic and social development of the province. There is no doubt that he envisioned B.C. Central as the head of that movement.

Polished and articulate, intense and gregarious, May had associations throughout British Columbia, and his friends included many in the business and political elite of Vancouver. He saw the movement as one of the key economic, social and political forces in the province's future. In some ways, he would be right, but his particular emphasis on how that might be achieved was not always greeted warmly, and never welcomed universally.

By instinct, May was a centralist who sought to maximize the power of the province's credit unions through an aggressive Central. For him, Central was the hub of the provincial movement: it would provide services to local credit unions and co-operatives and in that sense was at their command. But it was also in the vanguard, providing information, initiating new services and activities, forcefully projecting

15. Annual Report, B.C. Central Credit Union, 1978, pp. 26-27.

the "co-operative way" on the provincial economy. In his approach, May made several linked and important assumptions: there would be fewer and larger credit unions; there would be a continuous shortage of deposits because of the rapid expansion of the movement; credit unions would play a broader role in their communities; the nature of membership was changing; and credit unions had to provide a full range of financial services.[16] These assumptions help to explain many of the changes that occurred at Central during the 1970s.

Under May, B.C. Central grew at an even faster rate than the B.C. movement. In terms of assets, Central grew from $52-million in 1970 to $661-million in 1978.[17] Only VanCity, which had $718-million in assets in the latter year, was larger. But Central's real growth was not in assets; it was in people and services. By 1978, more than 300 people worked for the organization, a major increase from the approximately 90 employed when the League and Central were united in 1970.

It was the range of services, though, that made Central unique. With the board's approval, the expansion of services began soon after May assumed office in 1970. He was particularly supported in his expansionist endeavours by Rod Glen, although their motivations were somewhat different. Starting in 1971, May and the board went through an extensive annual planning process and Central's activities were all restructured under a management-by-objectives approach, then the dominant school in management theory.

Under the new regime, Central's essential services remained the same: management of the movement's liquidity reserves and provision of financial services, such as cheque-clearing, loans, investments, and advice on interest rates and economic trends. These activities were undertaken by the Administration and Finance Division, headed after 1972 by Aj Gill.

During the 1970-78 period, this division was hard pressed to meet the financial needs of Central and the credit unions. The year 1974 was particularly difficult as the demand for funds outstripped the supply. Central had access to only $30-million from a chartered bank, not enough when all of the credit union deposits in Central were tied up. To meet the demand, Central successfully co-ordinated a province-wide "super saver" account, its first large-scale intervention in a major marketing campaign. George May also went to Europe and raised

The Wizard of Central

The fine art of economic forecasting was lampooned in this cartoon in *Enterprise*, February 1970.

16. George May to E.R. Brann, September 7, 1973, BCCCU Archives.

17. Annual Report, B.C. Central Credit Union, 1978, p. 23.

173

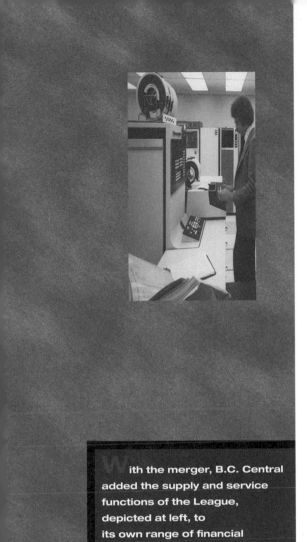

Central's first off-shore loan, largely from co-operative banks. These accomplishments significantly boosted Central's confidence in its capacity to lead the provincial movement.

The confidence was also natural because growth seemed, for most of this period, to be automatic. For most of the seventies, inflation consistently hovered between 5% and 8%. In the later years, however, trouble began to threaten as the spread between lending and deposit rates declined, meaning that local credit unions were particularly keen to receive a good interest rate on their deposits in Central.

Providing that return became difficult. Managing liquidity, for example, became more complex. One aspect of the problem was simply that the amounts of money being managed were becoming larger. By 1978, Central had over $550-million in credit union deposits, which required much improved forecasting and controlling capabilities, a better understanding of the financial markets, and increased technological sophistication. Perhaps even more importantly, it required consensus within the provincial movement as to what was a reasonable return on the moneys invested in Central. What was the acceptable interest rate? How much risk should be taken to achieve it? They were not questions that could be easily or even permanently answered.

During this period, Central also became a leader in defining the types of financial products that local credit unions should offer their members. From a small beginning in 1967, Central became a major provider of registered retirement savings plans in the 1970s. Through a subsidiary, Central Financial Corporation, it also served as a mortgage lender to members of local credit unions when those credit unions were too small or did not have the funds to make the loans. In short, the financial capacities of Central were rapidly developed, but they were hard pressed to keep up with the growing and diversified demands of credit unions.

The other side of Central was split into two groups, the Services Division and the Development Division. Both expanded rapidly, initially with the strong support of most credit unions. Early in 1972, a Market Research and Development Department was created, largely to cater to the needs of local credit unions. It was particularly concerned with marketing issues, and it carried out four kinds of studies on a fee-for-service basis: market analyses, member analyses, member surveys, and image or awareness surveys.

This department was also responsible for the expansion of Plan 24, the demand deposit savings account that was purchased from VanCity and distributed throughout the system. Plan 24 was administered for local credit unions through Central Data Systems, and the number of credit unions participating in the program had grown to 69 by 1978. It was a particularly popular service for credit unions around the province, and its distinctive features would not be duplicated by the banks until the 1980s.

The second department within the Development Division was Promotion and Communications. It was responsible for all the publications, particularly *Enterprise*, as the *B.C. Credit Unionist* had been renamed in 1967. It also conducted the province-wide advertising campaign, which included radio and newspapers throughout most of the province and television in the main metropolitan areas. Finally, it was responsible for meeting the growing educational and training needs of local credit unions. It was particularly interested in training, reflecting George May's belief that the chief need was for fully qualified employees and directors.

The Services Division included an array of departments. One was Personnel Services, which operated a placement service for credit union staff and advised local credit unions on employee benefits. Another was Printing and Supply, which supplied cheques and stationery for credit unions, printed reports and manuals on a fee-for-service basis, and handled mail-outs.

Another major activity for Central was the operation of Central Data Systems (CDS), a wholly-owned computer service corporation. Central assumed ownership of this company during the merger process when CDS was encountering financial and operational difficulties. Although management continued to be complex, CDS was able to expand its user base with reasonable speed. By mid-decade, local credit unions were joining CDS at a rate of between 20 and 30 a year. This enabled them to offer Plan 24 to their members, and they gained daily activity reports, month-end trial balances, and better monitoring of delinquency. Starting in 1970, CDS began to examine the development of on-line computing systems, a major initiative, but a necessity if credit unions were to remain efficient. It moved slowly in making decisions about the on-line system because there were contrasting views and needs among credit unions. Moreover, the continuing challenge of coping with the daily demands of an expanding system understandably, but unfortunately, distracted attention from the larger question of what might be best for future needs.

In 1972, Central began a consulting service, also on a fee-for-service basis. It advised on computer issues, the preparation of manuals for credit union staff, and planning for new branches.

All these departments went through a continuous evolution as old services were expanded and new ones added. But one program was discontinued: the field service. George May believed that credit unions should be more independent of Central, that they should accept more responsibility for their own future. As long as fieldmen were around, he reasoned, credit unions could rely too much on them, thereby perpetuating a kind of unhealthy dependency. In some ways, he may have been correct, but there was also a heavy price that would be paid: without fieldmen, there would be infrequent and limited contact with credit unions "on the ground." In the long run, this declining contact may have contributed to the separation that ultimately occurred between Central and some of its members as the seventies came to an end.

The closure of the field service also produced a quick response from smaller credit unions in need of assistance. Consequently, a department was added in 1974, under the direction of Philip Moore, to serve the needs of small credit unions. At the same time, Central began to provide contract managerial services to local credit unions, although the demand was never very strong. In 1975, a new subsidiary, Greentree Developments, was added to help credit unions develop their office buildings. Greentree became very active, serving the needs of housing co-operatives as well as credit unions; its work is readily evident in credit unions throughout the province, even two decades later.

In the same years, May and Glen began to look outside the financial industry for opportunities. Both were impressed by the emergence of "the leisure society." Their speeches and the annual reports in the 1970s frequently referred to the declining hours of work in many industries, the growth of pension plans, and the increasing affordability of travel. During the mid-seventies, Central investigated several possible holiday/convention sites, particularly Bowen Island, before purchasing land for those purposes near Penticton. The dream never materialized, even in Penticton, but it was not an idea that necessarily was doomed to failure – it just did not "fit" the movement at that time.

Central and interested credit unions also began to look into tourism and, specifically, into travel as a supplementary business. In 1972, Central purchased a travel agency in Vancouver. The long-term idea was to make its services available throughout the credit union system, partly as a way to attract non-members to credit unions. A few credit unions responded to this initiative, notably Nanaimo, but the idea, which had promise considering the size of the movement's membership, was not greeted enthusiastically. Without enthusiasm, it was doomed.

Central also attempted to reach out to the broader community in B.C. by formalizing its relations with co-operatives. Between 75 and 90 co-operatives, mostly consumer co-ops, were members of Central during this period. In 1971, the provincial organization, the British Columbia Co-operative Union, ran into economic and managerial difficulties. At the meeting called to wind it up, the representatives of co-operatives present voted to offer its assets to Central, in hopes that Central would assume responsibility for the general development of co-operatives in the province. After some debate, and in view of its large number of co-operative members and its significant co-op loans portfolio, Central accepted the responsibility.

In 1972, Central created a Co-operative Services Office. Its purpose was to encourage the general development of co-ops in the province. It undertook "growth services" to established co-operatives; assisted groups interested in forming co-ops; provided general information on co-operatives; and helped lobby government on behalf of the movement.

An artist's impression in 1977 envisioned Central's new office building on False Creek.

The Office undertook two main initiatives during the seventies. The first was the promotion of co-operative housing. In 1972, the federal government had introduced funding for mixed-income co-operative housing as a way to help build self-sustaining, healthy communities for the poorly housed, particularly in the larger cities. In British Columbia, co-operative housing advocates, especially Shirley Schmid, who was strongly supported by George May and Rod Glen, were among the most successful organizers of this new form of housing.

The other possible area for significant co-operative growth was in consumer co-operatives. There were three dimensions to this possibility, all of them promising for at least a part of the seventies. On Vancouver Island, direct charge co-operatives were prospering and new ones were being formed. Rod Glen, for one, dreamed of expanding them to the mainland. Second, the New Democratic Party, when it formed the provincial government in 1972, promised to foster the development of consumer co-ops as a way of combatting the rising cost of food, always a problem for people on low- or fixed-incomes in inflationary periods. Third, Federated Co-operatives, with its headquarters in Saskatoon, was in an expansionist mood, partly because its rural base in B.C. and especially in the Prairies was losing its younger population. The Co-operative Services Office, then, had considerable potential when it opened, and it had the support of many of Central's most important leaders.

To ensure that the Office and the co-operative members of Central were adequately heard within the boardroom and at Central's meetings, the rules were changed in 1975 to make way for one representative elected by and from the co-operative members. In many ways, though, this was also an acknowledgement of Central's co-operative roots and an expression of a desire to ensure that the provincial credit union movement retained its co-operative associations as it evolved.

As Central grew, finding space for its employees became a problem. Shortly after he became CEO in 1970, May began to search for an appropriate location for a new head office. After failing to find a site in downtown Vancouver, in 1972 he located a six-acre parcel of land on the south side of False Creek, near the docks of a large commercial fishing fleet. The area was undeveloped, poorly served by buses, and removed from the downtown business community. The land was purchased for just under $1-million, and May and his associates started to work on a plan for the area's development.

It was not an easy process. There was little development in the area to guide the city planners and there were complicated negotiations over rezoning.[18] The final plans would not be adopted until 1977 and the political hurdles were overcome only with the assistance of Ron Basford, a federal cabinet minister, who helped in discussions with the National Harbours Board, and Mike Harcourt (then a city councillor and later the Premier of British Columbia), who assisted in negotiations with the city.[19] All of these thrusts were accompanied by a series of senior management changes within Central. As the staff of the organization expanded to over 300, a bureaucracy began to emerge, with the senior executives becoming well paid and sometimes appearing to be removed from the local credit unions. As Central became more active in commercial loans and involved with large loans, some of its leaders became closely associated with prominent Vancouver land developers, such as Nelson Skalbania. This association was unwelcome to many local credit union leaders around the province, and would contribute to dissatisfaction with Central in the coming years.

Central became much more politically active in the 1970s. May had many contacts with politicians, particularly within the Liberal Party, nationally and provincially, while others on the board or in local credit unions had close contacts with the New Democratic, Social Credit and Conservative parties. May and the board's leadership met regularly with provincial politicians, in government and in opposition. Annually, a delegation from Central went to Ottawa to meet with cabinet ministers and B.C. Members of Parliament. In 1974, Central formally adopted a legislative relations program. It included regular visits with politicians, special contact programs with candidates during elections, and continuous contact with key public servants.[20] It was a process that would continue indefinitely.

This increased emphasis on government relations was partly an indication of the growing maturity of the provincial movement, a recognition that the state significantly determined the ways in which credit unions operated. During the early seventies, there was a long and

18. "Credit Union Centre Development," May 27, 1972, BCCCU Board Minutes.

19. Podovinikoff interview.

20. "Establishment of Formal Program for Legislative Relations," May 30, 1974, BCCCU Board Minutes.

complex set of negotiations with Ottawa over the taxation of credit unions. As credit unions had grown larger, not only in British Columbia but in other provinces as well, banks, trust companies and the federal government began to question the way credit unions were taxed. They attacked the fact that credit unions did not have to pay tax on the dividends returned to members and they wanted the larger credit unions to be taxed more heavily.

In 1971, the federal government introduced Bill C-259, which would have taxed co-operative dividends to members and treated credit unions in the same manner as any other small business. This last measure, in effect, would have imposed a 50% tax on credit unions whenever they had annual surpluses of $400,000 or more. This would have severely limited the capacity of credit unions to grow. Another proposal would have increased the taxation of central credit unions while allowing banks to obtain a tax benefit if they were to lend to credit unions; this would have seriously undermined centrals across the country. Yet another serious proposal was to ignore credit union deposits in a central when calculating the reserve levels of local credit unions. In short, it appeared Ottawa did not understand the way in which credit unions organized their affairs.

Various B.C. credit union leaders, but especially George May, Rod Glen, Bob McMaster and Fred Graham, played crucial roles in contesting these proposals. The latter two, in particular, contributed significantly to preparing and presenting briefs outlining the credit union position. All of them made frequent trips to Ottawa to plead the case of credit unions and caisses populaires before politicians and bureaucrats. They also encouraged local credit unionists to contact their Members of Parliament, an approach that proved very effective in British Columbia and especially in Quebec. By the time it ended in 1972, it had become the largest sustained campaign ever launched by credit union and co-operative members in the history of the national movement. It was an example of how such organizations could mobilize social and political power when they had the will to do so.

The proposed Income Tax Act was finally amended in the wake of this lobbying. The resulting amendments were complicated and made it more difficult for credit unions to calculate taxes, particularly in how reserves were treated and how subsidiaries could be established. More importantly, though, credit unions would not be seriously restricted by increased taxes as they continued to grow. The significance of this victory can scarcely be overestimated as far as the B.C. movement was concerned. It would have developed in an entirely different direction if credit unions had not prevailed in Ottawa.

Central also became more active within the provincial sphere. The New Democratic Party government, between 1972 and 1975, was very sympathetic to credit unions and co-operatives, but it was frequently unpredictable. Many of its members, like many members of the Social Credit governments before and after, were unfamiliar with the movement. Consequently, the NDP never developed a consistent policy towards co-operatives despite its sympathies, and too many of its members, in the classic social democratic tradition, considered co-ops to be just another variant of public enterprise.

Towards the end of the NDP mandate, however, there was a flurry of activity associated with the possible reconfiguration of the inspection system. A government-commissioned study undertaken by Fred Graham in 1976 recommended placing the inspection service with CURB, a decision that would have emasculated the Superintendent's Office (as the Inspector's Office was called after 1975). This approach was greeted warmly by most of the leaders in the movement because it would have been a step toward self-regulation, and a move away from what was often perceived as government interference. By the time the report was available for serious consideration, however, a new Social Credit government had been elected and it speedily rejected the report. The idea of self-regulation would nevertheless remain alive, to be resurrected a decade later.

As for relations between Central, the Inspector's Office and CURB, the mid-seventies were particularly cordial. Under Geoff Hook, CURB had become a well-operated organization, and his replacement in 1975, Ross Montgomery, had worked at Central as George May's assistant. Until late in the decade, CURB dealt with between 20 to 30 credit unions each year, most of them small; indeed, most of the problems were resolved through joint efforts between Central and CURB. In the mid-seventies, too, the Chief Inspector was Dick Monrufet, who had joined the government from Central in 1973 when George McCulloch retired. Thus, though there were distinct institutional differences and responsibilities, regulatory activities were carried out by people who had grown up within the system, knew its key leaders, and were sympathetic to the movement's objectives. Similarly, all the ministers responsible for credit unions throughout the decade, New Democratic and Social Credit, were supportive and co-operative.

During 1975 and 1976, however, the provincial government imposed a hiring freeze that unfortunately affected the Superintendent's Office seriously; several of its staff had decided for various reasons to leave the Office at about the same time, and were not replaced. The result was a decline in the quality of inspection of local credit unions. In view of the problems that started to accumulate as the decade came to an end, this decline was particularly serious, contributing to the animosity that invariably developed between the Office and the province's credit unions.

Despite Central's accomplishments, its rapid and diverse growth had critics. Many of them were to be found within the larger credit unions. Beneath the tension lay a question that would permeate the movement for the next 20 years: who should have primary responsibility for the movement's growth? May, Glen and others looked to Central. An increasing number of credit union managers, especially in the larger and more aggressive organizations, believed it should rest with the local credit unions.

One of the most convinced advocates of the dominance of local credit unions was Rodger Lutz, who had become manager of Westcoast Savings Credit Union in Victoria in 1971. Under his management, Westcoast Savings became one of the most rapidly growing credit unions in the province. In 1970, it had assets of just over $1-million; by 1978, it had $225-million. The credit union had pioneered in serving senior citizens, appropriately enough for the community it served, and it had developed one of the best marketing strategies in the province. Lutz was impressed by the activities of several of the savings and loans associations in the western United States. He liked their emphasis on wealthy clients and he thought their diversified investment strategy was a wise approach. By 1975, he was wrestling uncomfortably with the structures of a provincial system and complaining about the costs of Central.[21] It was a perspective that had limited support initially, but would gain adherents in the years ahead.

There were other critics, though none as vocal or publicly persistent as Lutz. Geoff Hook, who had managed the Credit Union Reserve Board since 1970, became the manager of VanCity in 1976, shortly after the death of Don Bentley. Hook was a conservative manager who entered into new business activities cautiously. At CURB he had sometimes found himself at odds with George May's flamboyant style, and was critical of Central's expansionism. He saw few reasons to change that assessment when he managed VanCity. Above all, Hook thought that the momentum for growth should be based in the local credit unions, a view that was also increasingly shared by Wayne Carpenter, the manager of Surrey Credit Union in that period. Prior to 1978, they expressed these views but rarely pressed them; within a few years both men would become more vocal.

It would be misleading, though, to think that there was little general reaction to the rapid growth of the period and the associated domination of entrepreneurial instincts. Some of the problems were well-summarized in two papers presented to meetings of the "Big 20" credit unions in January, 1974, by Bob Hornal, the manager of Central's Development Division.[22] Since only a few credit unions and Central were actively engaged in annual planning exercises, Hornal called for more planning by all credit unions, and specifically planning that would address the issue

21. "Manager's Report to the Executive Committee," January 22, 1975, BCCCU Board Minutes.

22. Bob Hornal, "What is the Business of a Credit Union?" and "What We Need is a Philosophy," January 23, 1974, BCCCU Archives.

Over the years, representatives from credit unions and B.C. Central have met regularly with politicians at the municipal, provincial, and federal levels to protect the interests of credit unions and to demonstrate how the movement can assist individuals and communities to meet economic and social needs. *Top*, a credit union delegation meets with Tommy Douglas, leader of the federal New Democratic Party (*centre*). In the second photo, leaders of the movement huddle with B.C. Premier Dave Barrett (*centre, right*).

(bottom)

In the early 1970s, relations between the Credit Union Reserve Board and the credit union system were particularly cordial and constructive. Seen here are the board's five members of the time: *back row, from left:* Geoff Hook and Peter Podovinikoff; *front row, from left,* Ian Strang, Stan Stonier, and Wiata Winiata.

of credit union distinctiveness. He stressed that credit unions should have social and psychological purposes as well as economic objectives.

Equally, Hornal stressed that credit unions had to be competently operated, arguing that those critical of "philosophy" had mistakenly blamed idealism for the problems some credit unions had encountered. In his view, they should have blamed incompetence, for him a much more common cause. Above all, he argued that providing "banking" services was not the end purpose of a credit union; rather, a credit union was the means whereby individuals, "in a trustworthy world," could develop economically and socially, even psychologically.

Hornal's first solution was to create more credit unions, not fewer, essentially by transforming branches into new credit unions. In this vision, Central would become the chief support for local credit unions, and it would be the main instigator of new initiatives. His diagnosis had much to recommend it, but his proposed solution came too late to gain much acceptance. The same fate befell a later and rather innovative suggestion by Hornal that credit unions consider franchising branches so that they could retain considerable community involvement.[23] It was too radical an idea, however, and raised questions about how to preserve managerial efficiencies. There was no stopping the drive to fewer and larger credit unions.

There were also growing concerns about the declining role being played by elected leaders in the movement. Within the most rapidly expanding credit unions, directors were increasingly finding it difficult to maintain control over their organizations. Within Central, it was also becoming apparent that control of the board had passed to managers, particularly those from the larger credit unions. In 1975, for example, 13 of the 15 members of Central's board were managers, all of them drawn from among the 40 largest credit unions.[24]

Moreover, the 80 smallest credit unions rarely sent representatives to Central's general meetings. Their directors or secretary-treasurers seldom appeared because they were unable to attend the five-day sessions; in many instances, too, the credit union just could not afford to send a delegate. In the view of one observer, "control of the 'bureaucratic apparatus' in the B.C. Credit Union Movement [had] passed to the professional elite."[25] Consequently, he warned that "the end could be similar to that of George Orwell's *Animal Farm* where in the final scenes, the animals (the members) can distinguish no difference between their leaders, the pigs (the Managerial elite) and the humans (the Private Banks)."[26]

Several suggestions were put forward to help deal with these problems, some of which were adopted immediately or subsequently. These included Central paying the costs of delegates attending its meetings and the use of mail-in ballots to make greater participation possible.

23. "Co-operation or Competition – Common Bond or Open Warfare," August 24-25, 1974, BCCCU Board Minutes.

24. Moore, "Towards 2000 – With Participation," p. 23.

25. Ibid., p. 9.

26. Ibid., p. 10.

Others advocated increased regional activities for Central, and discussions began about how to restructure Central's board to ensure better regional representation – an idea that helped spark a two-decade preoccupation with the board's structure. Some suggested that there be two Central meetings each year, one a business session, the other a convention – an idea that found considerable support and was adopted. All of these suggestions were an effort to bring Central closer to its members and to stimulate discussion among delegates. They were a reaction to a perceived (and probably partly correct) view that Central was dominated by an ever-smaller number of increasingly powerful "movers and shakers."

At the same time, there was a growing concern about the health of democratic procedures within local credit unions. Attendance at annual meetings was declining, and, as credit unions grew larger, a small minority could easily gain control. Moreover, at many credit union annual meetings, staff outnumbered other members. Staff members, therefore, could determine who sat on the board, potentially a very unhealthy situation. There were also concerns in larger credit unions about the roles of branches in the democratic process: Should they elect directors? Should members vote at the branches over a period of days, rather than at the annual meeting? All of these ideas were debated in many credit unions, starting in the later 1970s. Many of them would be implemented by certain credit unions in the 1980s.

While, in many respects, the B.C. economy was strong and growing, there were equally significant social and economic problems confronting many British Columbians. Indeed, many who criticized the way credit unions expanded in this period believed that expansion had resulted in the movement ignoring a major part of its real constituency – the poor and nearly poor. It was a difficult and often ideological issue. Those who reacted to the criticism argued that credit unions generally had simply used most of their assets to meet a most basic and vital need: housing. But that answer did not satisfy everyone.

In a broader perspective, credit unions were caught somewhere between the desperation of poverty and the glamour of the new entrepreneurship. On the poverty side of the ledger, there was a considerable social conscience – beyond a concern for housing – evident in the movement in the 1970s. Much of this social concern could be found in local credit unions.

In 1976, for example, a credit union was established by the Lower Mainland Community Congress for Economic Change. The Congress, which included many Americans influenced by the urban reform movements of the 1960s and early 1970s, defined its "community" as a grouping of self-help organizations. The credit union they established, called CCEC Credit Union, was unique for B.C. but was

During the late 1960s but particularly the 1970s, leaders of the B.C. movement became active in the international credit union movement. Their efforts were recognized by this World Award, presented to the B.C. League by CUNA International.

Rod Glen was especially involved in the worldwide movement. In this 1979 photo, *below*, he receives an ovation at a World Council of Credit Unions meeting in Australia for his work on behalf of credit unions in Latin America. Adding congratulations is Chris Hansen, left, chairman of CCCS, Canada's national credit union organization.

As the B.C. movement emerged as an important player on the world stage, it was maturing into an essential element of the society and economy in its home province. The opening of the nine-storey Credit Union Centre in 1978 symbolized this progress, and the building remains a prominent landmark in British Columbia's largest city, *right*.

BC Central Credit Union

patterned after similar experiments in Quebec. Using a federal government employment grant, the organizers reached out to groups of unemployed people and community organizations. In fact, 30 of the new credit union's early members were organizations active among the urban poor, women's groups and Natives. An unusual feature of the credit union was that it initially paid its members no interest on their deposits and used the accumulated savings for community economic and social development.[27] The experiment would come to have an impact well beyond British Columbia.

In the same period, a credit union was started among Native peoples, but its members were too diverse and too poor to make it successful. Other credit unions with an obvious commitment to social issues channelled their interests into providing housing, particularly for low-income people. While most projects were undertaken with the assistance of government funding, several were not.

Central, too, clearly demonstrated a desire to mobilize credit union resources to deal with pressing social issues. One of the projects it undertook was to develop a "limited income or low-cost credit facility." The underlying rationale was that most local credit unions, preoccupied with making a good return for their members, would find it difficult to lend to low-income earners at the going rates. Moreover, it was becoming recognized, particularly in the United States, that lending to people with low incomes was a specialized activity. In 1972, Central established CUPAC Services Society to make loans to people with low incomes, charging them on the basis of "ability to pay" rather than the conventional market rate. Under this program, credit unions would refer such applicants to Central, where a small group of qualified lenders would see if loans were possible. By the middle of the decade, about 100 applicants were successful each year.

By 1978, then, B.C. Central had become a large, aggressive organization. Early in the year, George May was appointed chief executive officer of the Canadian Co-operative Credit Society (CCCS), the national central based in Toronto. CCCS had been reorganized in 1977, its capitalization had been increased by credit union centrals and its major member co-operatives, and there seemed to be a desire within the Canadian co-operative movement to create a true national liquidity pool. May was attracted by the possibilities, and he hoped to replicate the kind of growth for which he had been largely responsible at Central.

He was replaced by Peter Podovinikoff, then the president of Central's Board of Directors and chief executive officer of Delta Credit Union. Podovinikoff inherited a large, some would say bloated, organization that for a year or so continued to grow under his leadership. Unfortunately, he started the job as the economy began to decline. In

27. "CCEC Credit Union," October 3, 1975, BCCCU Board Minutes.

fact, starting in 1976, B.C. credit unions had seen their margins begin to shrink. That is, the difference between the rate at which credit unions loaned money to their members, regardless of type of loan, and the rate they paid on deposits, had narrowed. In fact, margins had shrunk from about 4% at the start of the decade to little over 2%. One of the main reasons for this change was that Central, under pressure from local credit unions, had begun to switch its investments from high-yielding personal and commercial loans to mortgages, which earned significantly less. The impact on Central and credit unions, especially those particularly sensitive to market trends, was serious, although the full effect would not be understood for a few years.

Nonetheless, 1978 ended optimistically. In November, Central moved into its new quarters on False Creek. An attractive building, a pleasant mixture of brick, glass and plants, it rose nine stories. It offered magnificent views of the ocean, the city and the mountains beyond. A large fleet of fishing boats anchored just beyond its front door, a daily reminder of the role played by fishing people in founding the movement. In the fields nearby, only partly filled, there was room for housing. Across the water, beyond the fishing fleet, lay Granville Island, soon to be a key symbol of the city's vitality. If one looked, there were ample reminders of where credit unions had come from; there were also signs of the places where they yet might go.

"Nanoosing"
1978-1984

Business

COR
Week

PLOYERS, IWA SIGN TWO-YEAR PACT

First local sawmill clos

ENTERPRISE
A MAGAZINE FOR CREDIT UNION OFFICERS   January/February 1980

CO-OP

mployers' negotiator Keith Bennett   est industry and the sector's largest union Friday in Hotel Vancou
Munro signing two-year accord between for-   ver. Contract ends six-week strike.

HINTERLAND HOUSING

Prices join languishing Vancouver

By BRIAN POWER
Sun Business Writer

A heavy dose of high interest rates is now dragging down housing prices throughout B.C. as municipalities slip into the same doldrums that Vancouver has languished in for months.

The downturn has been less dramatic than Vancouver's because the outside municipalities did not experience the same wild surge that affected the big city last fall.

Still watchers throughout B.C. say that the panic in Vancouver has in some ways affected the whole province.

People watched housing quickly become unaffordable in Vancouver and started buying, an attitude that helped drive up the prices from September at a 61 per cent increase from March and by at least $25,000 in Kamloops during the same period.

Or they tell...

on the Sechelt Peninsula has skyrocketed 400 per cent in the past year, says Ken Wells, of the Sunshine Coast Real Estate association. They sell for up to $35,000 around Sechelt or Gibson's while waterfront property goes for up to $50,000 and more.

Said Gibson Realty manager Ken Cosby: "Our normal sales are up in the summer time but we have almost followed Vancouver to a dead halt."

NANAIMO: Things have died down in this boom city. Prices are being cut weekly, says Vancouver Island Real Estate board manager Bill Wynne.

their homes in Calgary or Edmonton, buy an identical house in Kelowna and walk away with $20,000 in their pockets," said Dennis. "Now they will probably have to make up the difference.

He quoted high land costs — $60,000 for a typical Kelowna home — a large number of developers and a fundamental market shift before interest rates jumped and the market is now glutted with them.

Okanagan prices vary widely with a three-bedroom house selling for in Kelowna for $100,000 to June and $89,000 in Vernon.

You can buy a three-bedroom bungalow in the city for $108 not to $110,000, about $12,000 less than in May, says Black Bros. Realty manager Bill Wynne.

The city has new lots onto the market and one in a modern subdivision can be picked up for under $50,000.

PRINCE RUPERT: In what may be a...

Stanle
Va

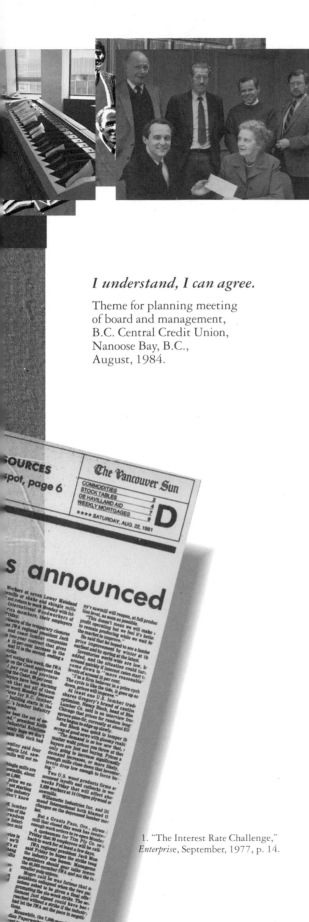

I understand, I can agree.

Theme for planning meeting
of board and management,
B.C. Central Credit Union,
Nanoose Bay, B.C.,
August, 1984.

1. "The Interest Rate Challenge,"
Enterprise, September, 1977, p. 14.

*L*ATE IN 1977, ROSS MONTGOMERY, THEN GENERAL MANAGER of the Credit Union Reserve Board, issued a warning. He was alarmed about the interest rates that credit unions were paying members for deposits; in some instances, their rates were 2% higher than their competitors'. He was equally alarmed that some credit unions were charging up to 2% less than the going market rate for mortgages.

These were dangerous practices and his explanation was straightforward:

> Obviously, credit unions are not operating as thrift institutions in the province of British Columbia. They are encouraging people to borrow, not to fill the "needs" of their members; instead, they try to create "wants" so that there will be an outlet for their surplus funds. Because of the growth syndrome, credit unions are competing with other credit unions, not with the competition, the other financial institutions in the market place. It seems that credit unions are not interested in helping others, or really helping their members. They are merely concerned with their own growth.[1]

He had struck a chord. The growth of the preceding decade or so had come at a cost. It had been so rapid that the institutional culture of most of the larger credit unions, especially in the metropolitan areas, had been dramatically altered. Moreover, their capacity to co-operate with each other had declined alarmingly. Over the next six years, the most difficult in the history of the B.C. movement, that already strained capacity would be stretched even further.

The specific issue addressed by Montgomery was the change brought about by amendments in the Credit Union Act in 1975, which allowed local credit unions to set their own interest rates. Previously, they had had to submit proposed changes to the Inspector, who traditionally (and in keeping with Canadian views on rates) tended to permit few changes. After 1975, the Superintendent (as the chief regulator was renamed in the amendments of that year) would not be involved in rate changes unless the credit union was under supervision.

Given this new freedom, some credit unions adopted what came to be inappropriate rate structures in order to gain temporary advantages in specific marketplaces. They made such decisions either because they did not have managers with adequate expertise, or because ambition had overcome their common sense. In that sense, the rates issue was symptomatic of the kinds of changes wrought by the 1975 and 1976 revisions of the Act. Those revisions, largely written by credit union leaders and Bill Wright (the successor to Bob McMaster as the pre-eminent co-operative lawyer in the province), gave immense freedom to credit unions.

In particular, the revisions allowed credit unions to undertake virtually every kind of "banking" activity. The corollary of this freedom, of course, was that they would have to achieve increased discipline. It would take some years – and some mistakes – before the need for that discipline was learned.

In fact, the deeper issue embedded in Montgomery's comments was that credit unions were not being as cautious as they should have been. The general expansion of the 1970s, when credit unions had such a significant advantage in mortgage lending, had made a few of them over-confident to the point of recklessness. More to the point, some of them did not employ the requisite trained people when starting new initiatives, perhaps understandably since many of the managers in the seventies were people who had learned most of their skills on the job.

Montgomery's appeal was also necessary because the competition for deposits and for loans to people of medium income was increasing rapidly. In 1976, the chartered banks had begun to compete fully for mortgage loans to Canadians of all income levels. It was a change that would ultimately draw credit unions out of the secluded niches they had created for themselves.

In the increasingly competitive mortgage business that resulted, credit unions briefly maintained their advantages. Through their open-ended payment privileges, rapid approval procedures, and convenient hours of service, they were initially able to offer better services. But as the decade came to an end, the banks responded, in some instances imitating the open-ended payment feature, but competing primarily on the basis of lower interest rates on mortgage loans.

This competition, along with steadily rising interest rates, meant that local credit unions and Central itself were facing a serious margin squeeze by the later seventies. In 1978, the net income of all the credit unions in British Columbia was $26.4-million; in 1979, it was $13.5-million, and it would not exceed $20-million again until 1982. This meant that the capacity of the local credit unions to build reserves declined seriously, even though the movement continued to grow at a steady pace. Similarly, in the same period, Central's assets grew at the rate of $30- to $50-million a year, but its net earnings did not. In 1981, Central's net income declined by almost 30% from the previous year, dropping from $6.8-million to $4.9-million. Central did not start to recover until 1983, and even that recovery was short-lived, as interest rates hurt Central's net income again in 1984.

In fact, between 1978 and 1984, the credit union movement was buffeted by economic crises beyond anything it had known before. For nearly all of their history in the province, credit unions had known only growth and profitability. When there had been difficulties, they had been caused by local problems, such as the closure of a mine, the occasional case of fraud, and errors made by managers and boards. Until 1978, credit unions had not had to deal with the turmoil caused by structural problems and the decline of an entire economy. Understandably, they were not particularly well prepared to cope when the serious problems appeared.

The main problem of the period – and by far the most important reason for the turmoil that erupted – was the economic crisis that beset Canada and particularly British Columbia. A principal villain was inflation, which reached unparalleled heights, but it was aided and abetted by the unlikely twin of economic stagnation.

In the later 1970s, after an upward blip in the middle of the decade, interest rates had apparently stabilized at 7%. In fact, like many investors of the period, the investment managers at Central thought it a good idea to purchase government bonds. In the late 1970s, particularly 1978, they invested $170-million in bonds; as it turned out (and as critics long reminded Central), this was not the best of investments. In a little over 20 months, between March, 1978, and December, 1979, interest rates rose 11 times, and reached 14%. In the early 1980s, rates soared to 23%.

Like most managers of Canadian financial institutions, the managers of B.C. credit unions were unprepared for this type of change, which could occur, and ultimately usually did, each Thursday when the government announced its treasury bill rate. Some credit unions even moved their monthly (as times worsened, sometimes bi-weekly) meetings to Thursday night so they could react to the latest changes. Unlike the early seventies, the years that followed in the late seventies and, especially, the early eighties were not happy times to have responsibility for managing a credit union.

But if the impact of the inflationary spiral was troublesome for credit unions, it was disastrous for many British Columbians. Of course, those who had funds on deposit benefited significantly as deposit rates rose to the high teens. The vast majority, however – people who thought of themselves as the middle class – were all too often soon facing the kinds of economic troubles not seen since the Great Depression. In fact, it is arguable that the decline of the Canadian middle class (on whose prosperity most of the post-war expansion had been based) began in the "stagflation" of the early eighties. And with that decline, the country began to experience fundamental change.

On a more immediate level, for many members of B.C. credit unions, the economic pressures of the period put their housing at risk. Between 60% and 70% of the total amount lent by credit unions at that time was in mortgages, almost entirely in first mortgages. When most of those mortgage loans were made, the assumption was that borrowers could afford to pay about 30% of their gross income for housing costs. In keeping with human nature, most borrowers pressed that rule to the limit.

As mortgage rates doubled and then tripled, the pressures on those with large mortgages became torturous, as their payments rose to 50% or even 60% of their original income. Mortgage renewal could be agony; for some, although only a very few, it meant walking away from their homes, along with all the consequences that entailed.

It is difficult to know with certainty how credit unions collectively treated their members during these crises. But the anecdotal evidence suggests that most credit unions worked hard to renegotiate mortgages and to be patient with families who could pay only a portion of their mortgage payment.

Perhaps, then, the two affluent members of Lake View Credit Union who accepted no return on their large share accounts, as a contribution to younger families facing hardships, were not unique.[2] There is also the case of one credit union in the Victoria area that, despite a seriously worsening financial situation, only foreclosed on a handful of mortgages, far fewer than traditionally "prudent" practice would have dictated.

In fact, the general trend within credit unions, as members faced problems in making loan payments, was to renegotiate the loan so the payments could be met. In that respect, they broke one of the fundamental rules of banking: "the first loss is the least loss." It was a rule that deserved to be broken in the early eighties, and it often was, to the benefit of both members and credit unions.

In the final analysis, though, the only way British Columbians could meet such pressures was by having two or more jobs in a single household. By the late seventies, over half of all married women were working for pay outside the home; the numbers of young people working in service jobs had increased dramatically; college and university students had started to take longer to complete their studies; and domestic violence had increased amid growing social pressures.

As conditions tightened in the middle and later seventies, B.C. Central began to examine the possibilities of commercial lending. Between 1944 and the early seventies, commercial loans had been made only to fishing and consumer co-operatives. While there had been some problems with these loans, they had usually been profitable and free from losses. One reason why the experiences had been generally positive was that the leaders of local co-ops were typically well-connected to credit union leaders; this meant that bad experiences were usually known about long before the situation became desperate. At the same time, though, some of these associations could mean that credit unions were loath to take strong action when loans to co-operatives were in trouble.

During the earlier and mid-seventies, two types of consumer co-operatives began to appear in British Columbia. One was a group of

uring the 1970s and early 1980s, Central worked very closely with its consumer co-operative members to promote the co-operative movement. Each year it published a special issue of *Enterprise* devoted to co-operative activities around the province. Central, and local credit unions, funded the construction of several co-operative stores, such as the one in Nanaimo, pictured on the right. Most of the stores on Vancouver Island were organized on a "service fee" basis, a system whereby members paid for the costs of operating the store on a weekly fee basis and then purchased goods at virtual cost prices.

2. Interview with David Griffeth, October 15, 1994.

ENTERPRISE

A MAGAZINE FOR CREDIT UNION OFFICERS   January/February 1980

CO-OP

health food co-ops loosely associated through their own wholesale organization, Fed-Up Co-op, a name that reflected in part their opposition to the ways in which the conventional co-operative system was operating through Federated Co-operatives. This group was particularly concerned about reforming the food distribution system in the interests of purer food. It was also concerned about how management structures could be democratized, a particularly challenging task in the food industry, where chains of command and tight discipline seem to be essential. Needless to say, its approach was at odds with that taken by the conventional co-operatives.

The second group consisted of direct charge or service fee co-operatives, most of which were located on Vancouver Island. Rod Glen was a tireless evangelist for this new form of co-operative, and he popularized them across Canada. In Atlantic Canada, his efforts assisted local enthusiasts in the development of the service fee concept, which found extensive support and grew to become a significant element in the region's retailing system.

Glen even had a modest international impact, and the "Nanaimo experiment" became widely known in co-operative circles in Australia, South America, and even Europe. Glen nevertheless had little success in convincing the leaders of Federated Co-operatives, the wholesale organization serving some 300 traditionally-structured co-operatives in Western Canada, that the service fee approach could work on the Prairies or in British Columbia. Without Federated's strong support, it would be difficult to promote the service fee concept across British Columbia.

Thus, in 1978, when B.C. Central and Federated Co-operatives formed a joint committee to consider how they might expand the consumer co-operative movement in British Columbia, they worked on floating loans to develop conventional co-operatives.[3] When the committee reported in 1979, it outlined the problems confronting the establishment of new co-operatives and proposed that a new consumer society be organized in Kelowna, then thought to be the most fertile area for a new co-operative.[4] The new store opened in April, 1981.

In the early eighties, there were other major initiatives aimed at creating large, conventional consumer co-operatives, the loans usually being extended not through local credit unions but through Central. The most prominent of these loans was for an expansion of Surrey Co-op and the development of a new co-operative in Salmon Arm. In addition, Central lent funds for the development of new service fee co-operatives on Vancouver Island.

With the exception of some of the stores on the Island, these loans did not turn out well. The Kelowna and Salmon Arm co-ops failed,

3. For a fuller discussion of the efforts to create consumer co-operatives, see Brett Fairbairn, *Building a Dream: The Co-operative Retailing System in Western Canada, 1928-1988* (Saskatoon: Western Producer Prairie Books, 1989), pp. 238-245.

4. *Enterprise*, January-February, 1980, p. 6.

Surrey was overextended when interest rates moved upward, and two of the stores on the Island were forced to close. Central lost very little in these closures, its investments being well-secured. Nevertheless, the problems consumed considerable managerial time and, even more importantly, emotional energy during the early eighties. They also marked the end of Central's financial support for the consumer co-op movement. Henceforth, such co-ops would have to secure their funds on a local level, either from credit unions or, more commonly, from other financial institutions.

During the same period, though, and far more significantly, Central and local credit unions became involved with commercial loans to privately-owned businesses. Indeed, although a few credit unions had dabbled in commercial lending to non-co-operative businesses, it was B.C. Central that gave this activity a considerable stimulus, starting in 1977.

That year, Central organized a Business Loan Co-ordinating Service, which advised credit unions on business lending for a fee. Staffed initially by Bruce Higgs and William Clark, it gave advice on how to make mortgage, operating and term loans to businesses. It was a service worked out in conjunction with the Reserve Board, and it received a good response from credit unions, especially the medium-sized operations.[5]

Meanwhile, Central and the larger credit unions were beginning to write large commercial loans in significant amounts. Central's entry into non-co-operative commercial lending began in earnest shortly after the amalgamation. George May was widely known in Vancouver's business circles, and his vision was that Central should become a major financial player in the total economy. Central's board at the time, too, was largely made up of managers intrigued by the possibilities of commercial lending. Most supported the initiatives in the beginning, often with considerable enthusiasm. A few, notably Saanich Peninsula's manager, went home from the meetings to consider how their own credit unions could make such loans.

At the same time, the larger credit unions, especially VanCity, were also becoming interested. It was not long before the two organizations were pursuing the same clients, and that situation did not generate good feelings between Central and its largest member. In fact, it became one of the main reasons why Central had great difficulty in retaining the support of all the large credit unions through to the middle of the 1980s.

But it was not only the very largest credit unions that were interested in the business. Several medium-sized operations also became involved, especially after 1980, when credit unions were faced with deteriorating balance sheets. At that time, larger commercial loans

5. "Business loan service offered," *Enterprise*, October, 1977, pp. 17-19.

had to be approved by the Reserve Board. Indeed, some credit union boards became less diligent than they should have been in reviewing some of the larger commercial loans, since they thought approval by CURB was a sufficient safeguard.

The attractions of commercial lending were obvious for many credit unions. Such loans usually earned higher interest rates than most other loans, and they typically offered credit unions the immediate advantage of substantial up-front fees. Moreover, many commercial loans seemed to create a meaningful social benefit in that they stimulated local economies, thereby providing employment and encouraging growth. In an era when many local economies were in trouble and when many credit unions were enduring reduced incomes, these loans seemed like a god-send.

Between 1978 and 1982, CURB approved more than 300 large commercial loans annually, an indication of how widespread the practice was becoming. The two largest credit unions in Victoria, Saanich Peninsula and Westcoast Savings, were among the most active participants. They were in a part of the province that, for a while, seemed insulated from economic distress because of government, military and university payrolls and because of the growing importance of tourism. They consequently had opportunities to attract deposits and to grow significantly, and they were given an incentive when the federal government created MURBS, a tax shelter to encourage investors to build lower-cost housing. Buoyed by its early successes, Westcoast Savings began to make loans throughout the province, going as far afield as Fort St. John, Dawson Creek and the Okanagan Valley.

In fact, both credit unions moved too aggressively into this kind of financial activity, believing that the diversity of their new investments would ensure a stable return for their memberships and a basis for growth. Unfortunately, their boards did not have sufficient training or experience to monitor this new kind of business effectively. Nor were they sufficiently resolute to curtail the enthusiasms of their managers – one of the chief duties of any board. The result was that, by 1984, both credit unions were accumulating large deficits as their commercial investments, particularly in MURBS, ran into difficulty. The full extent of their problems would become apparent in the next two years.

This experience in commercial lending was salutary (although ultimately expensive) for several reasons. First, it reflected the strong, if sometimes misapplied, entrepreneurial spirit within credit unions. Second, it demonstrated the importance of ensuring that boards had sufficient experience and training, so that they could properly monitor and, when necessary, curtail management. Third, it pointed out the crucial importance of entering into new business ventures slowly, after ensuring the credit union had the appropriate expertise and leadership. Credit unions had to recognize that each new enterprise would likely have unexpected "learning" costs. Fourth, especially in light of the Victoria situation, it showed the importance of limiting the amount invested in commercial lending, so that only strong borrowers were attracted and potential losses were stemmed. For all those reasons, the experience had lessons for future diversification.

In retrospect, though, it is easy to exaggerate the importance of commercial lending and the economic problems of the time. The most important point was that the credit unions of the period dealt with their adversity well. No credit union depositor in British Columbia lost money. Most of the mergers that occurred were essentially the absorptions of weaker credit unions by the more prosperous; almost all were voluntary and amicable. Most were encouraged, if not arranged, by CURB; none precipitated deep public dissatisfaction. The reserve fund, while under pressure, was not exhausted. The government, while worried about potential liability, was never called upon for assistance, as were the governments of Alberta and Manitoba by their credit union movements.

It is also important to realize that other financial institutions across Canada, and perhaps in British Columbia, suffered proportionately greater losses. Three small western banks were closed, the first Canadian banks to meet that fate in 70 years. The federal deposit insurance fund for the chartered banks, which were supposedly better managed, exhausted its reserves and required extensive assistance from Ottawa to cover the losses incurred by the banks. More than 10 years later, the fund was still burdened with a $1.7-billion deficit. Moreover, the trust companies, which had expanded their business almost as much as credit unions in the 1960s and 1970s, started to decline significantly. The economic crisis of the early eighties showed clearly that credit unions, particularly in British Columbia, had become permanent, stable and effective participants, even leaders, in the economy.

Nevertheless, the financial problems encountered by the movement in the late seventies and early eighties were important. The problems forced upon credit unions a type of discipline they had not known before. They forced credit unions to examine their practices and even question the previously automatic assumption that growth was a benefit. No longer could new initiatives be undertaken without careful research, meticulous preparation and knowledgeable personnel. The days of fearless overconfidence had drawn to a close.

The problems also forced the B.C. movement to re-examine its provincial structures. In particular, they exacerbated the debate over how Central was controlled by its members, particularly its member

he Credit Union Foundation was established in 1958 as the Westcu Foundation. In the early years, it was promoted and cared for by a handful, most notably Lucille Sutherland and Wes Darling, for whom it was a work of love. From the beginning, the Foundation had a strong commitment to helping young people gain their education. It also helped people who had particularly difficult challenges in their daily lives, such as single parents and seniors on reduced incomes.

In more recent years, the Foundation has grown steadily under the leadership of people such as Ross Montgomery, Bill Wright, Phil and Rose Moore, and Bert Gladu.

From its earliest years, the Foundation has also assumed the role of funding co-operative banking projects overseas. In this 1984 picture, Lucille Sutherland presents a cheque to Bruce Thordarson of the Co-operative Union of Canada for a project in Latin America. Behind her, left to right, are trustees Ron Briggs, Wes Darling, Phil Moore and Bill Wright.

credit unions. That issue had started to emerge in the earlier seventies as the movement began to be differentiated according to the size of credit unions. It would continue for a decade to be one of the most difficult problems the movement had to face.

As the larger credit unions became more sophisticated, as they employed more specialists in marketing, investing and personnel than Central itself, their need for Central's services declined. Consequently, they began to question the amount of dues they were paying to Central each year, dues that some believed were supporting services they did not require.

In fact, one of the problems in the relationship between Central and local credit unions involved the lack of clarity in how Central raised and spent its funds. To some extent, the fuzziness was explained by the two differing visions that existed when the League and Central amalgamated. Glen, May and their associates saw the revised Central as the hub of the movement, the centre of a powerful force in the provincial economy. They wanted, therefore, to maximize the power of Central and, necessarily, its capacity to raise funds. They did not care particularly where the funds came from since, in their view, the funds were all of a piece – the consequences of movement solidarity. The result was that the financial statements presented by Central did not clearly differentiate where funds came from and where they were spent. In a movement increasingly sophisticated in its accounting procedures, such ambiguities were unacceptable.

Many Central advocates, such as Rip Robinson and Geoff Hook (by the late seventies the manager of VanCity), never believed in a broad mission for Central in the first place. They believed Central had two distinct roles: a limited set of "trade association" activities and a cheque-clearing/liquidity management function. That view gained increasing support as some credit unions became larger and more concerned about how their investments in Central and their annual dues were used.

These were two distinct views, which would clash for a decade and would be forced to contest with each other in a period of economic adversity. At the same time, there was growing resentment over Central's activities in commercial lending. Some, for ideological reasons, did not support making loans to co-operatives, reflecting a lingering belief that most co-operatives were refuges for left-wingers. More importantly, opponents resented Central's increasing involvement with other commercial lending, particularly in the Greater Vancouver area. For those most aroused, the only way to limit, if not end, such lending activities was to increase the influence of the largest credit unions over B.C. Central. It would be a long, debilitating and cantankerous debate.

Central had tried to react to the growing concerns of some of the larger credit unions by organizing regular meetings of representatives from the largest 20, starting in 1974. Those meetings had partly alleviated the concerns, but by 1976 some of the more aroused credit unions, particularly VanCity, Westcoast Savings and Richmond Savings, were pressing for a reconsideration of the way in which credit unions exercised control over B.C. Central. They sparked brief but acrimonious debates at the 1976 and 1977 annual meetings, when motions calling for proportional voting based on the size of credit unions (by assets or members) were put – and defeated.

In some ways, the control issue was rather simple. From Central's beginning in 1944, each member credit union had possessed one vote. This practice was in accordance with what was widely assumed to be the norm (one member, one vote) within the international co-operative movement. That assumption was dubious, but deeply felt, meaning that considerable passion could be aroused by questioning it.[6] Between 1975 and 1985, every annual meeting witnessed a significant debate over voting entitlements and the meaning of democracy.

There were a number of questions inevitably involved whenever proportional voting was discussed. Was it an appropriate way to control co-operative organizations? How might it be implemented? How could the interests of small credit unions be recognized? Particularly in the context of the ongoing debates over branching and commercial lending, such questions could not be debated calmly or openly.

Nor was it an issue peculiar to British Columbia. Around the world, the one-member, one-vote principle was virtually unchallenged within the local or first-tier co-operatives, but, from the early twentieth century, there was a range of voting practices in second-tier organizations such as B.C. Central. In fact, in 1966, the International Co-operative Alliance, the international organization for co-operatives, had formally adopted as a "Principle" that co-operatives at other than the first tier could be organized on an "appropriate democratic basis." The challenge, of course, was to decide what was "appropriate."

Among B.C. credit unions, the issue became particularly emotional for readily understandable reasons. For those who held to the traditional assumptions of one vote for each credit union, the issue was partly self interest: that is, the desire to retain as much power as possible. But, equally, it was a question of ensuring that different voices would be heard, that those preoccupied with simplistic notions of growth for its own sake would not debase the movement. For those who wanted some form of proportional voting, the issue was how to ensure that difficult business decisions were made effectively, so that those credit unions that contributed considerable capital could be confident it would be employed to maximum advantage.

There was another dimension to the debate, less obvious but critically important. The increasing sophistication of the larger credit unions inevitably meant that they were influenced markedly by conventional thinking in North American business circles. That thinking had little precedent to contribute to a discussion of how Central had to be organized if it was going to live up to its co-operative mandate.

For most observers of North American business structures, only two models were really acceptable. There was the contractual approach to obtaining specific services, or there was ownership through subsidiary operations. Neither model fitted exactly a second-tier co-operative structure, in which power was shared, sometimes informally. That ambiguity was a structural problem for co-operatives operating amid the conventional management theory of the North Atlantic capitalist world. It perhaps explains why the most successful second-

6. Joe Weremchuk, "Problems Aired at Common Bond Hearings," *Enterprise*, April, 1978, pp. 18-19.

and third-tier co-operative enterprises since the 1970s have been in Asia, southern Europe, and South America, where ambiguous relationships are more accepted and their benefits more readily understood. In British Columbia, the lack of a readily sanctioned model for the relationships basic to Central would long remain a cause of discord.

Late in 1977, at the same time as it became known that George May was leaving Central, the leaders of the largest 20 credit unions stepped up their demands for reconsidering Central's control structure. Some spoke out at meetings of the Common Bond Committee as it met with credit union leaders in its travels around the province that year. They also passed a motion at the formal meeting of the Big 20 credit unions that autumn. Thus, when Peter Podovinikoff became Central's chief executive officer on January 1, 1978, one of his first tasks was to propose that a committee be struck to reconsider Central's control structure.

The Board of Directors appointed a committee, chaired by Wayne Carpenter, manager of Surrey Credit Union. It prepared a draft report and met with credit union representatives throughout the province, finally completing its report in January, 1979. The report was a compromise that gave one vote in Central elections to all credit unions with up to 2,000 members and 10 votes to VanCity, with its nearly 42,000 members; the 15 next largest credit unions each had between five and seven votes. Looked at in another way, the 140 smallest credit unions (out of the 168 that belonged to Central) had over 60% of the voting entitlement. The report was debated and adopted at an extraordinary meeting in late 1979. It did not end the debate, however, since it was a compromise that only partly placated the largest credit unions and antagonized many of the smaller ones.

Within two years, as the economy worsened and margins narrowed, the larger credit unions again pushed for reconsideration of the control structure. In 1982, yet another committee was appointed, and its deliberations would consume considerable time and energy over the next two years. The control structure issue, a hardy perennial amid the staple co-operative debates, had arrived and it would not soon disappear.

There were similar questions of control and purpose within the national system. In part, these emerged out of the challenges created by changes occurring within the Canadian payments system. The system was moving steadily from an almost exclusive reliance on cash and paper transactions toward electronic transactions. That change posed several difficult questions for the national credit union movement. Who should manage the new system? Should there be several systems? Who should be included in the system? How should it be funded? How should the new system be governed?

In a series of reports between 1975 and 1978, the federal government decided that there should be one system, funded by "qualified users" on a user-fee basis. It ultimately insisted that non-bank financial institutions be included in the group, since they accounted for over 20% of the Canadian financial system.[7] But their inclusion was not automatic and required considerable lobbying from the leaders of the caisses populaires and credit unions during the later seventies. George May, Peter Podovinikoff and Fred Graham played important roles in helping to define and to promote the position of credit unions in this campaign. In fact, it was May's involvement in national issues that led him to join the Canadian Co-operative Credit Society.

Indeed, the payments issue encouraged many people to take a greater interest in the possibilities of a national organization. In response to this growing interest, CCCS expanded its membership from five to nine credit union centrals and from seven to twelve major co-operatives in 1977. This expansion demonstrated that the long-standing differences of opinion over insurance and philosophy were gradually abating. Some of the older protagonists had retired, and it was possible once again to dream of creating a national financial co-operative centre.

In part, too, the increased support for a stronger national entity emanated from two growing fears. One was what could happen if a provincial system were to fail, perhaps because of circumstances beyond its control. In fact, during the mid-seventies, two credit union centrals, Alberta and Ontario, neither of which was a member of CCCS at the time, encountered severe liquidity crises. They were assisted by nearby centrals to overcome their temporary problems, but only on the condition that they would join the national organization.

The second fear was related to what might happen as the Canadian Payments Association evolved. The negotiations for the CPA's forma-tion were complex and forced an unprecedented degree of information sharing, joint activity and co-ordination among the provincial centrals, a process led by CCCS. Much of the leadership also came from the pro-vincial centrals; Peter Podovinikoff, in particular, played a major role.

The significance of the CPA initiative cannot be overestimated, though it was seldom discussed in public forums in British Columbia. Because of it, credit unions became members of the association as full-fledged direct clearers. Because of it, credit union leaders started to play important roles in the Canadian banking industry. Norm Bromberger, Saskatchewan Central's chief executive officer, was appointed to the CPA's board, while other credit union leaders sat on some of its key committees.

The impact of these negotiations was particularly important. With the exception of only two, or at times three, of the larger credit unions, the English-Canadian movement was united through CCCS, thereby maximizing its strength on the national level. This integration, in

7. Reports on the Canadian Payments System, April, 1983, BCCCU Board Minutes.

turn, meant that the provincial centrals had to develop a strong communication system so they could assemble the information in a "timely" fashion. Once accomplished in the early eighties, this collaboration, in turn, was a significant factor in promoting greater co-operation across provincial barriers.

This growing unity soon impressed governments and other financial institutions. For the first time, the credit union system was perceived as a national force in the financial services industry, and it was able to negotiate satisfactory terms for participation in the CPA. Subsequently, credit union leaders were more frequently asked for opinions by government leaders, and CCCS became a much more aggressive lobbying organization in Ottawa. As in the past, B.C. Central played an important role, through continuing annual visits with the Members of Parliament elected from B.C. and promotional activities during elections.

The growing national presence also encouraged some of the national leaders to advocate even greater development of a national co-operative financial system. Much of the initiative, naturally enough, came from CCCS. During the later seventies, it prepared a series of reports that outlined how it could become a strong national liquidity organization. While provincial credit union systems varied somewhat in the depth of their support for these proposals, the studies were generally well-received and ultimately accepted. By the later seventies, CCCS was responsible for lobbying with the federal government. It was increasingly more active in providing liquidity for the national system. It was negotiating for loans from co-operative banks in Europe and credit union organizations in the United States.[8] Thus, for a few years in the late 1970s, some 25 years after it had been organized, credit union and co-operative leaders from across the country were giving CCCS the attention it deserved.

As in the past, B.C. representatives played a major role in shaping the evolving national system. At various times, George May and Peter Podovinikoff, along with Rod Glen and Geoff Hook, were deeply involved. Podovinikoff also played an instrumental role in an associated project: the blending of the activities of CCCS and the National Association of Canadian Credit Unions. This project unfolded between 1975 and 1978 and led to the integration of the boards of the two organizations in the latter year under the CCCS umbrella. It was a somewhat similar process, with a similar rationale, as the one that had led to the amalgamation of leagues and centrals in several provinces, a process that had started in British Columbia in 1970.

British Columbia's leaders also played a major role in the development of The Co-operators, a national insurance company owned principally by co-operative organizations, including credit union centrals.

8. Ed Grad, "National Financial Systems for Credit Unions," *Enterprise*, February, 1978, pp. 4-6.

This was a dream that had been around since the late 1940s. It was fulfilled, at least institutionally, in 1976, when Co-operative Insurance Services, based in Regina, was amalgamated with Co-operators Insurance Association, based in Guelph.

For the remainder of the decade, The Co-operators grew rapidly, especially in Ontario and on the Prairies. In fact, it became the second-largest multi-line, general insurance company in Canada, an indication that the underlying dream on which it had been based was feasible and had merit.

George Viereck played a very significant role in The Co-operators in this period. He was one of the key individuals responsible for bringing about the amalgamation in 1976, and he served in a variety of executive posts with the new organization. He also tirelessly promoted The Co-operators across Canada, especially in British Columbia. In a long career, it was his most significant contribution to the national movement.

While a number of B.C. credit unions supported The Co-operators faithfully, Viereck faced a rather difficult "sell" in his home province. Some of the leaders of the B.C. credit union movement remained suspicious of The Co-operators because of the old struggles between CUNA and co-op supporters. Indeed, one suspects, the suspicions remained long after people had forgotten what had caused them.

In reality, though, the old divisions were starting to heal. In the United States, community-bond credit unions were no longer viewed with deep suspicion. Between 8% and 10% of that country's credit unions, measured in both assets and membership, were "residential" credit unions, as community-bond organizations were called there. They were no longer unusual, and they were no longer regarded as a dangerous aberration.

In 1976, too, CUNA Mutual's Canadian operations were incorporated as a substantially independent Canadian firm, CUMIS Life Insurance Company. This was a major step that helped placate those who resented perceived domination by the Americans. Within two years, representatives from CUMIS and The Co-operators were starting to consider, as many had long advocated, how a single co-operative insurance program could be developed for the national credit union movement. Playing important roles in this initiative were British Columbia's representatives on the boards of the two companies – George Viereck in the case of The Co-operators, Helmut Krueger and Susanne Raschdorf (both from Central's board) and Bernie Proft, general manager of East Chilliwack Credit Union, in the case of CUMIS.

There were reasons, however, why some B.C. credit unions, especially the larger ones, remained suspicious of automatic association with any

DATA
SOURCES

MIS DATA
BASE

MODELS

REPORTS

External data
economic
financial

Forecasts and
assumptions about
the future

Change
forecasts

LOAN
PROJECTIONS

"What if"
analysis

General
ledger system

Current general
ledger data

Calculations
and
analysis

TERM
DEPOSIT
PROJECTIONS

External data
economic
financial

Existing
loan/term
deposits
portfolio data

FINANCIAL
MARGIN
PROJECTIONS

BUDGET
PROJECTIONS

Computing has totally revolutionized credit unions since the early 1970s. It has changed the workplace, dramatically increased the range of services for members, challenged management and boards alike with complicated and expensive decisions, brought a network of specialists to the system, and enhanced decision-making capabilities extensively. Within Central, the cheque-clearing function was a key activity to benefit from computers and other advances in technology.

This conceptual diagram from 1981 gives an overview of a computerized system for financial decision-making.

insurance organization, even one they could influence if they chose to do so. Thus, although most of the 15 credit unions that had started to sell general insurance services to their members by the early eighties were selling The Co-operators' products, their commitment to the Guelph-based company was not as deep as might have been expected.

In the final analysis, only a few of British Columbia's leaders shared the dream of creating powerful co-operative insurance companies, stretching across Canada. Not enough of them thought it was possible to create a co-operative insurance company that ultimately could dominate the Canadian insurance industry. Not enough believed there was an opportunity for co-operatives to capture the commanding heights of a key national industry — or even that it was important to do so. For them, insurance was an adjunct, one they hoped would be a profitable service for their organizations, but not one of the central purposes for their existence.

To an even greater degree, B.C. credit unionists were less enthusiastic than they might have been in welcoming Co-operative Trust. That company, after its formation in Saskatchewan in 1952, had had a difficult time developing into a profitable, national trust company. In British Columbia, it made some gains by working with B.C. Central in offering registered savings plans, but progress in working with credit unions was slower than expected. In large part, this was because of potential competition between Co-op Trust and local credit unions: both wanted to attract capital and investments from credit union supporters — the question was whether there was enough to go around. In time, the same issue would emerge with both The Co-operators and CUMIS. Conceptualizing and creating an effective, integrated and mutually-sustaining national financial co-operative system would not be easily achieved.

During the late 1970s and especially the early 1980s, the national co-operative picture became even more blurred as both CCCS and Co-operative Trust encountered serious financial problems. Both organizations became deeply involved in commercial lending and in the Western Canadian real estate boom. They therefore suffered from the unparalleled drop in real estate prices in that period, particularly in Alberta.

From a B.C. perspective, the resulting problems were very serious. B.C. Central had invested $34-million in CCCS, an investment on which the national association was unable to pay dividends at anywhere near a market rate. That low return, in turn, seriously undermined the capacity of Central to declare dividends at competitive rates to its members. In a way, then, the investment had a double impact, inevitably magnified by those who were not sympathetic to CCCS or who wished to criticize George May, its manager after 1978.

In the case of Co-op Trust, British Columbia's credit unions had a limited investment, but its serious difficulties raised the question of how the national movement might best be structured. Consequently, during the early 1980s, considerable thought was given to amalgamating CCCS and Co-op Trust, possibly even with some of the centrals, to form a stronger national organization. It was not an idea that could be achieved, but its very discussion reduced confidence in the national organizations.

Meanwhile, local credit unions in British Columbia were also facing serious economic adversity. Ironically, given their tendency sometimes to belittle smaller credit unions, the largest credit unions were the most vulnerable. Their problem was that they were the most completely integrated into the financial marketplace. As that market fluctuated, therefore, they experienced the greatest difficulties. No less than five of the ten largest credit unions came under supervision at different times in the early eighties, in every case because of delinquent loans or inadequate reserves. All of them, too, were forced to make management changes, a measure of how difficult it was for managers to "grow" with their credit unions, particularly when the economy was deteriorating.

In contrast, most smaller credit unions weathered the storms with relatively few difficulties. With secure memberships and limited risks, they were able to sustain their reserves and maintain their services. It was only in communities where the local economies suffered, such as Port Alberni, Kimberley and Fort St. John, that smaller credit unions encountered structural problems. When the local economy collapsed, not even strong management could save a credit union; in those instances, some support was necessary from the provincial credit union system.

Regardless of size, though, the relationship between boards and management became much more complex during the early eighties. As in the boom period of the 1970s – but for different reasons – the most prominent issue was how boards could effectively monitor the activities of management. During the 1970s and 1980s, Central trainers, representatives of the Credit Union Reserve Board, and credit union writers devoted considerable effort to upgrading the skills of directors. In many ways, though, it was a race against time, because untrained directors responsible for aggressive managers could easily find themselves facing disaster.

The main change directors had to make was to learn how to step back from the daily operations of the credit union and focus instead on assessing general trends. In particular, this meant that they had to examine comparative data over periods of time rather than just review the monthly reports. It also meant that they had to approve lending

The B.C. movement's central organizations have displayed various logos over the years. The first, borrowed from the American credit union movement, was the "little man under the umbrella." It was widely popular and captured well the populist sentiments of B.C. credit unions in the "emancipatory phase."

The second logo, created in 1972, played on the letters in B.C. Central's name, a device used commonly by designers of that period.

The third, which became widely used by credit unions from the 1970s onward, was the "Hands & Globe," the symbol of the international credit union movement adopted by the World Council of Credit Unions.

9. For examples of the kind of training and advice given to directors during this period, see the February, 1978, issue of *Enterprise*.

policies rather than concentrating on individual loans, although they had to remain vigilant when large loans were made, especially commercial loans. And it meant they had to be able to assess the mix of capital, to analyze delinquency, and to employ ratios that would allow them to monitor trends better.[9] Above all, they had to be trained so they could plan for their credit unions on a regular basis, a lesson not learned well enough until the middle or even the later 1980s.

At the same time, directors and, even more so, managers had to try to make sense of the unfolding world of technological change. The banking industry was a technology consultant's dream in the early 1980s. Banking is a data-intensive industry, characterized by considerable routine tabulations, and governed by the flow of information. In fact, as it had long been and long will be, the banking industry is not so much about money as it is about the effective use of reliable information. For that reason, it was an industry ripe for computerization.

During the 1970s and early 1980s, the impact of the computer was incredible. It made possible the diversification of customer or member services. It allowed credit union managers to analyze deposit trends, to better match deposits with loans, to segment their markets, and to compete in a widening range of financial services. In time, virtually every aspect of credit union business would be irreversibly altered by the cybernetic revolution.

Credit unions differed, however, in how they adapted to technology, depending on their size, the commitment of their leaders, and the markets within which they functioned. This difference was both a blessing and a curse. It was a blessing in that it sparked an array of interest in the almost limitless possibilities for computerization. It was a curse because, like some forms of religion, computers created fanatics convinced that theirs was the only true way.

On a local level, the most obvious transition occurred as credit unions went "on-line." This meant that the local credit union was linked through communication lines to a central computing facility. For most of them, that entailed joining Central Data Systems, which had begun as an independent company owned by credit unions but became a subsidiary of B.C. Central in 1972.

In 1977, Metro Credit Union became the first to go on-line through this company. During the next year, another 31 credit unions or branches went on-line. This development, a natural progression within the computing industry, gave credit unions instantaneous access to up-to-date records. It meant, for example, that credit unions did not have to wait for overnight processing of statements, as had been required under the old batch data processing systems.

Installing the terminals and training the staff, however, was a challenging task, especially when it was conceived as a province-wide project. Converting a typical credit union to the new system took about four months in total and involved considerable training of staff. In fact, conversions were major job-revolutionizing events for anyone involved with them. The pace of installations also stretched Central Data to the limits of its capabilities, and often meant "power downs," events that badly disrupted services in some credit unions.

Nevertheless, the attractions of the new technology were many. For members, its most obvious impact was that it made possible the introduction of automated teller machines (ATMs). These had been invented in the 1930s, but could not be widely installed until extensive computing systems were in operation. Although that had occurred in the 1960s, it was not until the 1970s that a rather skeptical banking industry began installing ATMs extensively. The credit union movement was not far behind the banks in this process. In B.C., some local credit unions, such as Saanich Peninsula and Alberni District, were among the first institutions to embrace the new technology enthusiastically. Nationally, amid some misgivings, the movement took steps to create its own access card, the CUE Card, in 1977.

For members, ATMs offered easy access to cash at all times of the day. They also offered members another way to pay bills and to transfer money from one kind of account to another. For credit unions whose members used a specific ATM more than 2,000 times per month, the processing costs were lower than for over-the-counter service. It was a development from which members and credit unions both benefited.

Central was hard pressed to meet the challenges of the rapidly unfolding technology. Its capacity to respond was blunted by the demands created by so many credit unions trying to join at roughly the same time. Once committed to one system, there was so much to do in meeting those requests that there was little time to step back and see if a better avenue was available.

Central's efforts to create an integrated technological system received a blow when VanCity and Nanaimo District Savings decided to go their own separate ways and develop their own computing services with other suppliers.

Their objectives were commendable enough: they were searching for data systems that would allow them to deal with members on a very individualized basis, more so than the systems of CDS would permit. VanCity selected the Geac system, a "real-time," on-line banking system that permitted it to introduce Plan 24. That account, which paid interest daily, was a major change in the Canadian financial services industry. Soon VanCity's lead was followed by a number of other credit unions: Surrey, Richmond Savings, Westminster, First Heritage Savings, B.C. Teachers and Island Savings.

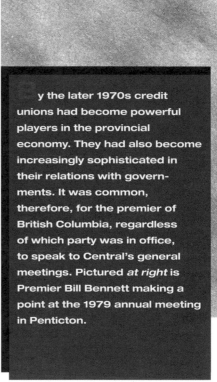

y the later 1970s credit unions had become powerful players in the provincial economy. They had also become increasingly sophisticated in their relations with governments. It was common, therefore, for the premier of British Columbia, regardless of which party was in office, to speak to Central's general meetings. Pictured *at right* is Premier Bill Bennett making a point at the 1979 annual meeting in Penticton.

ATMs offered members easy access to cash.

In 1980, partly in an effort to replicate the flexibility which VanCity and others were achieving with their new systems, Central switched to the Geac real-time, on-line system. It turned out to be a costly and difficult migration. Old contracts had to be cancelled, incurring heavy penalties, and the expenses for the conversion, as is so often the case with computers, were higher than expected.

By 1982, the additional costs had reached $3.6-million. The problem was that not all of Central's credit union membership was involved, and that made raising the necessary funds difficult. Moreover, the members participating in the programs were soon quarrelling among themselves as to the extent of their responsibilities and commitments. It was a difficult issue, one that eroded confidence in Central throughout the late seventies and early eighties, until it was ended by creating an independent company, CUE Datawest Ltd., to provide data processing services.

The preoccupation with technology also arguably undermined the credit unions' traditional concentration on members' needs and interests. Somewhat ironically, concerns about technology meant that credit unions tended to become passive "servants" of their memberships. The emphasis was on managing the over-all assets of credit unions, on letting new financial "products" sell themselves, on searching for niches in local markets. This was a marked shift in emphasis from a perspective that began with members' needs and sought imaginatively for ways to meet those needs. Returning to a more "member-focused" approach to credit unionism would, therefore, become an issue in the later eighties – an issue in which computers ironically could ultimately become an ally.

Computerization also contributed to some growing tensions within credit unions. It increased the pressures on staff by forcing them to learn new skills (and not all could do so easily), it threatened job losses as automated teller machines became commonplace, and it changed relationships between managers and other employees. Moreover, as interest rates rose and as credit unions began to encounter serious problems because of the mismatching of their portfolios, tensions grew within boards and, more particularly, among employee groups. The eighties would not always be pleasant for those working in credit unions.

At the same time, the province was swept by labour unrest triggered by the restraint program of Premier Bill Bennett's Social Credit government. Trade union militancy increased and there were several efforts to unionize more credit unions beyond the 20 where labour unions were already certified. Most of these efforts failed because, like most people in the banking industry, credit union employees were either unsympathetic to unions or found that management and boards responded satisfactorily to whatever concerns they had.

At Fraser Valley Credit Union, however, a particularly vicious controversy broke out in 1982 when one of its branches, located in Mission, was certified. A long, acrimonious debate over the wording of the collective agreement led to a strike in December. The strike dragged on for nearly six months and led to the emergence of a "Save Our Credit Union" Committee, consisting of members who supported the unionization effort. At the annual general meeting in April, 1993, leaders from this committee successfully proposed a motion (which was ultra vires) to remove the entire Board of Directors.

In the resulting confusion, the Credit Union Reserve Board appointed an administrator, John Charlesworth. Succeeding court decisions returned the existing board to office and led to an election for four vacant positions in August. The election was contested by representatives from the Save Our Credit Union Committee and from a "Concerned Credit Union Members" Committee, consisting of people unsympathetic to the unionization drive and concerned about the disruptions of the previous year. In a heavy turnout of members, the latter committee's candidates were elected, albeit closely. The controversy within the credit union soon died down; nevertheless, it had created tensions within the B.C. system between trade union advocates and others less sympathetic to unions.

Some trade union leaders also criticized credit unions because of a particularly bitter confrontation resulting from the construction of condominiums on land adjoining Central's building on False Creek. The apartments were part of the Pennyfarthing complex in which Central had once had an influential investment. When it became known that the second phase of the project was to be built by a high-profile, non-unionized firm given enhanced opportunities by recent, controversial changes in labour legislation, some trade unionists criticized Central for not opposing the development. The project was among the very first to see multiple-unit residential buildings constructed by non-union labour and became a surrogate battleground over the prospect of the provincial government's show-piece, Expo 86, being built on an open-shop basis, with union and non-union labour working on the same site. It was an issue that fomented considerable controversy and, for a while, embroiled Central directly in the tumultuous political struggles of the early 1980s.

The pressures associated with technological change, social disruptions and political controversy also contributed to an emerging debate over how Central should be organized. That debate was intertwined with yet another complex problem in the early 1980s: the share capital and credit union deposit requirements of Central.

Credit unions made two main kinds of investments in Central. As a condition of membership, they were required to invest between 1% and 2% of their assets in the share capital of Central. Because of the amounts involved, larger credit unions were required to invest less than 2%, with any credit unions having assets of $1-billion or more required to invest only 1%. Depending on its financial results each year, Central would pay a dividend on these share investments, dividends that were often crucial to the economic performance of local credit unions.

During the difficult later seventies and early eighties, Central paid dividends on these investments that were below the market rate. The reasons for the low returns were many: the new building initially had high carrying costs, there were some poorly performing commercial loans, and the bond portfolio was earning a below-market rate, as were the CCCS investments. Member credit unions, particularly the larger ones, were inevitably dissatisfied about the low return on their investments in Central, and some began to look elsewhere for higher returns. Westcoast Savings defied Central's rules and did not keep its shares at the required levels, while it invested more of its liquidity reserves outside the system.

Under the Credit Union Act, each credit union was required to deposit at least 10% of its liabilities in another institution. This money was to serve as insurance against a sudden need for funds. It was, therefore, to be "liquid," deposited on terms that would allow the credit union to have ready access to it. Most credit unions deposited all of their liquidity in Central, but as they grew larger (and the sums amounted to tens of millions of dollars), they began to look elsewhere for better rates. A few found them with banks and other institutions.

In an effort to keep the deposits of the larger credit unions, Central started to make individual arrangements with them in the later seventies. It proved to be a bad practice. It led inevitably to distrust and the circulation of misinformation throughout the system. By the mid-eighties, many credit unions were unhappy, either because they were not able to earn the highest rate or because of what they had heard another credit union was receiving. It was an impossible situation for Central, one that could not be tolerated for long.

The deposit issue must also be seen within the context of the general instability of the period. Not only were credit unions, for the first time in their history, confronting serious problems in meeting their reserve requirements. They were also increasingly perturbed by the serious problems and instability confronting the credit union systems in Ontario, Manitoba and Alberta, as a result of fluctuating provincial economies.

Indeed, the collapse of Alberta's real estate market was nearly a fatal blow to the Alberta credit union movement, and it was an experience well-known throughout British Columbia. In Manitoba and Ontario, the credit union system was fragmented and hard pressed to cope with rapidly fluctuating interest rates and irregular housing markets. All three provincial systems suffered deeply and all three had to seek assistance, either from the national credit union system or from provincial governments.

In British Columbia, the provincial government was well aware of the problems and began to monitor the B.C. movement more closely. In one sense, increased government interest was welcomed by some within the movement: in 1981, after some adroit lobbying by Central, the government amended the Credit Union Act to allow credit unions to raise at-risk, non-guaranteed "equity" shares from their members, leaving all investments in "non-equity" shares fully guaranteed. In return, the government insisted that credit unions build up statutory reserve accounts equal to 5% of loans and investments within 10 years.

The change in reserve requirements was triggered by a growing set of problems within local credit unions. By the early 1980s, the Credit Union Reserve Board regularly had between 25 and 30 credit unions under supervision. This led CURB, as it did Central, to question the effectiveness – the quality and the timeliness – of the inspections being undertaken by the Superintendent's Office. CURB therefore again requested that government transfer the inspection service to it, in the belief that this would help identify problems earlier. These proposals did not gain government support, but they were indicative of a general understanding that many problems experienced by credit unions could be counteracted if recognized early enough.

All three organizations – the Superintendent's Office, CURB and Central – did agree generally that avoiding problems would require fewer, and more efficient and professionally-operated, credit unions. Between 1978 and 1984, the number of credit unions declined from 176 to 136, mostly attributable to mergers or "buy-sells" encouraged by CURB. More than 20 of the credit unions that were absorbed had closed bonds, indicating that the trend begun in the 1960s was continuing. More and more, it seemed that the future belonged to large community credit unions.

At the same time, the number of credit union locations increased from 296 to 314, because of branching. When one considers that various small credit union offices were closed down in this period, this was a significant increase. Almost all of the new locations were opened by community credit unions, especially those in the Victoria and Greater Vancouver areas. Many of the new branches soon grew larger than most small credit unions; almost invariably, it seemed, the new branches were financially viable. It is little wonder that the leaders of the day saw the way of the future as larger credit unions serving more people in a variety of locations.

All of these changes within credit unions meant that Central itself was being forced to change. Amid the growing economic pressures and the evident expectation of the larger credit unions that Central curtail its activities, its first reaction was to try to gain additional revenue through investments and commercial lending. When those two initiatives failed, largely because of the nature of the economy, Central was forced to listen to its largest members and to embark upon significant cuts in its operations. Among the first to go were the travel service and the collection agency, both of which had started in the expansionist days of the early 1970s. They were followed soon after by Greentree Developments.

Another area to be cut was education, at least in the way education had been thought of since the movement's beginnings in the 1930s. In fact, the decline in educational activities had actually started during the 1970s. George May was convinced that the credit union movement needed to move aggressively into the marketplace. He believed the best way to do this was to train management and staff in local credit unions so they could adjust to changing market practice and evolving technology. Consequently, May shifted the emphasis of Central's educational programs away from directors and members and toward tellers (as they were still called) and managers. Central particularly concentrated its training efforts on tellers because of the pressures they were facing as technology changed so quickly.

Jac Schroeder was asked to prepare a special program for tellers, a task which he completed in the late 1970s. It was a considerable success and was widely imitated by credit union systems in other parts of North America. He also completed two handbooks focused on the roles and responsibilities of directors, which became widely known in other provinces and especially outside Canada. Ironically, because of the shift in emphasis in British Columbia, they were not well used at home. To some degree, the problems that subsequently appeared can arguably be attributed to that fact.

The Co-operative Services Office was also cut. It had never been popular with some of Central's credit union members, and many of the new co-operatives opened in the mid-seventies were in difficulty as interest rates soared. In some instances, too, the groundwork for some of the new co-operatives had not been laid properly, meaning that some of Central's co-operative loans were in difficulty. Faced with its other problems, and sensitive to the pressures of some of its members, Central opted to shut the Office down.

One survivor of the shutdown was Camp Rainbow, organized by credit unions and other co-operatives in 1976. The camp's development had been facilitated by Central and ultimately controlled by the Co-operative Services Office. Camp Rainbow's first purpose was to teach young people about the benefits of co-operatives and co-operation. As time went by, it came to focus more on developing their leadership skills. It became, for some credit unions and co-operatives, and more importantly for hundreds of young people each year, a concrete manifestation of how credit unions were and could be different.

Amid the cutbacks, Central's senior personnel began to change significantly. In 1981, Aj Gill resigned as chief financial officer, and was replaced by Wayne Nygren, a native of Springside, Saskatchewan, where co-operatives were the main businesses and the credit union the main financial institution. After university, he had worked briefly in bank branches in Western Canada, moving to the Bank of Canada in 1972, where he managed chartered bank reserves and assisted with the Canada Savings Bond campaign. Between 1976 and 1982, he had worked for Credit Union Central of Saskatchewan as director of capital development services.

When Nygren joined B.C. Central, therefore, he had well-rounded experience in banking and a good understanding of the major strategic issues confronting credit unions. But perhaps above all, he brought with him a transparent honesty and a quiet determination to do well. One of his first acts was to end the practice whereby large credit unions negotiated special rates on their deposits with Central. The decision was not well-received in all quarters, but it was the correct decision for the organization and the movement.

Among the others who joined Central in this period was Richard Thomas, who became executive assistant to the CEO in 1980. A 1976 graduate in public administration from the University of Victoria, he had been employed as a research officer and policy analyst by the provincial government, most recently in the Ministry of Consumer and Corporate Affairs. In the two years prior to joining Central, he had been involved in drafting amendments to the Credit Union Act. He was, therefore, well-suited to helping credit unions learn how to adjust under the new regulations. Even more importantly, he brought to Central a deeper understanding of the internal workings of the provincial government, a vitally important quality for the coming years.

Richard McAlary came to Central in 1981 as an economist in the Finance Division. A dynamic and controversial commentator on British Columbia's economy, he soon became widely known through the provincial media. He was, to some extent, the movement's first media personality. In 1981, he started to publish *Economic Analysis of British Columbia*, a monthly overview of the province's economy. Each issue of the newsletter concentrated on a different aspect of the economy, with a continuing watch on key variables such as population shifts and changes in the largest industries. It was very well received and widely quoted, though McAlary's views did not always win support, either inside or outside the movement.

These additions took place even though the cuts were continuing; indeed, they would still be taking place through the mid-eighties. When they were over, the number of employees at Central was barely 200, a substantial drop from the heyday of expansion in 1976, when over 300 had been employed.

An underlying rationale for the cuts was a desire to clarify the accounting practices at Central, pressed by the larger credit unions. They wanted to separate Central's financial services, which they believed should be provided on a fee-for-service basis, from its "trade association" functions, which could be funded by dues. From their point-of-view, this approach would simplify accountability and control expenses. From Central's perspective, however, this would restrict the organization's autonomy and curtail its initiatives. It was an issue that could not be resolved without considerable controversy.

The shift in how Central reported its operations and raised dues and deposits, the difficulties imposed by the fluctuating marketplace, and the divisions among the province's credit unions meant that the vision of Central as the dominating, driving force for a provincial co-operative sector was fading. In its purest form, as the vision of a powerful provincial co-operative nexus, it was Rod Glen's dream. Ultimately, it was one that only a few could embrace.

Sadly, too, it was a dream that was obviously fading as Glen himself was dying. In 1978, he learned he had cancer. For the next two years, until his death in April, 1980, he fought both the disease and the eclipse of the dream that had preoccupied him since the 1950s. In the end, he lost both battles and, for those who knew him well, it was difficult to know which hurt more.

As Central carried out its cutbacks, two broad conceptions of its future became discernible. Peter Podovinikoff summarized these two visions in 1982: One approach, held by leaders from some of the largest credit unions, was that the number of credit unions would steadily decline because of amalgamations and buy-outs. At the end, only one would remain. That remaining credit union would be very much like a bank, although the ways in which branches related to their communities could be structured differently. However it was organized, though, its emergence would make B.C. Central redundant.

Rod Glen embodied a pioneering vision of credit unionism at the local, provincial, national and international levels. For his outstanding life-long contribution, he was posthumously recognized with the movement's highest honour, the Distinguished Service Award of the World Council of Credit Unions, presented at a ceremony in London, England, in 1986.

The other approach envisioned two groupings of credit unions bound to Central. One group would consist of a small number of larger credit unions, probably organized on a regional basis, relying on Central for only a few services. This group would operate numerous branches, provide many of its own services and associate with other credit unions, perhaps through Central, only to stabilize the system or to gain obvious economies of scale. A second group would be formed by 100 or so credit unions. They would be associated through networks and, above all, through their connection with Central. It was a vision that saw the creation of two types of credit unions meeting essentially two kinds of needs.[10]

This view of how the movement might develop emerged as the tensions within Central and among its members were continuing to grow. In reality, although there was much blaming of individuals, most of the deepening tensions were caused by the continuing economic difficulties. And, as in the late 1970s, most of those problems were to be found in the larger credit unions.

In Victoria, for example, as the housing market declined sharply, the two largest credit unions, Westcoast Savings and First Pacific, faced deepening problems. In the Lower Mainland, Surrey and Richmond Savings encountered similar difficulties. Inevitably, their problems were projected onto Central. By 1982, Surrey, Richmond and Westcoast, along with VanCity, were meeting regularly, in part to consider the possibility of forming their own central. They began to look at alternatives for their cheque-clearing and they started their own lobbying efforts with governments.

In an effort to respond to these pressures and to placate the less militant among the leaders of the largest credit unions, Central established a Financial Advisory Committee in the autumn of 1981. It essentially included representatives from those credit unions, and its main task was to monitor the financial operations of Central.

In particular, the committee concentrated on how Central's activities could be separated into those activities that would be funded by financial operations and those that would be funded by dues. The committee also undertook a careful analysis of the commercial loans Central had on its books, with an eye to decreasing them as rapidly as possible. In some ways, the committee rivalled the Board of Directors as a controlling factor in Central's operations. Whether that was true or not, Peter Podovinikoff had little choice but to pay close attention to its views, expressed in what became monthly meetings. Amid growing requests for reforming the system and repeated threats to withdraw from membership by a few credit unions, the committee was a strong impetus for the restructuring of B.C. Central.

10. Peter Podovinikoff, "A Look Ahead," Report to the Executive Committee, February 19-20, 1982, BCCCU Board Minutes.

By 1982, the demand for the reform of Central was picking up momentum. Some credit unions were concerned about the low dividend rates (relative to market rates of interest) paid on their investments in Central. Others were dissatisfied by the uncertainties over technology. Still others wanted to see the business of Central more clearly delineated and its involvement in commercial lending ended. Perhaps as much as anything, the accumulated tensions within the movement – as much local as provincial, and caused by several years of adverse experiences – were becoming focused on Central. As with all central co-operative organizations, adversity among members almost inevitably leads to a desire to change their second- and third-tier organizations.

It was within this growing unhappiness that a committee charged with reconsidering Central's control structure began its meetings in 1982. Chaired initially by Harley Biddlecombe and latterly by Ian MacPherson, the committee searched for a compromise between the one-member, one-vote approach (preferred generally by smaller and some medium-sized credit unions) and the more strictly proportional approach (preferred by the larger credit unions). It proved to be an unsuccessful attempt at compromise. Smaller credit unions were alarmed, most large credit unions were unsatisfied.

The failure to achieve a new basis for proportionality was serious in many respects. It increased dissatisfaction among the larger credit unions. It meant, too, that associated issues, especially the permanence of share capital and the rules governing withdrawal from Central, were left unclear. During the summer of 1983, as the general financial situation in the province continued to worsen, some members of Central became increasingly unhappy. One of them, Westcoast Savings, gave notice of its intention to withdraw, and actually did so. Very soon, though, Westcoast found that it could not maintain satisfactory clearing arrangements with the banks and it was forced to return to Central, a hard lesson that did not go unnoticed within the provincial movement.

As more credit unions, and Central itself, encountered difficulties, they tended to turn increasingly to management consultants. It was almost inevitable, then, that Central's board hired a consulting firm, Western Management, to review the role of Central within the provincial movement. In the late summer and autumn of 1983, the firm interviewed a broad cross-section of leaders and distributed a questionnaire widely throughout the provincial movement.

The consultant's report was delivered to Central's board in December, 1983. In some ways it was a positive report, commenting on how the movement had grown, both in assets and members, in the preceding decade. It was particularly positive in praising Central's performance in cheque-clearing, in managing liquidity, and in providing publications and economic analysis. It was positive, though less so, about Central's capacity to lobby government, to carry out provincial advertising, and to advise on the construction of credit union buildings.

On the other hand, and much more importantly, it criticized Central's leaders for some of the problems of the early eighties, particularly for their failure to revise Central's control structure, create a single technological system, and forge a consensus on the role Central should assume. It pointed out that Central's board had become seriously divided, largely because of uncertainties over the organization's role, but partly because of personality conflicts. It also criticized past investment decisions, particularly the investments in CCCS and in bonds, both of which seriously eroded Central's capacity to reward the investments of credit unions.

The report concluded with the recommendation that Central aggressively address the control issue, review all the services it offered, move to create a single electronic system, and tighten the over-all management of the organization. It was a strong, even harsh, report calling for a revitalization and reorganization of Central.

By early 1984, as some of the larger credit unions continued to apply pressure for rapid change, Peter Podovinikoff's position had become untenable. For eight years he had tried to apply the principles of compromise in a situation where fewer were willing to do so. As the economy worsened and as many of the larger credit unions encountered their own financial difficulties, "the centre would not hold."

During the spring of 1984, Central's board wrestled with the problems that had been accumulating, that had been revealed, and to some extent had been exacerbated by the consultant's report. In February, struggling to find a new perspective and a fresh personality, it hired James Thomson as chief executive officer. Thomson was a Scot who had held senior positions with the Workers' Compensation Boards in British Columbia and Alberta. He had a reputation as a strong manager and a conciliatory leader, two qualities the board thought were particularly required.

In August, the board headed for the small community of Nanoose Bay on Vancouver Island for what had become its annual planning retreat. It was a deceptive place for such a meeting. Tranquil, and blessed by the beaches and forests that make the provincial coast so alluring, it was hardly the place to stage a donnybrook.

And, indeed, despite all the tensions of the preceding period, all the threats to withdraw, the rumours of the creation of a second central, and the unhappiness in many credit unions, the underlying bonds remained strong. In many ways, they were personified by the chairperson of the day, George Viereck. A veteran of some 40 years in the movement, a simple and honest man with deep convictions, he made his greatest contribution to the provincial movement on that weekend. He recognized, much as he disliked some of the directions, that the provincial structure had to change. Aided by a remarkable facilitator, Bob Johnson of Vancouver, he did more than anyone else to make that change possible.

The board worked throughout the weekend of August 24-26. When it was finished, it had prepared what became known as "the Nanoose Accord." It was an 11-point agreement aimed at addressing many of the inequities, real and perceived, that had developed over the years.

Five recommendations were particularly important. It was recognized that Central was a voluntary organization, from which members could withdraw with appropriate notice and be repaid their investment in shares. Central was to be controlled essentially by credit unions, which would vote proportionally based on the size of their own memberships. All credit unions would pay dues, also in proportion to their memberships, an approach that placed significant demands on the larger credit unions, since a ceiling on the amount they had had to pay was lifted by the Accord. All credit unions would contribute equally to share capital, an important point for smaller credit unions, which had been contributing proportionally twice as much as the larger credit unions up to that point. There would be three important committees, dealing with legislative, finance and services issues, on which membership would be carefully distributed among different kinds and sizes of credit unions.

As is so often the case with co-operative organizations, the solution was itself a compromise. It was a victory for those who wanted to preserve the system, to keep alive the dream of a powerful co-operative financial presence in the province. It was achieved in that most co-operative of all places, a meeting room, following much animated, even bruising, discussion. Above all, it was practical and it was acceptable.

Only credit unionists could have found hope and reaffirmation in a place with the unlikely name of Nanoose. But, on the other hand, Nanoose was a place where the Coast Salish people gathered in the autumn to rejoice in the bounty the seas surrendered up to them. In 1984, it was the place where, despite the adversities, a generation of credit union leaders harvested the strengths of some 45 years of vitality.

10 Co-operation, Conflict and Consensus
Mainstreaming
1985-1994

ENTERPRISE

OCTOBER/NOVEMBER 1988

A MAGAZINE FOR CREDIT UNIONS

VOLATILE INTEREST
GLOBAL COMPETITION
RE-REGULATION
SECURITIZATION

CREDIT UNION

the CHANGING FINANCIAL CLIMATE

NATIONS UNIES

UNITED NATIONS

1. Typescript of Chief Executive Officer's Report to the 1986 Semi-Annual Meeting of B.C. Central Credit Union, p. 9.

2. As it turned out, there was little need for such caution. When the matter came to the floor of the 1991 annual general meeting, it carried with little discussion.

The basics of planning for success start with understanding our market place and realistically charting a course based on strengths and weaknesses. The basics end with a single-minded focus on a mission to serve our identified groups of members very well. In between are a myriad of decisions on people, products, pricing, delivery, technology and controls. As leaders we must manage the process by which daily decisions get made to ensure consistency of direction, of purpose and of vision. Together, as individual components of an integrated, co-operative financial system, we can and will be successful.

Wayne Nygren,
Chief Executive Officer,
B.C. Central Credit Union
November, 1986[1]

THE NANOOSE ACCORD USHERED in a more tranquil era for British Columbia's credit union movement. Indeed, when the compromise was brought to Central's semi-annual meeting in the autumn of 1984, it elicited little comment. It was almost as though the vast majority of delegates had tired of the discussions and wanted to move on to other issues. Rather cautiously, though, they accepted the proposal from the board with the caveat that it would be implemented on a trial basis, to be adopted finally, either in its original form or altered, at the 1991 annual general meeting.[2] Debates that had fractured the provincial movement off-and-on for more than a decade had been put to bed — at least for a while.

It was good for the movement that those debates had receded, for the province was on the verge of a decade of dramatic change that would affect British Columbians in often bewildering ways, many of them beneficial, some of them frightening. The Coquihalla Highway opened up the interior to easy access by tourists and businesses; a few even began to think of the Okanagan as a bedroom community of Vancouver, a revolutionary alteration to the province's commonly-accepted mental map. "Whistler" became an internationally recognized name as the glories of its ski hills and hiking trails became known around the world. Expo 86 brought dreams of becoming "world class," whatever that might mean. Vancouver's harbour provided even more vital links to the booming Asian economy, attested to almost every day by the line of freighters waiting to dock in the terminals; its airport struggled to meet the demands of an increasingly mobile population. Large shopping centres were built in the suburbs and downtown areas of the larger cities and in many of the larger towns — vigorous, if sometimes tacky, testimony to the pervasive power of consumerism.

The population grew steadily, mostly because of increased migration from the Prairies and central Canada, partly because of a relatively high birth rate and increased immigration from Asia. The newcomers needed homes and, as a result, the construction industry in many parts of the province boomed. Despite the Agricultural Land Reserve system, the rich farmlands of the Fraser Valley were swallowed up in a seemingly unending stream of suburbs. Older city streets were dramatically altered by the extensive development of condominiums, some by the addition of "monster houses." The cities of the Okanagan expanded rapidly as they welcomed retired people and families seeking less expensive housing. Along the scenic eastern shores of Vancouver Island, for much the same reason, the construction of retirement communities and service industries threatened the tranquility of what had been small towns and villages. In the interior, wherever the primary industries were thriving, communities grew, their housing and community facilities little different from what one could find in the cities. British Columbia had clearly entered into the mainstream of North American life, and, as will be discussed, credit unions were a part of that transformation.

Much of the growth was fuelled by the prosperity found among Canada's most privileged generation, people born between 1935 and 1955. While certainly not everyone in that age cohort was financially secure, an unprecedented number were. They had benefited from a bountiful labour market and the prosperity that had flowed when North America was the dominant force in the international economy. Over 60% of them had owned homes, consequently profiting from the almost uninterrupted rise in real estate values in most places. Most were enjoying or anticipating pensions that had been assured through trade union bargaining, government pensions, and retirement savings plans. Their health needs were not at risk thanks to the Canadian publicly-funded health-care system, and they were living long enough "to spend their kids' inheritance." They were the "Trillion Dollar" generation, whose needs and expenditures would fuel the economy and hide much of the economic peril of the 1990s – even if, ironically, their accumulated public debt increasingly became one of the preoccupations of the age.

The province was also changing rapidly because of its growing emphasis on the information and knowledge "industries." Five new universities were created. The established universities, conditioned to serving a small percentage of the population pursuing a narrow set of professional careers, could not cope with demands for increased access and a new range of career possibilities. New communication systems shortened distances and reduced the barriers that had separated the regions of British Columbia in the past. The ferry system became one of the best in the world, while highway construction and commuter air lines completed the transportation revolutions that had started a generation before. Many of the geographic barriers that had so strongly influenced the province's development in the past were no longer as important.

Yet, beneath the glitter and the general prosperity, social problems were growing at alarming rates. The provincial unemployment level seemed to be permanently fixed at between 10% and 12% of the population. In some interior and coastal communities where primary industries declined or needed fewer employees, the rate climbed above 20%.

Some groups within society were less employed than others. Among young people in their late teens or twenties, the unemployment rate typically approached 20%; in some times and places it exceeded that level. Among aboriginal peoples, the segment of the population with the highest birth rate, unemployment was often more than 40%; the results were evident in the Native communities and all too often on the streets of the province's major cities.

In nearly all the major towns and all the cities, food banks and soup kitchens became a way of life for thousands of people, most obviously single women with children or older women with limited incomes. By the early 1990s, too, an estimated 2,500 people lived on the streets of Vancouver and Victoria alone — a reality that would have been unthinkable and probably unacceptable in the preceding 40 years. They were one measure of how society was changing, and not for the better.

The nature of work was also changing. Computers and different management techniques meant a declining need for middle managers in larger firms. The result was a growing band of highly skilled, well-educated people, many of them male "breadwinners" in their fifties, men who had either become unemployable or were unable to find anything better than marginal jobs. They were some of the most obvious, most vocal, and most distressed refugees from the economic wars being lost by many in the middle class.

As for the newly-employed British Columbians, many found work with small companies requiring employees for only limited periods. All too often, too, they earned less than $10 an hour, not enough, especially in the larger urban areas, to enable people to exist satisfactorily on one or, in the case of families, even two incomes.

During the same period, too, traditional family life continued to undergo significant change. Divorce rates increased to the point that about one-half of all marriages were not permanent. Moreover, because of economic pressures, more young people were postponing starting a family until their later twenties. An increasing number of people, too, because of the pressures of careers or personal preference, opted not to have families or to defer having them, changes that significantly affected housing needs and community life, particularly in Vancouver.

The roles of women in the economy continued in the directions under way since at least the 1950s; the most obvious trend was that more were employed in the paid work force. In 1979, women had made up 40% of the work force; by 1989 they accounted for 45%. Moreover, women were increasingly successful in gaining managerial and professional positions. In 1979, women held 39% of such positions, but by 1989, they held 48%; this meant, in fact, that they occupied nearly two-thirds of all such positions created in the period. Women were also crucially important in the creation of new businesses and jobs. They started more businesses than men,[3] and were more successful in keeping them in operation.

During the decade, though, women's earnings relative to men's actually declined – from 66.2% to 63.7%[4] – largely because, in the managerial and professional positions, their salaries remained significantly lower. The main point, though, was that women were an increasingly variable force in the marketplace, fulfilling a wider range of jobs and reflecting widely different economic status among themselves. By the 1990s, there were several "market segments" among women, an increasingly important factor for any financial institution, including credit unions.

Indeed, all of these changes profoundly affected the movement. Increased wealth provided remarkable opportunities: even if credit unions only maintained their share of the market, they would grow. The communications revolution made greater integration possible among credit unions and reduced the regional tensions that had harmed the movement in the past. Each affluent "market segment" – the newly rich, the rising entrepreneurs, the retired, the growing number of women in the work force – was an important group to consider, perhaps to court. And, for those who were concerned or interested, there were the recently poor or the traditionally impoverished – if ways could be found to meet their needs in the prudent, cost-effective manner credit unions had once pioneered.

Such changes did not take place within some form of British Columbian or Canadian isolationism. They were part of a global economic and political transformation. The pressures on the middle class were directly linked to the growth of international corporations, the decline of tariff barriers, and the pervasive communication revolutions. The social revolutions affecting young people and women could be found in all industrialized societies. The ways in which governments changed their relationships with financial institutions were part of a worldwide restructuring of economic systems.

That restructuring was one of the main elements in what became known as the emergence of a global economy. In some respects, the "new economy" was not so much new as it was a marked intensification

3. *Market Smarts*, B.C. Central Credit Union, November, 1989, pp. 6-7.

4. *Economic Analysis of British Columbia*, B.C. Central Credit Union, November, 1990, pp. 3-4.

of what had been happening ever since capitalist structures had reached out from Europe in the seventeenth century. This intensification was possible because technology made it so easy to move capital around the world, because national governments competed vigorously with each other to attract capital, and because the rules governing the flows of capital were relaxed.

These economic changes greatly affected Canada in general, and British Columbia in particular, and they posed a challenge to governments. Most particularly, governments were concerned about how they should regulate financial institutions. The issue was forcibly brought home by the disasters involving savings-and-loans associations in the United States, which started to emerge in the middle of the 1980s. Savings-and-loans, or "thrifts," had been started during the Great Depression, as complementary financial institutions to credit unions. Initially, they were primarily concerned with mortgage lending, but they had expanded their activities over the years to include many other kinds of investments, some of them imprudently, a few dishonestly. As the losses grew into the trillions of dollars and governments became enmeshed in bailing out the thrifts and restructuring them, Canadian observers became alarmed.

In Canada, the federal government started a systematic review in 1986 of all its legislation regulating financial institutions. Inevitably, the provincial government had to follow suit. The two levels of government had three essential reasons for the reviews – expanding the economy, reassuring investors, and avoiding bail-outs. All three issues were complex; all were important.

First, from the perspective of economic growth, the provincial government was acutely aware that financial institutions were the engine of local, regional and national economies. In a world that was increasingly relaxing barriers to the movement of capital, it was crucially important that any jurisdiction have its own aggressive financial sector; the only really plausible option for a provincially-based financial sector was a credit union system. But, if it was to fulfil that role, it was essential that the system be efficient, competitive and resilient.

Mel Couvelier, who twice served as B.C.'s Minister of Finance between 1986 and 1991, was hardly a supporter of co-operatives, but nevertheless believed in a strong credit union system. He saw it as potentially key element in the unfolding provincial economy. It could be an effective way in which British Columbians might influence the province's economic development in the most fundamental manner, including ultimately raising the capital needed to compete internationally.

Second, the provincial government, particularly from the mid-1980s onward, was increasingly concerned about its contingent liability for the B.C. credit union system in the event the system encountered serious difficulties. It had been warned by the problems in Victoria and Fort St. John, although the resources of the Credit Union Reserve Board had been more than sufficient to meet the losses that had occurred. Nevertheless, the problems had been severe enough that the government changed the name of the Credit Union Reserve Board to the Credit Union Deposit Insurance Corporation in 1985. That change emphasized the insurance role – a subtle shift in emphasis away from the self-help, movement-inspired rationale upon which the organization had been based originally.

Third, and even more serious, the B.C. government was aware of the losses other governments in Canada had sustained in the failures of the Canadian Commercial and Northland banks, as well as the problems of the credit union systems in Ontario, Manitoba and, especially, Alberta. In the mid-1980s, too, it was faced with a problem closer to home when the Teachers' Investment and Housing Co-operative encountered difficulties.

In retrospect, this B.C.-based co-operative was an example of a good idea gone wrong. Originally designed as a savings institution for teachers that allowed them to help each other obtain housing, it moved into the general housing market in the early 1980s. It did so without adequate regulation, since it was incorporated under co-operative, not credit union, legislation: it was a disaster waiting to happen. The disaster came in 1985, when its investments in the Alberta and Arizona real estate markets collapsed. It was a sobering experience for the B.C. government, whose potential liabilities as the chief regulator amounted to many millions of dollars.

In the face of such difficulties, governments were hard pressed to maintain public faith in their financial institutions. Only a thorough review of those institutions and a reconsideration of the regulatory system could appear to accomplish that end. Such a review became a persistent preoccupation for some politicians and public servants and most leaders of the financial industry, including credit union leaders, in the late 1980s and early 1990s.

That reconsideration also occurred as the financial marketplace was being dramatically overhauled. During the 1980s, the federal government was ideologically committed to freeing the financial industry by breaking down the barriers that had historically differentiated its four major "pillars," or sectors: banking, trusts, insurance, and securities.

That breakdown was facilitated, even required, by technology. The computerization of the financial industry made it possible and advantageous for trust companies and banks to own insurance companies and for more ordinary Canadians to invest in the international stock market, perhaps through their registered retirement savings plans. Computerization also meant that financial institutions, including credit unions, would be drawn together through technological agreements and payment systems that encouraged homogenization, even uniformity. In the long run, it would mean that credit unions would have to consider carefully how they could maintain their distinctiveness. Technology is never neutral – it shapes people and institutions even as it serves them.

The federal government was equally committed to integrating the Canadian economy within the North American and, ultimately, the international economies. A key part of this initiative involved making the Canadian financial system more like those found elsewhere; as with technology, this initiative inevitably meant that credit unions were treated more and more like banks. It was a perspective that nevertheless found support among regulators in the provinces, including British Columbia; it was a perspective that gave B.C. credit unions an opportunity, even as it posed a long-term threat.

In October, 1986, the B.C. government embarked on a consultative process aimed at reorganizing the regulation of the province's financial institutions. The process was led by an aggressive Superintendent, Al Mulholland, who represented well his minister's wish to tighten the regulatory process for credit unions. In the spring of 1987, the government released a paper entitled *Credit Union Amendment Act, A Discussion Paper.*

The paper outlined proposals for reforming the Credit Union Act. The government pledged support for deposit insurance up to a limited but unspecified amount. It called for a single, high-quality inspection system, perhaps by combining the Credit Union Deposit Insurance Corporation and the office of the Superintendent of Financial Institutions. It recommended that credit unions be given more freedom in how they could raise capital, and it argued that significantly higher levels of capital would be required.

The government also advocated greater regional co-operation among credit unions, especially in the hiring of trained personnel for commercial lending. It called for more mergers and amalgamations, thereby confirming a government perspective evident for several years. Recognizing the blending of financial services occurring in the marketplace, the government proposed that credit unions be allowed to own trust companies. It even suggested that credit unions be allowed to convert themselves into trust companies when there was "substantial membership support." Finally, among its key recommendations, it called for a significant upgrading in director education and standards of care, even the appointment of outside "professional" directors. A credit union's board would also be required to appoint two committees,

5. See *Credit Union Amendment Act, A Discussion Paper*, (Victoria: Queen's Printer for British Columbia, 1987).

a finance committee to develop prudent financial policies, and an audit committee to provide better control over the credit union.[5]

These proposals marked a significant departure in the relations between the government and credit unions. Clearly, the government was attempting to expand its regulatory influence. In the past, most of the momentum for changing legislation had come from the movement. The reforms of the 1970s, in fact, had been almost entirely instigated and carried out by credit union leaders and their supporters, notably Ross Montgomery and Central's lead counsel, Bill Wright. In contrast, during the mid- and later-1980s, much of the impetus came from a provincial government seeking to expand its regulatory domain.

The government's proposals triggered a busy period for Central's Legislative Committee, chaired by Philip Moore of Greater Vancouver Community Credit Union, and for Richard Thomas, Central's director of government affairs. One issue immediately at the forefront of the discussions was the extent to which the government would continue to protect deposits in credit unions. Ever since the issue had become important in the later 1950s, the government arguably had had a "moral" commitment to guarantee deposits to their full amount. Given the size of the provincial movement, that relatively open-ended commitment was becoming unacceptable.

During late 1987 and early 1988, Central successfully negotiated a formal arrangement whereby the Minister of Finance would be empowered to guarantee borrowings by CUDIC, if necessary to repair the deposit insurance fund. The cost to credit unions of this arrangement was the imposition of a limit on their deposit guarantee – $100,000 per separate deposit. The unlimited guarantee that had existed for 20 years was no more.

Still, no government funding was involved in extending this guarantee. Rather, if CUDIC's reserve fund ever became impaired, and after a special assessment had been levied against credit unions, CUDIC could then replenish its resources by borrowing on the security of the government guarantee.

The $100,000 amount was nevertheless particularly important, in that it exceeded the $60,000 per single deposit guarantee of banks and trust companies provided by the Canada Deposit Insurance Corporation, a federal crown corporation. In making its case for this level of insurance, the credit union system argued that a chartered bank could "double-up" on insured deposits by placing deposits with both the bank proper and its mortgage corporation subsidiary. Altogether, the $100,000 figure was a significant step in calming any concerns among members about the security of their deposits – and it was a useful marketing tool for credit unions trying to attract members with larger deposits.

In October, 1988, the Ministry of Finance released a second discussion paper, entitled *Financial Institutions Act: Major Policy Proposals*. At the heart of that document was an initiative to abolish the separate statutes regulating credit unions, trust companies and insurance companies. All would be rolled into a single Financial Institutions Act.

After considerable discussion and consultation, the Legislative Committee prepared a response to the government's proposals, a response that was nearly unanimously endorsed by the province's credit unions. The essence of Central's position was that credit unions should not be mingled legislatively with trust and insurance company legislation; that they should have freedom to develop in several economic directions (especially in providing insurance); that more stringent rules concerning capital requirements should be developed; that directors should be better trained; and that credit unions should be required to pool their mandatory liquidity deposits in B.C. Central.[6]

A key concern, partly raised in the government's second paper, was how to stabilize credit unions in difficulty. The experience of the early eighties had demonstrated that it was necessary to have a significant pool of money available at all times in order to withstand difficulties. It had also shown the necessity of having adequate warning systems to identify problems; of having early intervention systems to address concerns; and of having regulatory authority to force credit unions, if necessary, to take remedial action.

Broadly speaking, there were two alternatives. One was that the government could continue to provide such services as it had in the past, the costs being borne through assessments paid by credit unions. The other, partly following the approach used by the Mouvement Desjardins in Quebec, would see the province's credit unions create their own stabilization organization. The committee, Central and the credit unions opted for the latter alternative (albeit with differing degrees of enthusiasm).

During 1988 and 1989, a long series of complicated negotiations led to the acceptance of Stabilization Central Credit Union as the principal vehicle for the stabilization of credit unions. It was part of a major restructuring of the financial regulatory system in British Columbia. In that restructuring, the provincial government created a new organization, the Financial Institutions Commission (FICOM), to regulate credit unions, insurance companies and other provincial financial institutions. In total, the creation of FICOM, the new legislation and the formation of Stabilization Central meant that the province's credit unions had entered a new age, characterized by new structural underpinnings and new responsibilities.

All of the maneuvering to find a new regulatory environment was one measure of how credit unions were entering into the mainstream of

6. For the complete position, see "The British Columbia Credit Union System's Response to Financial Institutions Act: Major Policy Proposals," (B.C. Central Credit Union, undated). The response was submitted to the Ministry of Finance and Corporate Relations on January 31, 1989.

the regional and, to a degree, the national economy. Another measure was the growth achieved by credit unions and the system since 1984. By 1994, the only credit unions finding it difficult to grow were those in communities based on a single resource whose chief industries had declined or closed. Everywhere else, credit unions grew steadily, often dramatically, largely because they were so successfully engaged in the mortgage business.

At the end of 1994, the provincial movement had almost 1,300,000 members and nearly $16.5-billion in assets. This was a remarkable increase from 10 years earlier, when the province's credit unions had 955,000 members and $6-billion in assets. The number of credit unions had continued to decline throughout the period, dropping from 136 to 101.[7] The number of "locations," though, had grown from 288 to 311; this was a result of credit unions opening new branches or maintaining locations gained through amalgamation.

When one looks beneath the patterns of growth and searches for trends, an obvious tendency was that big credit unions got bigger. The largest credit unions were concentrated in the Lower Mainland and on Vancouver Island, areas that benefited most from the prosperity of the period. The regions of greatest growth were in the Vancouver suburbs stretching along the Fraser River and its delta. Vancouver City Savings grew to over $3.5-billion in assets, partly because of its strategy of moving out to where the metropolis was expanding. Richmond Savings and Surrey Metro Savings, already concentrated in the communities whose populations were developing most rapidly, each grew to over $1-billion in assets for the same reason. Similarly, on Vancouver Island, Pacific Coast Savings achieved the billion-dollar plateau, largely by catering to the somewhat inflationary but nevertheless booming housing industry in the Greater Victoria area.

Credit unions, in fact, became the largest financial network in the province. Put another way, taken as a system, credit unions were larger than any of the banks or trust companies, and they enjoyed the steady support of between 15% and 20% of the population throughout the period. In some parts of the province – the suburbs of Vancouver, the Fraser Valley, and the Kootenays – credit unions collectively had a significantly larger share of the market than any of the chartered banks.[8]

As these changes became evident, B.C. Central and the provincial movement were confronted by the difficult question of how they should anticipate their long-term future. How should they strive to position themselves in a rapidly-changing world? Should they try to develop stable niches in communities, making the best independent arrangements they could to meet their technological and product needs? Should they strive to build, at the cost of lower short-term

7. At the end of 1984, there were 132 credit unions affiliated with Central; four credit unions were unaffiliated. *Enterprise*, May-June, 1985, pp. 30-32.

8. This discussion of member attitudes and composition is based on A. Wiggins, et al, *The Public Image of Credit Unions in British Columbia, A Marketing Research Report*, (B.C. Central Credit Union, 1987).

MERGER MAP

Of The

EIGHTIES

In the merger mania of the 1980s dozens of B.C. credit unions of all sizes and bonds have merged, amalgamated or purchased each other. Some were marriages of convenience, some were actively encouraged by CUDIC and a few were resisted by a significant number of their members. In some cases the partners were previously co-habitating, more often they were in direct competition. However, most would agree the credit union foundation has been strengthened by the various nuptial agreements.

Enderby & District Credit Union merged with Grindrod Credit Union 1981

Penticton & District Credit Union merged with Princeton Branch, Yale Credit Union 1982 changed name to Valley First Credit Union 1983

Nelson & District Credit Union amalgamated with Riondel & District Credit Union 1984

returns, the kinds of integrated structures that would give them as much regional, national and even international control as possible over their own destiny? Should they explore more systematically how they could combine with other financial co-operatives, in the rest of Canada, in North America, in Europe, and in Asia, in order to create an effective international co-operative financial system?

The problem with addressing such fundamental issues, though, was that the present kept getting in way of the future. For understandable reasons, most B.C. credit unionists focused almost invariably on another set of questions: How to maintain the appropriate level of equity? How to meet liquidity requirements? How to meet the competition down the street?

Answering those questions meant embracing new opportunities and accepting increased pressures. They meant responding to a steady, sometimes hectic, demand for housing, a growing need for retirement planning, and pressures from members wanting to invest their disposable income more profitably. Internally, it meant adding more sophisticated investors so that credit unions could manage their funds more effectively, for example, in mortgage-backed securities.

At the same time, advances in communications, including on-line systems, electronic mail, telephone conferencing, and fax machines, continued to revolutionize the workplace. As with all such revolutions, they involved considerable effort, worrisome costs, and difficult transitions. They required changing the "culture" of organizations, retraining (sometimes replacing) people, and creating new alliances. And so they did in the credit unions of the eighties and the nineties.

Despite the generally positive situation between 1985 and 1994, success was not enjoyed equally in all years, in all regions of the province, nor by all credit unions. Indeed, at the start of the period, British Columbia was still feeling the effects of the severe economic recession that had swept much of the world in the wake of the oil crisis of the previous decade. Inflation, as measured by the consumer price index, had declined, but remained high. In the early eighties, it hovered at the 12-14% range, but fell to 3-4% by the later eighties.

That decline, while ultimately beneficial to the economy and thus to most credit unions, nevertheless triggered a serious, short-term problem. Between 1983 and 1986, credit union growth slowed perceptibly. The growth in credit union assets, which had jumped 60% from 1980 to 1983, was only 4.6% in 1984, barely above the level of inflation. Indeed, in 1984, the province's credit unions lost $12.6-million, the first over-all annual loss in the movement's history, and the only loss to date.

There were, however, significant differences in how credit unions were affected by the vagaries of the provincial marketplace. When they served smaller communities, being the only institution to do so in some 20 to 30 places during the period, they were required to offer only essential services. Similarly, several credit unions serving closed-bond groups needed to offer only a limited range of services. The result was that many of the smaller and medium-sized credit unions were among the most successful organizations in the middle and later eighties.[9]

In contrast, and as in the early eighties, the bigger urban community credit unions were locked into arduous competition with the national banks and trust companies. They were forced to offer a broader range of financial services, such as credit card accounts, ATM cards, lines of credit, and investment products. They consequently had to wrestle more persistently with limited margins, as they made large investments in technology and buildings in order to meet the real and perceived needs of their memberships.

And who were their members? Credit union members differed from the customers of other financial institutions in that they tended to include somewhat larger percentages of lower-income and less-educated people, although, as the period progressed, a growing number of professional and more educated people became members. Much more importantly, though, surveys of credit union members and general evaluations of trends within the banking industry in the province showed that most British Columbians chose their financial institution for reasons of convenience: they wanted an institution close to where they lived or worked. Very few selected their financial institution on the basis of ideology. If there had ever been a significant class basis to credit unions membership (and it was never as monolithic as many had tended to think), it was rapidly declining by the later eighties.

Did members, then, see credit unions as being different?

In the major analyses of public attitudes towards financial institutions carried out by Central in the period, the approximately 50-60% who did perceive a difference emphasized "friendlier" service, more convenient hours, and lower service charges. This meant that between 40% and 50% of the people interviewed about financial services did not know, or could not identify, how credit unions were different from other financial institutions. It was a sobering reflection on how poorly the movement had communicated its message to the general public.

One must also wonder whether most people who did believe credit unions were different actually took that difference seriously. In particular, one must wonder about the attitudes of the members of most larger credit unions. Within such credit unions, members were usually

9. Philip Moore, "A Survey of the Recent Performance of 90 B.C. Credit Unions," prepared for a 1987 planning session of Greater Vancouver Community Credit Union.

"signed up" without the distinctive qualities of credit unions being fully explained to them. In other words, the occasion when members could be most easily "reached" – when they were making a commitment by joining the credit union – involved no more than completing an application form. In several instances, too, the words "credit union" disappeared from advertising, while member newsletters became little more than marketing instruments.

The larger credit unions, serving large segments of the population, were arguably most affected by the general trends. Like the banks and trust companies, they were profoundly shaken when the real incomes of most people declined, meaning that disposable income, upon which local economies depended so much, fell significantly. Housing starts, a vital statistic for credit unions, dropped from over 40,000 in 1981 to 16,000 in 1984. Between 1985 and 1987, they increased only slowly.[10] All of these trends meant reduced incomes for people and reduced growth for most credit unions. They also meant rapid adjustments for credit unions, especially in matching the rates paid on deposits with the rates paid on loans, adjustments that could not be made expeditiously in some instances.

In Victoria, both Westcoast Savings and First Pacific continued to deteriorate, pulled down largely by the collapse of their commercial loan portfolios. In 1987, majorities on the boards of the two organizations, with the urging of the Credit Union Deposit Insurance Corporation, proposed an amalgamation to their memberships.

The membership of Westcoast Savings approved the proposal with little controversy, with 93% of those members casting ballots voting in favour. Members of First Pacific, however, engaged in an intense debate. A few First Pacific board members were opposed to the merger, as were some management personnel. Within the membership, many were concerned because Westcoast, just prior to the amalgamation attempt, had embarked on a policy of reducing services to members with low deposits. Westcoast, too, had recently opened a real estate subsidiary, a matter of concern to First Pacific members involved in that kind of business. The result was that when 6,611 First Pacific members voted, 66.32% supported amalgamation, a fraction (14 votes) short of the 66.67% required for it to carry.[11]

The issue did not die. It brewed within the city's credit union movement throughout 1987 and 1988. Finally, Finance Minister Mel Couvelier, whose home riding was in the Victoria area, requested an official enquiry. On the basis of that enquiry, Couvelier ordered an amalgamation. It took place in March, 1988. Shortly afterward, the board of the new organization – Pacific Coast Savings Credit Union – hired Doug Enns as manager. A native of Regina, Enns had successfully merged 10 credit unions in Calgary in the wake of the difficulties

10. All statistics are from *Economic Analysis of British Columbia*, B.C. Central Credit Union, August, 1987.

11. *Vancouver Sun*, August 6, 1987.

encountered by the Alberta system in the early 1980s. Quiet, determined and independent, he was one of the best "merger" managers in the Canadian movement.

The creation of Pacific Coast Savings can be used to understand better some of the main developments in the mid- and late-eighties. It demonstrated two main trends that changed the movement significantly.

The first was that it was an amalgamation, albeit ultimately a forced one. In that respect, it was typical of the way many credit unions sought to resolve their problems or grow into new markets. Indeed, some 64 credit unions in existence in 1980 had merged into 22 by 1989. Central generally supported this trend, as it had for some years, believing that it would create a healthier system. Perhaps more importantly, so too did CUDIC, under the leadership of Gordon Wallace, who became its chief executive officer in December, 1986.

It is difficult to measure the impact of all the mergers. In virtually every instance, they created healthier economic organizations with more modern technology, rationalized banking systems, and a greater capacity to serve their members. They also contributed, though, to a sense of pessimism among smaller credit unions, a fear that their organizations had only a limited future.

The second trend, dramatically evident in the creation of Pacific Coast Savings, was that people suffered. The managers of both credit unions, for example, lost their jobs. Rodger Lutz of Westcoast Savings had built a strong credit union, indeed, for some years one of the largest in the province. He was innovative, aggressive and independent. Given to wearing cowboy boots, holding managerial retreats in Hawaii, and flying to Vancouver in chartered planes, he was a flamboyant example of the western entrepreneur operating a fiercely independent credit union. He served briefly on the boards of B.C. Central, Co-op Trust and the Canadian Co-operative Credit Society, in each case antagonizing several individuals committed to creating more integrated provincial and national credit union systems.

The other manager, Harry Down, had emerged somewhat in Lutz's shadow through the development of Saanich Peninsula Savings, a credit union originally located in the quiet suburban hamlet of Sidney. Deeply committed, much influenced by the model of Rod Glen, he managed a successful credit union that for several years competed vigorously and sometimes acrimoniously with Westcoast Savings. A supporter of co-operatives, Down helped start a consumer co-operative in Brentwood Bay and he was generally a strong supporter of The Co-operators. During Central's most difficult period in 1983 and 1984, he served for one year as its chairman, a task that in retrospect diverted too much of his attention from his own credit union.

The fate suffered by Lutz and Down was not unusual. All told, about 30 managers — approximately one-quarter of all the general managers in the system — lost their jobs in those difficult years. In most instances, too, their middle managers were also let go, either immediately or when new managers took over.

One could argue that in some instances the growth and change in credit unions had simply surpassed the capacity of the released managers to deal with evolving issues. More frequently, though, the main problem was that the movement, and particularly the directors, had let many managers down. They had failed to prepare managers properly during the rapid growth of the 1970s.

At the same time, many directors of troubled credit unions also paid a significant price. It was painful to deal with serious losses in an institution responsible for protecting and enhancing the wealth of neighbours, colleagues and family members. Firing managers, who in some instances had become friends, was harrowing, particularly for those who had never fired anyone before. Responding to queries and criticisms was unnerving. The mid-eighties were not pleasant years for many involved in the B.C. movement.

There was one way in which the "Pacific Coast solution" was unusual. The new manager, Doug Enns, was familiar with credit unions. In most other cases, the new chief executives and, just as importantly, the new senior managers of the larger credit unions came from banks.

They were not the first credit union employees to come from banks. Indeed, from the beginning, credit unions had hired employees from local bank branches, occasionally managers but more often loans officers and tellers. Never before, though, had so many come at one time; more importantly, never before had the recruits come from the higher levels of the banking industry. A few had worked in the head offices of smaller banks, some had been responsible for centralized marketing activities, while others had held significant regional positions in larger banks.

The impact of this new managerial factor was dramatic. It helped many credit unions develop new accounting and reporting systems, assisted in the development of new kinds of services, and altered personnel practices. Controls over lending became tighter. Several of the larger credit unions started to provide financial planning for their members, some of them reflecting the experiences and practices of the major banks.

The new managers also brought with them different concepts of remuneration, including significant incentive programs, which dramatically altered the terms of employment, not only of general managers, but all senior staff and ultimately all personnel. In the long run, such programs transformed the "workplace culture" of some credit unions, perhaps not in every way for the better.

Few of the new managers, however, had a deep understanding of the nature and distinctive qualities of credit unions. Many inevitably had difficulties, at least at first, in working with boards of directors. Accustomed to the rather rigid, daily, often impersonal control of superiors in banks, they could find the less frequent, less "professional" direction by boards less predictable, less informed and less intimidating.

Furthermore, the new managers fostered a greater sense of independence within many credit unions. Coming from the often controlled environment of banks, they rejoiced in the unprecedented freedom of their new positions. It was a kind of power they had never possessed before, a kind of freedom that was to be coveted and even expanded. This perspective reinforced a vision of credit unions as, at best, a series of independent "fiefdoms" perhaps associated to meet common needs – but only as long as the price was right. As far as Central was concerned, this view emphasized short-term results over long-range possibilities; it tended to diminish the prospects of synergy among credit unions, the kind of synergy upon which many past accomplishments had been based.

New managers, too, were more skeptical about the way that credit unions carried out their business. In particular, they questioned the democratic procedures of Central and they were easily frustrated by the difficulties in achieving consensus across the system. They also challenged the need for two general meetings of Central each year; these were seen as expensive and unproductive in terms of measurable results.

Most importantly, the new managers were advocates of rapid, continuous growth. They argued that only large credit unions could provide the kinds of services increasingly demanded by members. Only large credit unions could employ the kinds of sophisticated staff needed to make modern financial institutions profitable. Only large credit unions could keep pace with the banks and trust companies. They helped forge the rapid expansion that became so dramatic in the last five years of the period.

Much of that growth was built on mortgages. The return to that form of lending was natural following the rather mixed experiments with commercial lending in the 1980s. Mortgage loans were safer and easier, and B.C. credit unions had gained considerable expertise in providing them. Consequently, as the decade came to a close, many credit unions were back to making 80% of their loans in the form of residential mortgages. It was a type of business that clearly benefited members; it was a type of business at which credit unions excelled.

While credit unions in the Okanagan and some booming communities in the interior expanded their mortgage business substantially, it was the credit unions in the Vancouver and Victoria areas that made the largest investments. In particular, Surrey, Coquitlam and Richmond and the eastern end of the Fraser Valley grew as rapidly as any area in Canada.

Growth, however, had its costs. The most literal cost came with the securing of funds to finance growth. One alternative, of course, was to turn to members. Indeed, one of the "lessons" of the early eighties was that credit unions should not rely just on retained earnings to build up their equity. As the pressure for equity grew, however, credit unions sought new ways to attract equity from members: equity shares became one of the most popular alternatives.

This approach, pioneered by Alert Bay and Van-Isle credit unions, invited members to invest in non-voting, non-guaranteed shares. In return, they were offered either a fixed or variable rate of return that would be above the normal rates for the various kinds of deposits. In the credit unions that pursued this option, the members' response was remarkably positive. It was an expensive kind of equity, however, even though it was in many instances a very significant membership benefit.

A much more controversial approach was taken by Surrey Metro Savings.[12] Based in the fastest growing community in the province, Surrey Metro was strongly committed to a rapid growth strategy. Growth, however, strained the capacity of the credit union to build reserves fast enough. To confront the problem, therefore, CEO Lloyd Craig and his board turned to the approach used in capitalist firms when large amounts of funds were needed: using powers given credit unions in the legislative revisions proclaimed in 1990, Surrey Metro listed a non-voting share issue on the Toronto Stock Exchange in 1992.

The issue sparked a vigorous debate in the B.C. movement, partly because it could be seen as undermining the conventional control structures of credit unions, partly because it was such a new concept. A few co-operatives, notably agricultural co-ops in the United States and Europe, had pursued a similar policy, but to that point only one (partly) co-operative company, the United Grain Growers, had done so in Canada. For many in the B.C. credit union movement, it was a step that undermined the basic identity of credit unionism. Thus, while the innovation was ultimately tolerated by the majority of credit unions at Central's 1993 annual general meeting, it was vigorously resisted by others. Nor was the issue ended at that time: in fact, it promised to become even more significant as the period drew to a close.

Growth had another cost: it encouraged credit unions to compete more aggressively with each other. The most aggressive were the three largest in the province: Vancouver City Savings, Surrey Metro Savings,

12. Surrey Credit Union, formed in 1947, changed its name to Surrey Metro Savings Credit Union in 1991.

"the Great Fraser Valley Branching Rush"

and Richmond Savings. They leap-frogged over each other – and many other credit unions – to establish branches at as many advantageous locations as possible, especially in the suburbs south and east of Vancouver. Indeed, it was in that area that the most marked competition – "the Great Fraser Valley Branching Rush" – took place.

The three largest credit unions were not alone in expanding within the Fraser Valley. At the eastern end of the valley, First Heritage Savings grew at a rate that rivalled the big three. To the west, Fraser Valley, Delta, and Maple Ridge Community expanded rapidly, although they did not enter as freely as others into the construction of new branches. Nevertheless, the various credit unions expanded cumulatively by some dozen branches in the later eighties, and many of those branches were uncomfortably close to each other.

The intense competition became a divisive and difficult issue, in the same way as the expansion of the late 1970s and early 1980s had created animosities. The issue also emerged in the Okanagan Valley as the housing industry boomed and credit unions, most notably Valley First, started to build new branches. As the issue developed, again much like in the 1970s, credit union leaders requested that Central mediate; as before, it was an impossibly "political" task for Central to undertake.

Then, during June, 1993, representatives of Surrey Metro Savings and First Heritage Savings gathered for lunch, presumably to discuss "friendly consolidation." Within a few hours, Surrey Metro made an offer to, in effect, purchase First Heritage: it would offer First Heritage members a combination of Surrey Metro shares and cash totalling $2.25 for each First Heritage share. First Heritage directors considered this offer an unfriendly take-over bid reminiscent of the practices of capitalist enterprise. Certainly, it was different from the more than 100 mergers that had taken place previously within the provincial movement. They rejected it, refusing initially even to take it to their members for consideration.

Surrey Metro then tried to force a member decision by encouraging its staff to circulate a petition for a meeting among its own members who also belonged to First Heritage.[13] Ultimately, the First Heritage board did ask their credit union's members to vote on the issue. In October, it organized a membership meeting attended by 2,500, one of the largest gatherings of a credit union's membership ever held in the province. Balloting took place in the credit union's branches and nearly 16,000 voted, by far the largest turnout for any credit union vote in the movement's history. Only 650 supported the merger.[14] All told, it was a divisive and difficult episode that troubled many within the provincial system; it was an aberration from the "natural" way in which amalgamations had taken place over the previous 50 years; it was an aspect of "mainstreaming" that many wished had not occurred.

13. See "Messy takeover fight does no credit to industry," *The Province*, October, 31, 1993, p. A50; "Surrey Metro merger bid blasted," *The Vancouver Sun*, September 2, 1993, p.D1; and "Fraser Valley showdown," *The Financial Post*, October 2, 1993.

14. "Merger plan rejection sets Surrey Metro back," *The Vancouver Sun*, October 31, 1993.

Not all of the growth, of course, took place in the Lower Mainland, Victoria or the Okanagan. Across the province there were many economically strong communities. Prince Rupert and Prince George, for example, although affected by the decline in the primary industries, still grew, building upon the shipping and transportation industries, the service sectors, the tourist businesses and, in the case of Prince George, a new university. Dawson Creek grew steadily as its part of the North continued to open. Nelson regained momentum and parts of the Kootenays flourished amid growing tourism. Other communities, such as Grand Forks, remained economically stable as important service centres for their local economies.

When credit unions flourished in small communities (and many did even in depressed communities), they were very important institutions. Board members were important local figures. Managers were often among the most influential and best-paid people in town, while their other employees earned competitive salaries and had good fringe benefits. Credit union buildings, almost invariably located on prime land in the centre of town or in the new shopping centres, were among the most attractive in town. Credit unions were also sophisticated organizations: as they achieved $100-200-million in assets, they could offer the full range of financial services. In many ways, the medium-sized credit unions were among the movement's most obvious success stories.

Unfortunately, though, not all local economies flourished, even in the generally more affluent early-1990s. In the lumber industry, the work force fell by 20-30%, although production was stable, in some years even increasing, because of technological change. The major development was that aging lumber mills were closing, some to be replaced by more efficient mills that employed fewer people, others never to be opened again. In the woods, new tree-harvesting equipment made large numbers of workers redundant.

These changes profoundly affected most lumbering communities. They were also significant for the entire economy because they meant fewer high-paying jobs in a key sector of the provincial economy. For young people they meant that the chances of finding employment in one of the province's traditional industries were sadly reduced. And, for many credit unions, they meant reduced pay packets, fewer deposits, and greater instability.

Similarly, the mining industries were employing fewer people. The mines of the interior, though nurtured by generous transportation arrangements, were unable to compete in the glutted mineral markets of the eighties and the early nineties. Competition within the mining industry around the world continued to increase, just as many B.C. mines were becoming uneconomic, exploration for new deposits was slackening, and debates over ecological issues were restricting growth. The industry was facing an uncertain future and so were its associated credit unions and their members.

The fishing industry, too, faced periodic gluts and depressed prices. Even more ominously, there were alarming signs that the fish stock was declining. Many spawning streams, their shores abused by logging, mining, hydro-electric dams and suburbia, were no longer friendly to returning fish. Too much fishing, on the seas and at the river mouths, was exacting too high a tribute; too few fish were getting through. The once-rich waters of the western coast were no longer capable of sustaining the yields they had historically given.

With these changes, a century of British Columbian dependency upon primary industries was in decline. That change affected credit unions because, for 40 years, these industries had provided some of the most fertile growth for the movement. Their primary organizations — unions and company networks — had fostered credit unions; their members had provided considerable stability through their loyalty and their steady pay-packets. But by the later eighties, the voices of people from the forests, the mines and the sea were rarely heard at the meetings of Central. The perspectives of their trade union backgrounds were largely stilled.

Such changes within credit unions and around the province profoundly affected B.C. Central between 1985 and 1994. During those years, Central's Board of Directors went through two distinct phases. During the first four years, the board was in an essentially defensive posture, buffeted by the economic difficulties and the tensions surrounding the organization. Then, from 1989 onward, the board became more aggressive, though not aggressive enough for some.

The two chairs at the start of the period, George Viereck and Ian MacPherson, were primarily concerned with bringing the various factions together and retaining support for a strong provincial and national system. Tod Manrell, who became chair in 1988 and held that position until 1993, had a similar view, but as Central's economic situation improved, he was also able to help push Central into a somewhat more aggressive position. A successful businessman and a deeply-committed credit unionist, he possessed a wealth of experience and a talent for conciliation. Above all, he brought to the position his optimism and confidence, rather rare qualities among credit union volunteers of the period.

The board, particularly at the start of the period, was made up largely of volunteers, a change from the later seventies and eighties when the predominant group had consisted of managers. There were advantages and disadvantages to this pattern. Volunteers tend less to

George Viereck, whose service to the credit union and co-operative movements spanned some 50 years, made his greatest contribution by smoothing the way for the Nanoose Accord in 1984.

want to "manage" Central, whereas many managers find it difficult to resist wanting to "take over"; indeed, that was part of the problem in the late seventies and early eighties. On the other hand, the volunteers were less knowledgeable about technology and the details of the banking industry; as a result, some managers were unwilling to give them much power.

One feature of the board was that, in comparison to all other second- or third-tier co-operatives in the country, it had a significant number of women among its members. Throughout most of the later years, one-quarter to one-third of the board's members were women. They rarely served on the Executive Committee, however, although they played important roles on other committees. One of them, Cathy Manson, the manager of Grand Forks District Savings Credit Union, had the distinction of being the only candidate ever to receive support from every credit union voting on one particular occasion when she ran for office. Another, Susanne Raschdorf, a director of Nelson & District Credit Union, played a very effective role in several national organizations, notably the Co-operative College and CUMIS Insurance Company.

At the start of the period, the board hired Jim Thomson to be Central's chief executive officer. He joined in September, 1984. Thomson came to Central from the Workers' Compensation Board of Alberta, where he had been executive director of finance for nearly five years, following six years with the Workers' Compensation Board of B.C. His earlier career involved some 15 years in banking, starting in Glasgow, Scotland, and culminating in a position as an economist with the Bank of B.C. in Vancouver.

He assumed an immense, perhaps impossible, task. The movement was reluctantly united under the provisions of the Nanoose Accord, but there was still considerable dissatisfaction, particularly among larger credit unions, which were still searching for change. Thomson, moreover, was an outsider, a man whose occasionally rather abrasive style was not well received throughout the movement. In the autumn of 1985, the board decided that a change was necessary and relieved Thomson of his responsibilities; he was replaced by Wayne Nygren.

Nygren brought to the position a strong reputation for integrity and openness. Since his arrival from Saskatchewan, he had earned the support of groups in all kinds of credit unions, large and small, urban and rural. He was also a keen proponent of the "system," in both its provincial and federal manifestations; in that respect, Nygren reflected well the dominant view on the board.

Shortly after his appointment, he named Laurie Yaworski as senior vice-president of finance and chief financial officer. A former professional hockey player trained within the Saskatchewan credit union movement, Yaworski was a certified general accountant who also held a master's degree in business administration and had qualified as a chartered financial analyst. For the previous 10 years, he had worked for Credit Union Central of Saskatchewan in accounting and finance. Yaworski brought a fiscally conservative approach to his job, a strong commitment to the credit union system, and a reputation for insisting on clean, open negotiations.

Nygren's other key new appointment to Central's senior management was Teresa Freeborn, who became vice-president of services and communications in April, 1987. Freeborn had begun her career at Delta Credit Union, moving to Stry Credit Union as a branch manager at the age of 24. From 1980 to 1984, she had worked at Central, preparing operations manuals and serving as a consultant to credit unions. Between 1984 and 1987, she had overseen all branch operations for B.C. Teachers Credit Union.

These two individuals, along with Richard Thomas, who became corporate secretary in 1985 and vice-president of government relations in 1990, formed the senior management team, which remained intact throughout the period. Elsewhere in the organization, too, long-serving employees were the norm. Of particular note were Jim Dowling, the controller, Mervin Zabinsky, director of payment and information services, and Barbara Ciarniello, manager of payment services. All three had started in the early seventies and provided much of the long-term stability in Central's service areas. This continuity in itself was a reflection of the stability Central achieved after the economic problems of the early and mid-eighties. As the years went by, it was also a tribute to the kind of leadership Nygren provided.

Nygren's first priority was to earn increased support for Central from the province's credit unions. In a general sense, this objective was pursued by the way in which he thought about his job and about Central's role in general. For Nygren (and the board's leadership of the time), Central was essentially the servant and, as circumstances permitted, the catalyst for the provincial movement. It was not a head office or even a "hub"; but, on the other hand, it was equally not just a branch office of the credit unions — or of any particular group of credit unions.

This perspective was not easily implemented, particularly in the business climate of the 1980s. It required considerable listening, frequently to people with very strong views; it meant making choices from the often conflicting advice that was offered; and it usually involved proceeding with abundant caution. In short, it meant adopting a management style that contrasted sharply with the aggressive, highly centralized approach that characterized North American business circles in the 1980s. It was oriented towards process rather than control, again an unconventional maxim in the period and most particularly within banking structures.

Nygren and his staff also undertook a series of specific activities in an effort to gain more support from the province's credit unions. The first was maintaining the effectiveness of the support systems Central operated on behalf of the member credit unions. As in the past, the cheque-clearing activities were carried out in an efficient, cost-effective manner. Central's management of system liquidity continued to improve, an important activity given the volatility of the financial markets.

The second was improving communication between Central and its member credit unions. From the time of his appointment, Nygren, members of his senior staff, and board members, as appropriate, regularly visited credit unions. Central also expanded the kinds of information it distributed to credit unions. Under the leadership of Richard Allen, the chief economist, Central produced a growing range of bulletins on financial analysis. The Marketing Department provided regular background information on marketing issues, including *Market Smarts*, a well-received analysis of the provincial, national and international financial industries. *Enterprise* magazine, under the editorship of Gayle Stevenson, became a particularly successful, award-winning magazine devoted to discussions of credit unions and analyses of regional differences.

Third, throughout the first five years of the period, Central continued to cut back some of its own activities while it changed others. Among the services and activities to be cut was Greentree Developments, the subsidiary that had constructed credit union and other co-operative buildings around the province since 1976. While some credit unions supported this organization strongly, most of the larger credit unions preferred to hire independent developers; they were reluctant even to be morally obligated to use a central service whenever they were thinking of expansion. They preferred to be free to make their own decisions, even though, from an over-all system perspective, the result might be higher costs.

In the later eighties, too, CUPAC Services Society, which had been organized in 1972 to help low-income British Columbians generally not served by credit unions, ran into difficulties. During the 1980s, government policies changed, meaning that it was increasingly difficult to secure funds to help people with lower incomes. Moreover, Central's member credit unions increasingly insisted on a user-pay principle for all of its services, including CUPAC. It was closed in 1990. Henceforth, whatever could be done to assist low-income people would have to be done by individual credit unions; regrettably, few appear to have taken up the challenge.

The biggest change in Central, however, occurred in its investment policy. Essentially, Central became more completely a liquidity manager, rather than a mixture of liquidity manager and commercial lender. Its capacity to earn large surpluses was consequently reduced, but so too were the risks that it took with funds on deposit from member credit unions. The rate of return might be less, but it would be stable.

This change affected two areas of Central's traditional investments. The first was its bond portfolio. That portfolio had been a long-term irritant for many of Central's members. Perhaps unfairly, but nevertheless persistently, some repeatedly reminded Central about how bad the investments looked in retrospect, forgetting how good they had looked at the time they were made (as indeed they had to investment managers at many other institutions).

Consequently, as interest rates generally fell in the mid-eighties, Central took every reasonable opportunity to sell off its bond holdings. In 1985, it sold bonds worth $86-million (from a portfolio that in 1981 had been worth $158-million). It took a loss of nearly $3-million in effecting these sales (not counting lost-opportunity costs), but it had moved clearly in the direction of restoring the value of its portfolio and introducing a policy of much more closely matching the terms-to-maturity of its assets with those of its liabilities, the latter being primarily the liquidity deposits of its member credit unions.[15]

In 1986, Central also adopted a considerably more conservative investment policy. The policy was designed to ensure a stable return for the money invested in it by credit unions and to complement Central's role as a supplier of central banking services.[16]

At the same time as Central sought more support from credit unions, it cautiously became more aggressive in asserting a conciliatory leadership role. One of its initiatives was the sponsorship of the United Nations Pavilion at Expo 86, the international exposition held in Vancouver during 1986. This initiative was begun by Richard McAlary and, despite some reluctance from a few credit unions, was ultimately well supported. The association with the United Nations was especially appropriate because the international organization had promoted co-operatives throughout its history and had been particularly supportive of co-operative banking.

The central theme for the pavilion was "Peace through Communication." It was in keeping with Expo's general emphasis on communications and the UN's declaration of 1986 as the International Year of Peace. The pavilion proved to be a successful project, drawing 1.6-million visitors. It became noted for a particularly effective

15. *Executive Briefs*, B.C. Central Credit Union, December 23, 1985.

16. "B.C. Central Credit Union Investment Policy," adopted May 24, 1986, BCCCU Board Minutes.

blending of traditional art forms and modern interactive educational technology. It also clearly showed how Central might help the provincial movement become more visible as a significant element in the society and economy of British Columbia.

During the later 1980s, Central also undertook a few initiatives aimed at creating a more cohesive system. In 1986, the board authorized acquisition of CuNet Services, a payment card system owned by 46 credit unions. The company had never successfully entered into the business, and it needed greater support from the larger credit unions if it was to be successful; Central's task was to increase that support. Central purchased the company for a little over $16,000, gaining in the process some $528,000 in tax credits.[17]

More importantly, Central sought, and increasingly was asked to play, a leading role in helping credit unions adjust to a rapidly-changing market situation. The changes could be seen on all fronts, even though credit unions were generally prospering as the decade came to an end. The problem was that their competitors were thriving too. In fact, although assets and membership increased between 1987 and 1990, credit unions' share of the market for deposits declined from 19% to just over 16%. Studies of consumers' perceptions further revealed that credit unions, in comparison to banks, did not appear as successful in securing the best branching sites, in training their staffs, and in attracting the interest of young people.[18]

In 1987, Central responded to these concerns and undertook an extensive analysis that culminated in a report entitled *A Strategic Study of B.C. Credit Unions*. It examined 12 pairs of credit unions over a 10-year period, 1977-86 inclusive. The main issues raised in the study were explained in terms of a long list of needs: more sophisticated planning, better training of directors, more careful selection of managers, increased emphasis on marketing, diversification of financial activities, and better financial management. The study examined these needs from the viewpoints of different kinds of credit unions – small, large, rural, urban and "growth oriented." The study showed how significant these differences were, thereby providing an approach to understanding the complexity of the province's credit unions that would become increasingly important.

This attempt to think strategically and to address the fundamental issues confronting the various types of credit unions was well received. It helped to generate a belief that the provincial movement should try to evaluate and address its fundamental issues. Thus, in early 1989, largely through the initiative of Tod Manrell, Central's board decided

Credit unions, through B.C. Central, proudly participated in Expo 86 in Vancouver by sponsoring the United Nations Pavilion. It was a natural "fit" for the credit unions because of the long-standing relationships between the UN and co-operative organizations and because of the Pavilion's emphasis on a peace theme. During Expo, Central used the opportunity to recognize pioneers of the movement at a series of special gatherings, such as the one pictured above.

17. August 8-10, 1986, BCCCU Board Minutes.

18. "B.C. Credit Union System Strategic Planning Project, Situation Analysis, November 1990," (Vancouver: B.C. Central Credit Union, 1990), pp. 3-10.

Expo 86

that it was time to see if the provincial movement could plan more systematically for its own future.

Central's board and management had, for some years, regularly undertaken planning sessions for the organization's own activities, but in recent years had not tried to plan for the provincial movement. During the seventies, when some of Central's leaders had tried to plan for the provincial "system," many of the most powerful leaders in the province had discouraged them. In the early and mid-eighties, Central was unable to plan for the system because of its own internal problems, a significant loss of support among key credit unions, and widespread changeover among the most prominent managers. It was only as the decade drew to a close that Central could seriously return to the basic question of how the provincial system could plan for its future.

Late in 1989, Central appointed a System Strategic Planning Committee to develop a vision for the provincial movement in the next century. The committee was initially chaired by Don Tuline, the chief executive officer of Richmond Savings Credit Union. Tuline had become Richmond's manager in 1983, when that credit union, like so many others, was being buffeted by declining margins. After making a series of management changes, he embarked on an extensive marketing campaign, a risky endeavour for any troubled organization to undertake. He completely changed the credit union's approach to computing, introducing the Prologic system based on the emerging microcomputer; this allowed the credit union to analyze member needs quickly and efficiently on an individual basis. By the later eighties, Tuline had also gained a favourable reputation for the planning methods he had introduced at Richmond Savings, and it was for that reason he was selected to chair the committee.

The committee divided its work into three stages. The first, completed by November, 1990, was an analysis of the situation in which credit unions operated. It documented the difficult competitive environment surrounding credit unions, raised concerns about apparent inefficiencies and insufficient capital, and commented on the need to find ways in which credit unions could improve their image. If the report seemed unduly critical in some instances, it must be seen in the context of the problems of the mid-eighties and the need to focus attention on the most significant long-term issues.

The second phase, involving "focus groups" of credit union leaders, followed by discussions among delegates at the 1991 semi-annual meeting, created a vision of what British Columbia's credit unions hoped to achieve by the year 2001. It said:

> We will be:
>
> The premier provider of financial services to individuals and owner-operated businesses in B.C.

Value-driven, community focused, and responsive to our members.

A strong, unified system.

In coming to see this vision, the committee and the delegates to the 1991 meeting concentrated on four main issues: capital formation, the development of products and services, the image of credit unions, and "universal access," meaning that a B.C. credit union member should have access to basic services through any credit union in the system.

The capital issue, of course, had grown out of the discussions and experiments of the previous five years. It was one of the continuing ways in which the problems of the early 1980s remained. It was not going to disappear, even if the better economic situation allowed credit unions to build up equity through allocations from annual surpluses.

The other issues raised by the committee were equally fundamental. In fact, they had been evident in different forms since the beginning of the movement. What was the best way to develop products and services? Should the initiative remain largely in the hands of credit unions or coalitions of credit unions? Should it be with Central? Should the emphasis be on complete control, partnerships with other financial institutions, or purchasing services in the market? How should credit unions try to project their image? Did they want to be "different"? Should all credit unions offer the same services and products? Was a common denominator better than diversity? None of these questions could be answered simply: they would remain in the forefront for years, as they had been for decades in different forms. They would be taken up by a standing committee of Central's board, appointed after the 1991 meeting and chaired by Michael Tarr, who became the board's chairperson two years later.

In the wake of the system planning project, the question of Central's control structure once again became an issue. Some believed that Central's board was insufficiently in touch with the needs and aspirations of different types of credit unions. Others argued that Central needed to find ways to identify and to carry out a strong leadership mandate.

In January, 1992, Central appointed the System Structure Task Force, chaired by Ian MacPherson, to consider how Central might be restructured to meet its objectives more effectively. After reviewing suggestions put forward by various credit union leaders, the task force concluded that the primary need was for the province's credit unions to indicate clearly what they wanted Central to be and to do. It recommended that Central revise its existing mission statement, making it as specific as possible, so that credit unions could give Central a clear mandate.

To further ensure better communication between credit unions and Central, the task force recommended changes in how Central's directors would be chosen. It recommended that directors continue to be elected from the North, the Kootenays, the Okanagan, and Vancouver Island, since geography dictated common interests for credit unions in those areas. It recommended changes, however, in how other directors would be selected. It divided the remaining credit unions into four groups based on asset size, with each group responsible for electing one director. This approach, based partly on the system adopted by Alberta credit unions a few years earlier, recognized that most credit unions communicated most effectively with their peers. Credit unions of similar asset size typically had more in common with each other that they did with neighbouring credit unions that were significantly larger or smaller.

In fact, credit unions of different sizes had already started to meet informally, the most active being two groupings in Greater Vancouver, one of nine larger credit unions (NETCU) and the other of six medium-sized credit unions (MEDCU). In some ways, electing directors from asset groups was simply a recognition of a strong set of dynamics already becoming important.

To the regret of some of its members and others, the task force also recommended that the position of director elected by Class B shareholders (co-operatives other than credit unions) be discontinued. The main reason for such co-operatives to join Central – to borrow funds – had disappeared almost completely with Central's decision to withdraw from commercial lending. As a result, only 40 co-ops belonged to Central in 1992, down from 80 a decade earlier. The task force recommended, though, that Central retain its associations with other co-operatives in the province by playing a more active role in the B.C. Region of the Canadian Co-operative Association.

The recommendations were accepted by Central's members at the 1992 semi-annual meeting. Support for the compromise presented by the task force was strong, though some within the larger credit unions indicated that they would have preferred the creation of a stronger provincial entity. It is doubtful, though, that many credit unions, including the larger ones at the end of the day, would have accepted a greater concentration of power within the hands of a provincial organization. Rather, creating a structure whereby groupings of like credit unions could work together, influence Central directly, and collectively empower Central (if they really wished to do so) seemed to be the best practical option available.

Recognizing the need for high visibility with the public, B.C. credit unions launched a prominent TV advertising campaign in 1992, co-ordinated by Central. A scene from the first commercials is shown *above*.

Central had a key role in bringing B.C. credit unions into the nationwide Interac network of ATMs in 1987, *opposite centre*. The Member Card was created in B.C. and shared with credit unions across the country, as they prepared for the next Interac venture, electronic payment at the point of sale, *opposite bottom*.

Member Card®
5412 3456 7890 1234
00/99 00/99
LEE M. CARDHOLDER
ANYTOWN CREDIT UNION
Credit Union

Your guide to Coquitlam leisure
Inserted in today's News

THE Tri-City NEWS

Seeking golden hearts PG. 3

Wrapping up the season PG. 27

Covering: Coquitlam • Port Coquitlam • Port Moody

987-5511   Circulation 943-6397   35¢

Credit unions hook-up with Interac

British Columbia's credit union system has joined the nationwide Interac network of automated banking machines, enabling B.C. credit union members to withdraw money from most ABMs in Canada.

The Interac network links more than 4,500 ABMs of credit unions, banks and trust companies across Canada.

Customers of banks and t[...] Interac network will be abl[...] from some 140 ABMs o[...] B.C. credit union [...] Chequing [...] accessi [...]

In retrospect, the questions concerning the basic roles of Central and credit unions in British Columbia emanated essentially from three sources.

They were derived partly from credit unions' position in the marketplace. The problems of the mid-eighties, the increasing competition of the later eighties, and the uncertainties of the early nineties clearly showed that credit unions were creatures of the marketplace – they ignored its trends at their peril.

Partly, too, the debates flowed from the issues that are inevitable in any co-operative system. Discussions about the appropriate relationship between "locals" and "centrals" never ends within co-operative structures. There are never simple answers as to which level should predominate, nor are there permanent rules as to how democratic structures should operate.

Finally, there were also similar issues within the national credit union system. In fact, the Canadian Co-operative Credit Society, the national credit union organization,[19] faced even greater difficulties than did B.C. Central. Initially, most of these were attributable to its commercial loan portfolio. Two of its problem loans involved co-operatives, United Maritime Fishermen and United Co-operatives of Ontario. Both organizations were caught in the throes of expansion when inflation and high interest rates hit in the later seventies and earlier eighties. Most of CCCS's bad loans, though, were to privately-owned companies, part of a diversification program George May had undertaken shortly after he joined the organization.

By 1986, CCCS was in significant difficulty. Many B.C. leaders were particularly alarmed by these developments since B.C. Central, with $34-million invested in the organization, was receiving far less than competitive returns on its investment, that is, when it was receiving any return at all. For a while, there was some serious discussion within the province about winding down the national association and transferring its activities to one of the provincial centrals.

As if these problem loans were not enough, CCCS suffered a severe reversal in 1987 when Osler, Inc., one of the securities firms it used regularly, was unable to honour its commitments to repurchase government securities from CCCS. This left CCCS short by $38-million. The National Contingency Fund, the brokerage industry's investment protection fund, rather begrudgingly reimbursed CCCS with $10-million, still leaving a potentially crippling shortfall. The issue dragged on until the mid-1990s when Osler's principals were finally convicted on 13 counts of fraud for concealing investment losses in 1986 and 1987.

The Osler affair undermined much of the progress CCCS had made in recovering from the bad loans situation of a few years earlier. It also

19. In 1992, the Canadian Co-operative Credit Society was renamed Credit Union Central of Canada.

alarmed many within the B.C. movement since it meant that B.C. Central would not receive dividends on its $34-million investment in the national organization for years to come (ultimately, it took seven years). Support for a strong national credit union movement was at its lowest ebb.

And yet, in the long run, there was no alternative but to try and preserve a strong national system. The unfolding technological revolution demanded it. That process had started before the Osler affair, continued through it, and gained even greater momentum afterward. One obvious manifestation of the technological imperative could be seen on almost all major streets in Canada: it was the automated teller machine.

The machines offered convenience to depositors by making it possible for them to withdraw funds at any time; they ultimately were beneficial for financial institutions because the cost of withdrawal through the machines was cheaper than withdrawals involving tellers. It was a change that credit unions could not afford to miss.

ATMs forced even the banks to co-operate. As late as the early 1980s, it was difficult to imagine that Canada's largest financial institutions could ever unite to create a single ATM network. With the prodding of the federal government, however, and given the almost prohibitive costs of creating rival national networks, they saw the advantages of working together. By 1984, many of the country's major financial institutions had united to form the Interac Association, initially to pool their individual ATM networks to enable customers to withdraw cash from any of their machines anywhere in the country.

In January, 1986, after a rather lengthy debate, a large segment of the Canadian credit union system agreed to unite through CCCS to join the Interac Association. In doing so, the national system accepted the obligation of developing its own computer switch, or "node," by mid-1988 to connect credit unions with the other Interac participants. B.C. Central immediately entered into negotiations with Pacific Network Services, an organization made up primarily of a few large credit unions, to see if the province's credit unions could enter as a unit.

Most of the provincial system reached a consensus by the late spring of 1986, but several credit unions, anxious to protect their perceived autonomy, were reluctant to accept this proposal. Finally, after considerable discussion, the proposal was accepted, and B.C. Central entered the national system in October, 1986. In fact, the B.C. representatives on the CCCS board and finance committee successfully negotiated to have the switch, which would connect all the English-Canadian credit unions to the Interac network, located in British Columbia. In part, that decision was a symbol of the increasing role B.C. was playing in the national system.

In that sense, the decision marked a renewed commitment among at least some of the leadership of the B.C. movement to creating an integrated national co-operative financial system. In 1987 and 1988, further discussions were initiated that would result in the B.C. movement becoming more integrated into the national system. The leaders responsible, George Viereck, Tod Manrell, Wayne Nygren, Laurie Yaworski and Ian MacPherson, were acting in some ways contrary to the general mood in the province.

As the ATMs of B.C. credit unions were linked into the Interac network in September, 1987, another technological advance – electronic funds transfer at point of sale – was under serious discussion. EFT/POS essentially carried the technology of the automated teller machine to the cash registers of local stores. It meant that a customer, instead of writing a cheque or paying for goods and services in cash, could directly access his or her chequing and savings accounts through an ATM card and secret personal identification number ("PIN").

It was, nevertheless, a complex step, involving difficult negotiations among several data processing companies, the complete range of financial institutions, and officials of the federal government. It raised issues of privacy, the calculation of profits, and the ultimate value to the consumer. Within credit unions in particular, it forced the pace of technological change and seemed to threaten their independence. It meant centralized decisions would have to be made, it meant strict timetables would have to be set.[20] Neither agenda was easily met.

An important aspect of the groundwork for EFT/POS was the development of a new card that would allow members both to access automated teller machines and to make payments through point-of-sale machines. Credit unions could enter into the national EFT/POS network only as a system or through individual affiliations with other financial institutions – for a fee. There was relatively little debate, in British Columbia, about the desirability of credit unions entering as a system, but there was considerable debate over what the card should look like.

It was a typical debate within credit unions. The more independent credit unions wanted their own colours, logos and names to be predominant in the card's design, with only a portion of the card reserved for a small logo indicating affiliation with the credit union system. Others wanted a card whose design features would be essentially the same for all credit unions, seeing in the common symbols a way to indicate the unity of the movement.

The latter position essentially won out at the annual general meeting in the spring of 1991, when the members of Central adopted a design featuring the name "Member Card" and including the "Hands

20. For a discussion of the implications of EFT/POS for credit unions, see Filomena Tamburri, "Moving Closer to a Cashless Society," *Enterprise*, January-February, 1988, pp. 3-5.

& Globe" symbol of the international credit union movement. To outsiders it might have seemed a minor, even obvious, step. But in the context of the recent divisions and the institutional pride involved, it was a significant accomplishment, for which credit must go to Wayne Nygren, Laurie Yaworski, Teresa Freeborn and Gene Creelman of Central, and a group of committed credit union managers and marketing managers.

The appeal of the new card's design, particularly its name, proved irresistible to the movements beyond B.C.'s borders, and Member Card was soon adopted as the universal card for Canadian credit unions affiliated with the national system.

Just as the problems of the early and mid-1980s forced changes in the provincial and national credit union movement, they also made change inevitable in the national co-operative movement. In those years the English-Canadian co-op movement began to reconsider the way in which it organized its national institutions. Several problems had started to emerge. The most important was that, aside from housing co-operatives funded by Canada Mortgage and Housing Corporation, relatively few co-ops were being formed. Thus, as a co-operative disappeared, because of financial problems or because it had served its purpose, there was rarely another to take its place.

Another area of concern was that many co-ops, but especially farmers', marketing and consumer co-operatives, were not attracting a broad cross-section of the Canadian public. Almost invariably, it seemed, when one attended annual or other meetings, one would see only males, most in their fifties or sixties. Most of them, too, were oriented to rural values and issues. In a society that was over 90% urban and changing rapidly, this was an alarming development.

A third issue was that, with the exception of credit unions, co-operatives were not attracting the support of people who lived in cities. Somehow, it was believed, co-operatives had to find ways to become more useful to people coping with the pressures of large cities or struggling to ensure that suburbs became and remained satisfying places in which to live.

One possible solution to such problems was to try and create a stronger national co-operative institution for promotion and lobbying activities. At the time, there were two national organizations, the Co-operative Union of Canada, located in Ottawa, and the Co-operative College of Canada, located in Saskatoon. The Co-operative Union did not seem to figure significantly in the activities of most large co-ops, while the College was increasingly struggling to develop programs that could meet the educational and training needs of diverse and steadily more self-reliant large co-ops.

Representatives from the two national organizations met several times in 1985 and 1986 to consider how the national movement might be revitalized through amalgamating the two organizations. In the spring of 1986, the decision was made to carry out the amalgamation. Ian MacPherson, who had represented Central during these negotiations, became the first president of the new organization.

While the amalgamation ultimately did de-emphasize education, it permitted a revitalization of co-operative enthusiasm at the national level. The new organization blended its lobbying activities with the Canadian Co-operative Credit Society, and became significantly more successful in presenting the co-op perspective to federal bureaucrats and politicians. It also succeeded, through increased provincial activities, in fostering stronger associations among co-operatives at the local level. Certain B.C. credit unions, particularly Delta, Vancouver City Savings, Evergreen Savings, CCEC and Pacific Coast Savings, were especially involved in the general co-operative movement in the province.

During this period, too, other British Columbians played important roles in the national co-operative movement. George Viereck, David Lach and Peter Podovinikoff served on the board of The Co-operators, while Bernie Proft, Susanne Raschdorf, Renate Mueller, Phil Keller and Jack Bright served at different times on the board of CUMIS. All of these people worked to achieve the type of efficient integration that would allow these two companies to serve credit unions through CUIS, their joint venture. Brian Elliott and Barry Forbes served on the board of Co-op Trust, a company that also suffered during the economic problems of the 1980s.

Podovinikoff also played a vital role in the economic development of Arctic Co-operatives, an organization that primarily served aboriginals in the Arctic. He helped steer that organization through some early activities until it became one of the most remarkable co-op success stories of the period.

These increased activities at the national level were complemented by increased involvement at the international level. One of the most committed international activists was Tod Manrell. Manrell, who had become chairman of the Canadian Co-operative Credit Society in 1989, was elected to the board of the World Council of Credit Unions. He became WOCCU's treasurer in 1991, and second vice-president in 1993.

Like so many other Canadians given the opportunity to see the work being accomplished by the international movement, Manrell became an enthusiastic advocate of the "credit union way." He played a prominent role in the Canadian Co-operative Association's committee that managed English Canada's overseas development activities.

Together with Peter Podovinikoff, he was primarily responsible for the provincial movement increasing its contributions to international development in 1992.[21] In 1994, he capped his distinguished career in the international movement by succeeding to the presidency of the World Council, a position he was expected to hold through the 1997 International Forum of the World Council, to be held in Vancouver.

In the same years, Ian MacPherson played a role within the international co-operative movement, serving on the board of the International Co-operative Alliance as a representative of the Canadian Co-operative Association. Growing out of this involvement, he was asked to chair an international process to redefine the principles and practices upon which co-operatives around the world are based. It proved to be a complex activity, reflecting most of the main economic changes altering the world at the end of the twentieth century, the incredible diversity of co-operatives in different societies, and the varying experiences of different kinds of co-operatives. It was a task for which the diverse British Columbian and Canadian experience provided a rich grounding and unique vantage point.

Beneath all these international, national and provincial changes, though, the most important developments between 1985 and 1994 occurred at the local level. The march to increasing professionalism, evident since the 1950s, continued inexorably. As credit unions became larger, they employed more highly trained and specialized personnel. As they sought to meet an increasingly wider range of member needs, their dependence on technology expanded. More credit unions had multiple branches, the largest ones having between 12 and 30, so that administrative and managerial structures became more sophisticated, and inevitably more complicated. It was not difficult to think of there being a "credit union professional" by the end of the period.

The heart of the business remained residential mortgage lending, but a growing number of credit unions were also engaged in other kinds of businesses. By 1994, over 30 credit unions were involved in the insurance business through insurance subsidiaries. About the same number were involved in financial planning, including the marketing of mutual funds. Vancouver City Savings was one of the early advocates of financial planning, and its services were soon sold to a number of other credit unions.

At the end of the period, too, there was widespread discussion about introducing brokerage services.[22] In short, credit unions had largely achieved what some of their more foresighted dreamers had long envisioned: they were becoming full-service, one-stop financial institutions.

The development of mutual funds owed much to the ingenuity of the board and management of Vancouver City Savings. In 1986, in

21. This was accomplished by doubling the annual assessment that credit unions paid to the Credit Union Foundation of British Columbia, from five cents per member to ten cents; the increase was earmarked for international development initiatives through the Foundation.

22. On March 16, 1995, Credit Union Central of Canada and Midland Walwyn Inc. announced an agreement-in-principle to introduce a national credit union brokerage firm on a joint-venture basis, with the credit union system owning 80%.

large part because of the enthusiasm of David Levi, a board member, it introduced the Ethical Growth Fund, Canada's first "socially-responsible" mutual fund. That fund invested only in companies that met certain "progressive" standards regarding their employment and environmental practices and were not involved in the military weapons industry or with political regimes engaged in repressive activities. It proved to be successful, and in 1992 VanCity sold the fund to Credit Union Central of Canada (as CCCS had been renamed), where it became the core of a family of mutual funds for the national movement.

All of these technological and marketing changes inevitably meant that the employees of credit unions were significantly different at the end of the period from what they had been at the beginning. There was, for example, a much greater degree of specialization, and the largest credit unions led this trend. The personnel and marketing departments of the larger credit unions were considerably larger than those of B.C. Central. Similarly, the money managers of the larger credit unions had nearly as large deposit bases, as many options, and as much expertise as Central's specialists.

An increasingly large proportion of these highly-skilled employees were trained in community colleges and universities. In 1985, many managers had little in the way of formal qualifications; by the end of the period, that was uncommon. In 1985, there were still some financial officers who were not accountants, but by 1994 almost all of them were. In short, there were many pools of highly-paid and effective specialists in the system, a significant difference from a few years earlier.

The addition of so many specialized services managed by a growing number of professionally-trained people profoundly affected the ways in which member service representatives dealt with members. The computing systems available at each wicket allowed the representatives to have a complete overview of a member's dealings with the credit union; that overview permitted them to remind members of the services being offered and to engage in "cross-selling." Doing so, though, required more training and expertise on the part of the representatives and usually they experienced increased pressure to perform at a higher or different level of knowledge. They consequently had to become more flexible, and better informed than ever before, particularly as credit unions became more concerned about helping members to "manage their wealth" better. It had always been true that they were the most important staff in representing a credit union to its membership; as the 1990s wore on, they became steadily more important.[23]

Perhaps the most important short-term trend brought about by the addition of so many highly-trained people was an increased emphasis on marketing. Several credit union managers tried to create a "sales culture" among their employees. This trend was evident in the later

23. Interview with Debbie Ottenbreit, Vice-President, Human Resources, Pacific Coast Savings Credit Union, September 6, 1995.

eighties in the widespread popularity of "relationship banking," an approach originating in the United States that emphasized the cross-selling of products. It meant that member service representatives, in particular, were encouraged to promote different financial products to members. It also meant that credit unions scrambled, as the possibilities became evident, to find new products to sell.

The emphasis on cross-selling and a sales culture marked a move away from a passive service emphasis that had grown up within credit unions in the seventies. That emphasis on service had come naturally enough in a credit union milieu, but its passivity was in some ways a break from the beginnings of credit unions. After all, in the 1950s and 1960s, leaders had been anything but narrow in their conception of what credit unions could do for their members. In that sense, the desire to expand services and search for members' needs was a return to an older ethic. The only question, one that time alone would answer, was whether the new services would always be organized in the members' best interests.

As in the general population, women continued to play an increasingly important role in credit unions. By 1989, about one-fifth of the general managers or chief executive officers of credit unions were women, while one-third of the branch managers were women. Although it is difficult to make comparisons because of the different management structures of the major banks, this level was significantly higher than the norm in the industry.[24] Moreover, some of the female managers were responsible for managing important medium-sized and larger credit unions, individuals like Cathy Manson of Grand Forks District Savings, Donna Parker of Parksville & District, and, latterly, Pamela Marchant of Island Savings and Jane Milner of North Shore. This was a change from the past, when almost all female managers were to be found in smaller credit unions.

Like their male counterparts, these women managers were confronted by a different world of management than had prevailed in earlier times. Previously, most of the managers within the movement had learned their work on the job or they had earned their position because they possessed special skills. By the mid-1990s, that kind of background was rarely sufficient and, in fact, many of the managers who had learned on the job (often having learned about credit unions during prior stints as directors) had departed during the 1980s, either through retirement or because of economic crises. In many instances, they had been replaced by managers who possessed exceptional skills in lending or marketing, skills that frequently helped resolve existing problems.

A specialized skill set, however, would not be enough for the long run. Increasingly, managers had to possess general qualities that would

24. *Market Smarts*, B.C. Central Credit Union, November, 1989, pp. 5-7.

enable them to forge strong bonds of association among their colleagues, to foster a climate in which credit union employees and directors could develop a clear focus for the organization, and to insist on precise planning procedures. Rarely could they afford the luxury of being "hands-on" managers, the type of manager that had prevailed in earlier periods. Rarely could they afford to retain employees who were not well prepared and highly motivated. The margins for error were becoming increasingly narrow.

The widening of their activities and the increasing sophistication of their employees were two of the most obvious trends in local credit unions. The third was a nagging concern about their communities. Credit unions can never escape being concerned about the differing fates of the local economies on which they are based.

In essentially single-resource communities, like Port Alberni and Trail, the issue was quickly translated into how the local economy could be diversified. In the cities, like Vancouver and Victoria, the issue became to identify the responsibilities to groups — those on welfare, street kids, single parents with limited income, Natives with few marketable skills — suffering amid the rapid economic and social change.

It was an issue that troubled some credit union leaders more than others. Part of the problem came from a growing recognition that somehow credit unions had lost their capacity for dramatic self-help activities. While they were able to provide the kinds of services and advice that could benefit large numbers of upwardly-mobile people of all classes, they did not seem to be able to find a general formula for helping the downwardly-mobile or the permanently-trapped. Given the experiments with peer-lending in the United States (within credit unions and especially community banks), and the success of the Gambian banks in the Indian subcontinent, this failure rankled some and challenged others.

Throughout the eighties and nineties, therefore, there were periodic debates about how credit unions might address the problems of the "new realities." Much of the initiative in raising this debate came from the board of Vancouver City Savings. In fact, that credit union, through its $1-million community development fund, sought to find ways to stimulate economic growth among the economically less advantaged in Vancouver, particularly in the east side of the city.

In some ways, it was unfortunate that the leadership came so much from VanCity because it tended to politicize the issue. In 1983, a group within the membership of that credit union had sponsored a slate of candidates consisting of prominent members of the New Democratic Party. This event brought to the fore the question of political affiliation. What made Vancouver City Savings unusual was that it was so openly associated with one political party. Board members of other credit unions were prominently associated with one party or another, but the ties, while known, were always informal. It was a contentious issue that ultimately affected, at least in part, how the movement dealt with the community development issue.

When representatives of VanCity raised that broad issue, as they did at various times in the eighties and the nineties, some considered it to be an "NDP issue." The bulk of credit unions – either for that reason, or because they thought it an issue only the marketplace could resolve – did not engage it seriously. This lukewarm reaction, too, emanated from the very real problem of how simultaneously to pay a competitive return on members' deposits while funding the riskier activities generally associated with community economic development. It was a difficult, unresolved issue, and predictably one that would not disappear.

Continuing...

If we are not compassionate going into the next generation, we will be toast. Institutions that do not focus on relations with their communities and with the people they serve will not last... and they do not deserve to do so.

Michael Tarr,
Chairperson, B.C. Central Credit Union[1]

CREDIT UNIONS IN BRITISH COLUMBIA HAVE BEEN IN EXISTENCE for less than 60 years; their "central bank," B.C. Central Credit Union, is barely 50 years old. They have nevertheless become the province's main indigenous financial system. Their penetration of the provincial population is exceeded in Canada only by the Quebec and Saskatchewan movements. Within English Canada, the B.C. movement has often been the leader in credit union circles, especially in the formation and development of community credit unions. Of the 10 largest credit unions in the country, for example, five are community credit unions in British Columbia. Many of the most important innovations within the national system – from daily savings accounts and risk equity to mutual funds and open-ended mortgages – have their origin in British Columbia.

Within the province, credit unions are represented in more communities than any bank or trust company; in more than 30 communities, they are the only financial institution. They have nearly 1.3 million members, meaning that they serve a considerable portion of the province's three-million-plus people.[2] By the end of 1994, the provincial system had nearly $16.5-billion in assets, making it a powerful factor in the provincial economy, indeed, the most important regional financial institution. And, beyond such numbers, many credit unions are powerful forces in their communities, perhaps most obviously in the small towns and villages where they are the engines of economic growth. The movement has grown far beyond the dreams of even the most optimistic visionaries of 50 years earlier.

What accounts for this success? The most obvious point is that credit unions have efficiently met some essential needs for a growing number of British Columbians. In particular, for the past 30 years, they have responded effectively to an apparently unending demand for mortgages. In fact, credit unions have become leaders in B.C.'s mortgage industry, institutions of choice for both members and realtors. They have pioneered in flexible pay-out features, allowing borrowers to pay out their mortgages at their own pace, in numerous instances a benefit of immense value. They have also been particularly responsive to mortgage borrowers by making decisions on mortgage applications quickly and easily. And many credit unions have become known for their willingness, in times of economic hardship, to help members work through difficulties.

1. Interview with Michael Tarr, February 18, 1995

2. It is difficult to measure the precise extent of credit union membership within the population. On the one hand, the 1,270,000 memberships at the end of 1994 would include many people who belong to more than one credit union. On the other hand, a single membership may serve a number of people, for example, in a family. Thus the oft-quoted claim that credit unions serve a third of the province's population may not be wide of the mark.

Credit unions, though, have never been monolithic. And today, despite the immense, almost unrelenting, pressures of the financial services industry and regulators to insist on uniformity in operations and policies, credit unions have retained a considerable degree of diversity. For example, at one end of the spectrum, Al-Pine Credit Union has 89 members and $178,500 in assets; at the other end, Vancouver City Savings Credit Union, has 207,000 members and nearly $3.6-billion in assets.[3] There are credit unions in the heart of downtown Vancouver, on Howe Street and Georgia Street; there are others on rural routes in small interior villages. There are credit unions primarily serving affluent suburbanites; there are others serving people of limited income. There are credit unions whose memberships are drawn entirely from one kind of employment; there are some whose bonds are based on ethnicity or religion.

In short, one cannot find today a "typical" credit union within the province; nor could one be found at any time in the past. In most respects, that diversity has been a tremendous asset. It will continue to be so in the future, as long as credit union leaders and regulators fully appreciate its value; as long as leaders of large credit unions do not patronize or ignore small credit unions; as long as small credit unions remain efficient, rejoice in their own worth, and recognize the distinctive problems that confront their larger brethren.

The truth is that large, medium and small credit unions have their own reasons for existence, their own ways of making useful contributions. Larger credit unions, especially if they work together, can help to maximize the strength of the system and expand the possibilities of the movement. They can influence pricing, service delivery and marketing within the financial services industry; they can expand, as they have so often done in the past, on the kinds of services they provide the consuming public. They have the advantages that relative autonomy can bring, while they have sufficient size to afford new initiatives; they largely represent the side of the movement that can reach out for significant power within the provincial economy.

On the other hand, small and medium-sized credit unions have the capacity and commitment to serve and cultivate specific groups of people, defined by community, unique market niches, or bonds of association. Typically, they can respond quickly to member needs, can be more approachable and less intimidating, and they are generally more open to traditional credit union markets among lower-income people.[4] By their nature, small and medium-sized credit unions also tend to question the common premise that growth for its own sake is always beneficial. It is a question that might have been asked more searchingly during the past 50 years; it is question that might be more important to ask in the future; it is the perspective that asks why power is desired.

Along with some of Canada's largest credit unions, the B.C. movement embraces very small closed-bond operations that meet the needs of distinct memberships. Al-Pine Credit Union serves employees of a forest products firm; treasurer Marjorie Filipovic is seen with Al-Pine's certificate of membership in the B.C. League, dated 1954.

3. Figures as at December 31, 1994.

4. See Tom Gies, "Are Mid-sized Credit Unions an Endangered Species?", *Enterprise*, May-June, 1995, pp. 3-5.

Whether credit unions are small, medium-sized or large, one "lesson" is clear from the past: there is no reason to expect tranquility. As one looks back on the history of the provincial movement, it is clear that British Columbia's credit unions have never experienced a "quiet time," and they should not expect one in the future. Partly, the continuing disquiet is explained by the fact that the financial industry has undergone continual change in the past half-century, particularly the past 20 years. More fundamentally, though, credit unions are financial co-operatives that, by their nature, must be sensitive to the social and economic changes that affect members and their communities; regardless of size or circumstance, they are extensions of members, they are parts of communities. It is not to be expected, therefore, that they can ever be static or somnolent institutions: that is why they are always interesting organizations; that is why being involved in them — as managers, employees, elected officers or concerned members — is perpetually challenging and fascinating.

The disquiet is also explained by the general patterns evident over the movement's 50-year history. In a somewhat imprecise yet compelling way, one can discern three periods amid all the diversity and complexity. The periods are not completely separated, however, although the divisions are important; rather, there is considerable continuity — continuity that provides permanent challenges for the movement and its institutions.

The first period lasted from the late 1930s until the early 1960s; it might be called the "emancipatory era." It was characterized by a co-operative search for ways to emancipate ordinary British Columbians from limited incomes and restricted opportunities. It was a period when small organizations provided valuable services to their members, and credit unions were clearly different from any other kind of financial institution. It was a time when the League and its activities were preeminent, when the volunteers were clearly dominant and the secretary-treasurers were as much public servants as they were entrepreneurs.

During this period, the essential co-operative nature of the local credit unions was obvious and pervasive; leaders shared similar backgrounds and a general commitment to what was generally accepted as a "movement." It was a time of remarkably ambitious and innovative thought and action, perhaps the most genuinely creative period in the movement's history. It was a time when British Columbia's credit union leaders played a significant role in helping to create a national credit union/co-operative movement, when they dreamed of — and to some extent accomplished — the creation of a broad movement responding to a wide array of human needs.

There were nevertheless some significant differences among leaders and credit unions; those differences were the consequences of political

A credit union forms part of the fabric of Vancouver's Polish community; manager/treasurer Alojzy Wojcik poses at the door.

ideology, local loyalties and geographic affiliations. Sometimes they were expressed in terms of party politics; more often, they were associated with geography, such as the classic division between Vancouver and the rest of the province; most often, they were manifested in the difficulties leaders encountered in trying to forge a truly integrated provincial system.

The second period might be called "the entrepreneurial era." It lasted from the early sixties to the early eighties and was characterized by powerful entrepreneurial impulses across the movement, at Central and particularly within some credit unions. Broadly speaking, there were two kinds of entrepreneurship. One, centred in some of the large and growing credit unions, was pushed by a handful of managers exhilarated by the freedom and possibilities credit unions offered. Partly western capitalist in style, often imitative of American community banks, this form of entrepreneurship drove credit unions in new directions and emphasized their independence from provincial and national initiatives.

The other kind of entrepreneurship, personified by Rod Glen and, to a lesser but still significant extent, by George May, embraced a form of co-operative entrepreneurship. Its focus was the movement, its vehicle was Central, its vision was universal. It was a complex vision that faced a difficult road in a society dominated by an unshakeable faith in the capacities of capitalist forms of enterprise.

Throughout the seventies and early eighties, these two visions struggled for supremacy. In the early eighties, when the economy deteriorated and confidence within the credit union movement ebbed, the more conventional form of entrepreneurship won a nearly complete and, in retrospect, unforgiving victory. Whatever remained of the other and broader vision survived provincially in the efforts of some to create a truly national co-operative financial system, and locally in a few credit unions devoted to a co-operative ethos.

The third phase started in the early eighties and has lasted until the present; it might be called the "mainstreaming era." It has been characterized by a search for how credit unions might become even more prominent leaders in the provincial financial industry, perhaps even dominant players in British Columbia's economy. There are many, and sometimes conflicting, visions as to how such a system might evolve; there are also many inherent questions – related to such issues as technological systems, management structures and capital formation – that have inevitably arisen as people have sought to prepare for the future.

Over the past decade, Central has consistently sought the role of the honest broker among the various alternatives, searching for ways in which it can usefully serve the greater good; in short, it has been

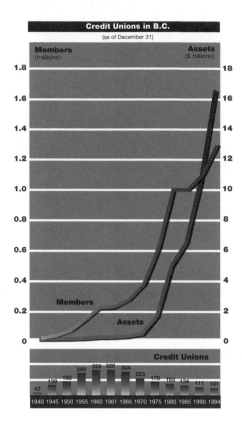

While the number of individual credit unions peaked in the early sixties, assets and membership have grown dramatically since that time. For the precise figures depicted in this chart, see Appendix 4.

Enterprise magazine continues the award-winning tradition of its predecessor, the *B.C. Credit Unionist*, with a focus on the most significant contemporary issues facing the system.

primarily concerned about achieving a new consensus after the disruption of the early eighties. In many instances, it has successfully played this role, a tribute to the diplomatic skills of many who have led the organization, both in management and on the Board of Directors. The vision is simple enough: to work for the creation of a single, strong credit union system in the province, linked together by distinctive organizational structures, a united front before governments, shared technological and marketing strategies whenever possible, and a strong commitment to communities throughout B.C.

In many ways, Central is the chief inheritor of the belief that there are advantages, usually immediate, sometimes future, in working together. In that sense, it carries into the modern period the perspective of the visionaries from the past who grasped what the potential of amassed strength could represent for members, their communities, the province and the nation.

Central's vision, however, is not the only version of consequence for the provincial system. Increasingly, government has also advocated ways in which the movement can be made into a more organized set of financial institutions. Strongly influenced by the collapse of financial institutions across North America in the 1980s, it envisions a strongly regulated, prudently managed system in which risks are minimized and deposits are secure. It is a vision that inevitably encourages having relatively few credit unions; it tends to prefer credit unions governed by the same practices and principles that shape the banking industry in general.

This governmental vision conforms, albeit somewhat roughly, with the vision most obviously found within the larger community credit unions. In many ways, those organizations have absorbed the culture, motivations and values of community banks. They are managed by very sophisticated professionals, many of them drawn from the mainstream banks. They are fiercely independent, as reflected in their loyalty to their own technologies, their own distinctive management "cultures," and their often ambivalent support for provincial initiatives. Without exception, they are extremely sophisticated organizations, often using their freedom in the marketplace to be more innovative than banks and trust companies.

The larger credit unions are also wrestling most obviously with one of the most difficult challenges confronting co-operatively-based institutions in the contemporary world: how to retain the co-operative ethos and structures as organizations grow and become increasingly integrated into the general economy. In doing so, they are not different from medium-sized and smaller credit unions, but the dilemmas and challenges inherent in the question often seem to be more perplexing when organizations become large and specialization becomes the norm.

271

Faced with this challenge, some within the larger credit unions adopt the easy way out and assume that eventually credit unions will become indistinguishable from banks. It is a seductive alternative, fostered by the assumptions of the Canadian financial industry in general; made attractive by the prestige and financial rewards normal to that industry; sanctioned by all the business schools; and uncomplicated by the "politics" of co-operative enterprise. It is also short-sighted, denying the rich potential that properly-run and motivated co-operatives can provide.

The issue of distinctiveness is not new; it has been apparent in the provincial movement since the Great Depression. It has been evident internationally since at least the nineteenth century. Within the B.C. credit union movement, the answers were more obvious in the emancipatory phase, and the alternatives appeared to be clearer in the entrepreneurial period. They are more diffused, less obvious in an age of mainstreaming; they are also of greater significance to the survival of the movement.

The first key to the answers rests within the traditional bases upon which credit unions have grown: membership, democracy and community. The second key is how credit unions will build upon these bases through their operating strategies – for example, their marketing systems, their adaptations of technology, and their capital formation. The test will be whether those strategies are developed so that they enhance member benefits over the short and long term, or whether they manipulate members in the short-term interests of "profitability" and employee benefits. Passing the test will require a particular kind of vision and a willingness to think of members in ways that are different from how other financial institutions think of customers.

The concept of membership is at the heart of credit union distinctiveness: credit unions are unique essentially because members are users and owners and because they can be investors. These unique qualities have not been emphasized in recent years as they might have been. When credit unions expand largely because of the great popularity of their mortgage programs, there is little need and little apparent direct benefit in stressing such relationships. That was true in the past and it remains true in the present. It is a widespread attitude that will have to change if credit unions are to reach their full potential in the future.

Membership inevitably raises questions about democracy. As with most co-operative systems, the credit union movement in British Columbia has tended to define democracy in terms of attendance at annual meetings and the percentage of members who vote in elections. To a point, this is appropriate, and it leads almost all observers to suggest there is a need to increase member participation. Indeed, that should be a priority for virtually all credit unions.

Democracy, however, is more than a matter of elections. It is really about relationships, about creating a feeling of belonging, of offering opportunities to influence decisions. The democratic impulse within credit unions, therefore, should not be evaluated exclusively through analyzing annual election results. It must also be measured by considering the way in which credit unions treat members on a daily basis, the ways in which they expand to meet members' needs and, above all, the integrity with which they provide their services. To some extent, it is like "relationship banking," but its real roots lie in 150 years of co-operative thought and not just in the enthusiasms of some adroit bank marketing specialists a decade ago.

Perhaps the most important part of that emerging, potentially "democratic," relationship is how credit unions will work to establish better bonds with their members. At least two approaches will be necessary. On the one hand, credit unions will have to work hard, through training and policies, to ensure that they treat members appropriately: courteous, efficient and informed service will be a significant key for future success. On the other hand, credit unions will have to expand the variety of services they provide. In doing so, they have a natural advantage in selecting and developing new services because they can make use of the member relationship; they can take advantage of the best traditions of co-operative entrepreneurship.

At its best, co-operative entrepreneurship is an almost certain recipe for economic success. Starting with members' needs, it brings together capital, labour and technology to meet those needs efficiently and fairly. The key in doing so lies in working with members so that needs are clearly understood, alternative ways of meeting those needs are explored, and new initiatives can be undertaken prudently and honestly. It is a form of entrepreneurship that should never be allowed to ossify, to become too burdened by organizational structures and personal agendas.

During the past 30 years, the B.C. credit union movement has boomed partly because it applied that approach to a limited range of economic needs, most obviously mortgages. In the present and in the future, the movement, largely because of technological and legislative changes, has the capacity to use that approach in a broadening range of financial activities. There are even opportunities, if the movement wishes to seize them, to move beyond those activities and to meet other needs; in that sense Rod Glen's dreams need not be dead, although his way of trying to achieve them certainly is.

There is a third dimension to co-operative entrepreneurship: it functions within a heightened and subtle appreciation of the importance of communities. In credit union circles, just as in general usage, the word "community" is not easily defined: different people mean different things when they employ it; the same person can use it in various ways and yet find important meaning in each usage.

At the simplest level, community refers to a specific geographic place, the place where people live, the place they walk about in the evening. For credit unions that clearly serve that type of community, the bonds can strike very deep; indeed, such credit unions are often powerful manifestations of local pride and concrete efforts to maximize control over local economies. Similarly, credit unions that unite communities on the basis of ethnicity, religion or workplace represent readily definable communities, even though those communities might stretch over considerable geographic space.

The complexities arise when credit unions reach over vast areas and their members appear to have very little in common. Leaders in such credit union "communities" understandably tend to think their members are really "customers," individuals who, for a variety of reasons, have joined their organizations searching for efficient, competitive financial services at convenient locations. In fact, many leaders do not even think that the attitude of such customers can ever be changed — some even argue no one should try to do so. The bonds of the resultant "communities" are usually not very strong; the benefits of being a credit union member are not always readily evident, especially if no one takes the time to explain them.

And yet the benefits of credit unionism for even the most loosely united credit unions are considerable. Members can reap meaningful direct benefits because of local control and quick decision-making. They can be the beneficiaries of all the services that have been built up over the years — from insurance to property management — by local credit unions and the co-operative movement. Indirectly, they benefit because a strong set of regional financial institutions makes continuous, significant contributions to the provincial economy. Indirectly, too, they benefit because credit unions have an independent voice expressing an alternative view on financial and economic matters before provincial and federal governments. And, in nearly every case, credit unions make major contributions to their "communities," particularly in assisting young people with their education, but also in major contributions to health-care and organized sports.

There is no doubt, however, that large community credit unions have to devote more thought and resources to identifying the nature of the community they serve. They must build on the membership connection so that common bonds and interests are encouraged, so

The two newest credit unions in B.C. serve members of particular ethnic or religious groups, in their own language. Khalsa Credit Union was started in 1986 to provide financial service to the growing Sikh community in the Lower Mainland; several of its leaders are seen at top. Sharons Credit Union, created in 1988, serves the Korean community, *above*.

To ensure continuing growth, credit unions must attract tomorrow's adults as members — and future leaders. Programs to involve young people in credit unions are becoming increasingly common, *right*.

that being a member can mean something more than merely doing business.

British Columbia is yet another "community" that the province's credit unions must consider. Some credit unionists over the years have thought about how credit unions can contribute to that community; for the most part, their efforts were premature. If credit unions continue to grow, if they expand into the kinds of financial activities that are available to them, however, it will soon be appropriate – even necessary – to start thinking in those terms. There is no reason why credit unions cannot be the heart of the B.C. provincial economy, much in the same way that the movements in Quebec and Saskatchewan influence their economies. Credit unions already have immense influence and power – they should strive for more. And they should give more thought to what they would do with that power once they have it.

B.C. credit unions are also associated with other kinds of communities. They are, for example, part of the Canadian family of credit unions; indeed, they have a long and distinguished record of contributing to that family's development – albeit not always without controversy. The national movement is undergoing remarkable change as the impact of technology and legislative reform unfolds. That change will inevitably lead to restructuring and reorganization, rethinking and re-engineering. As always, such changes will be painful, but they can be very beneficial; for example, the result could be, finally, an aggressive national movement that can play a powerful role across the country. B.C. credit unionists continue to have an obligation – arguably, it is greater than ever before – in helping to make sure that potential is fully realized.

Similarly, there is a strong and potentially much stronger co-operative movement within the province and across the country that provides yet another community of common interest. The provincial credit union system, and particularly some individuals and a few credit unions, has played a significant role in that movement. The potential has barely been tapped and the possible benefits for British Columbians – and ultimately credit unions – could be impressive.

There is also the international community of credit unions and similar financial co-operatives. Again, British Columbians have a long and distinguished record in support of the international movement. Several individuals have played key roles in helping to develop financial co-operatives in other countries; many have had the opportunity to visit some of the tens of thousands of credit co-operatives that exist all around the world. Those who have had either experience have gained a different perspective on their own movement; almost invariably, they have also understood more clearly why the credit union experiment is ultimately valuable.

Moreover, the global perspective suggests that the future for co-operative forms of enterprise, particularly financial co-operatives, can only be positive. As transnational corporations grow more powerful and interconnected, as nation states lose their influence, the capacity of most communities to control their destiny will decline. They can at least partly offset this trend by uniting in their own best interests and mobilizing their collective influence. Although financial co-operatives have enjoyed their greatest period of expansion around the world in the past two decades, the future promises even greater possibilities.

British Columbia's experience with credit unions is also important within the international perspective because of what it has done directly for its members and indirectly for the province. That record is clear and needs no further elaboration: the ways in which British Columbians have gone about building their movement could provide positive and negative models for others wishing to pursue similar goals.

The provincial movement is also important because it is a unique and significant experiment in the history of co-operative enterprise. Whether or not all understand, recognize and acknowledge it, the province's credit unions have been — and are — part of an historical quest that began over 150 years ago. It is a quest with a disarmingly simple objective: to work for the development of an honestly-operated economy based on a respect for human personality, a commitment to democratic practices, and a concern for the various communities in which people live.

For 50-plus years, British Columbia's credit unionists have been a part of that quest. In the process, they have shaped their own movement, with its own distinct structures and perspectives. Their experiences and solutions, are not completely transferable — and, indeed, would probably not be welcomed by everyone — but they offer insights from which others can learn.

And so it will continue in the future. For some within and without the credit union world, the constant struggle to apply the co-operative values and principles among imperfect people in an unrelenting marketplace is invariably doomed. For others, those who stress the materialism of human beings (and they can be found on both the ideological left and right), the effort will be seen as foolish. But for those who believe that it is possible to combine values and principles with economic action, it will be the only alternative. They will be the true inheritors of the people who, for more than 50 years, have tried to create financial institutions that are different.

THERE IS A LIMITED BUT GROWING LITERATURE ON THE HISTORY of credit unions in Canada, but, to this point, there has never been a history of credit unions in British Columbia. Consequently, the sources for this study have essentially been found within the large archives created by B.C. Central Credit Union, particularly in the early 1980s. Miriam McTiernan, then the archivist for B.C. Central, undertook an extensive survey of the credit unions in the province searching for records; fortunately, many credit unions responded to her enquiries and supplied her with records. In addition, she carefully preserved many of the reports that, along with the records of Board meetings, form the main resources from which this study was written. Ms. McTiernan also undertook, often with the assistance of Jac Schroeder, to interview many credit union leaders. The result is an excellent set of interviews that greatly informed the earlier chapters of this book.

Researchers wishing to explore further any of the themes discussed in this book could best do so by examining the B.C. Central Archives; it is hoped that the citations in the text will assist them in their enquiries. The author would be pleased to help in any way that he can.

Photo credits

Photograph of Alphonse Desjardins, courtesy of Credit Union National Association Inc., on book jacket, title page and page 15.

Food line photograph, courtesy of City of Vancouver Archives, photograph # RE P.5, N.4 #3, on book jacket, title page and page 19.

Photograph of George Keen, courtesy of National Archives of Canada, C-51906, on page 26.

Photograph of E.K. DeBeck, courtesy of B.C. Provincial Archives, Victoria, B.C., on page 37.

Photograph of Food Industries War Bond float, courtesy of City of Vancouver Archives, photograph # CVA 298-11, on book jacket, title page and on pages 38 and 46.

Panoramic photograph of Vancouver, courtesy of City of Vancouver Archives, photograph # CVA 296-37, on pages 106-107.

Exuberant youth photograph by R. Mort/Tony Stone Images, pages 266-267.

Other photographs are from the B.C. Central Archives, the *B.C. Credit Unionist* and *Enterprise*, archives of credit unions and individuals.

The author thanks all those who granted permission for use of photographs.

International Credit Union Operating Principles

THESE CREDIT UNION OPERATING PRINCIPLES ARE FOUNDED IN the philosophy of co-operation and its central values of equality, equity and mutual self-help. Recognizing the varied practices in the implementation of credit union philosophy around the world, at the heart of these principles is the concept of human development and the brotherhood of man expressed through people working together to achieve a better life for themselves and their community.

Democratic Structure

Open and Voluntary Membership Membership in a credit union is voluntary and open to all within the accepted common bond of association that can make use of its services and are willing to accept the corresponding responsibilities.

Democratic Control Credit union members enjoy equal rights to vote (one member, one vote) and participate in decisions affecting the credit union, without regard to the amount of savings or deposits or the volume of business. Voting in credit union support organizations or associations may be proportional or representational, in keeping with democratic principles. The credit union is autonomous, within the framework of law and regulation, recognizing the credit union as a co-operative enterprise serving and controlled by its members. Credit union elected offices are voluntary in nature and incumbents should not receive a salary. However, credit unions may reimburse legitimate expenses incurred by elected officials.

Non-discrimination Credit unions are non-discriminatory in relation to race, nationality, sex, religion and politics.

Service to Members

Service to Members Credit union services are directed to improve the economic and social well-being of all members.

Distribution to Members To encourage thrift through savings and thus to provide loans and other services, a fair rate of interest is paid on savings and deposits, within the capability of the credit union.

The surplus arising out of the operations of the credit union, after ensuring appropriate reserve levels and after payment of limited dividends on permanent equity capital where it exists, belongs to and benefits all members with no member or group of members benefiting to the detriment of others. This surplus may be distributed among members in proportion to their transactions with the credit union as interest or patronage refunds, or directed to improved or additional services required by the members.

Building Financial Stability A prime concern of the credit union is to build the financial strength, including adequate reserves and internal controls, that will ensure continued service to membership.

Social Goals

On-going Education Credit unions actively promote the education of their members, officers and employees, along with the public in general, in the economic, social, democratic and mutual self-help principles of credit unions. The promotion of thrift and the wise use of credit, as well as education on the rights and responsibilities of members, are essential to the dual social and economic character of credit unions in serving member needs.

Co-operation Among Co-operatives In keeping with their philosophy and the pooling practices of co-operatives, credit unions within their capability actively co-operate with other credit unions, co-operatives and their associations at local, national, and international levels in order to best serve the interests of their members and their communities.

Social Responsibility Continuing the ideals and beliefs of co-operative pioneers, credit unions seek to bring about human and social development. Their vision of social justice extends both to the individual members and to the larger community in which they work and reside. The credit union ideal is to extend service to all who need and can use it. Every person is either a member or a potential member and appropriately part of the credit union sphere of interest and concern. Decisions should be taken with full regard for the interest of the broader community within which the credit union and its members reside.

Members of the Board of Directors B.C. Central Credit Union 1944-1995

Affleck, R., 1947

Allan, G.K., 1955-65

Anderson, E., 1986-89

Armstrong, L., 1984-86

Aussant, J., 1979-80

Bentley, D.W., 1952-1956, 1959-68, 1974-76

Berner, L., 1982-85

Betts, M., 1981-90

Biddlecombe, H., 1980-83

Biech, L.H., 1978-84

Brown, H.H., 1944-45

Burdak, S., 1983-85

Byron, J.A. 1944-45

Charlesworth, J., 1988-91

Chausse, J.C., 1947-49

Corsbie, J.H., 1955-56

Cross, E.T., 1974-80

Dandeno, T., 1988-94

Darling, J.W., 1957-80

Davies, R.E., 1978-79

Dew, W.J., 1953-65

Dick, H., 1960-63

Dickinson, F.B., 1946-61

Dolsen, L., 1947

Down, H.A., 1974-85

Fanthorpe, H.A.L., 1966-67

Farnden, A.J., 1951-56

Forbes, B., 1985-88

Fox, L.W., 1959-60

Gatto, L., 1990-94

Gaunt, J.B. 1946-47

Gentleman, R., 1983-86

Gill, A.S., 1968-70

Girdwood, W.K., 1972-78

Glen, A.R., 1966-80

Goepel, P.A., 1947-49

Gorden, E., 1950-51

Gore, R.C., 1954-59

Graham, P., 1994-

Griffeth, D., 1984-

Harvey, H., 1948-49

Hastings, J., 1949-54

Hauck, C., 1948-51

Hewitt, J.J., 1967-73

Heyming, P.J., 1973-83

Holtby, G.N., 1944-1956

Hood, R., 1984-88

Hornal, R.J., 1977-78

Humphries, D., 1986-90

Insley, V., 1946-61

Iverson, W.D., 1973-76

Jansen, H., 1986-

Jones, D., 1993-95

Kaulius, E., 1976-83

Keith, D.A., 1946-51

Kellington, J.H., 1944-45

Kelly, J., 1993-

Krueger, H., 1957-70, 1974-79

Lach, D., 1985-93

Lucas, J.H., 1954-74

Lukash, L.R., 1967-71

Lutz, R., 1980-84

MacPherson, I., 1983-92

Magoon, R., 1991-

Manrell, T.T., 1985-

Manson, C., 1987-

Marzari, D., 1985-86

Mason, S., 1965-66

May, G.S., 1966-70

May, K., 1981-88

McCulloch, G.T., 1974-77

Miles, B., 1992-

Moore, E.C., 1944-45

Moore, P., 1979-84, 1987-

Morrison, L., 1948-53

Munn, G., 1995-

Munro, E., 1948-49

Nicholas, A.L., 1944-1953

Nunn, C.R., 1968-70

O'Connor, T., 1960-66

Parkin, R., 1983-

Phillips, B., 1980-83

Podovinikoff, P.P., 1970-1977

Pratt, J.H., 1961-67

Pritchard, S., 1989-

Prowse, C.A., 1952

Quail, J.F., 1970-74

Ramsell, G.W., 1949-55

Raschdorf, S., 1976-91

Read, G.J., 1965-67

Reid, M., 1991-93

Richards, P.B., 1961-70, 1974-77

Robinson, J.R., 1948-50, 1953-54

Russell, N.J., 1950-60

Sankey, T.R., 1978-81

Shepherd, G., 1979-82

Simpson, E.J., 1965-78

Simpson, J.O., 1974-76

Stonier, S., 1970-72

Strang, I.L., 1959-70

Strandberg, C.T., 1991-

Sutherland, S.D., 1976-81

Tarr, M.J., 1991-

Taylor, W.E., 1973-76,
  1977-78, 1980-84

Todd, E.J., 1963-68

Tovee, H.E., 1944-45

Treasurer, R.N., 1953-59

Turner, H.E., 1970-73

Viereck, G., 1970-72, 1977-86

Waddell, S., 1988-91

Webber, H., 1984-86

Welch, C.B., 1970-73

Weremchuk, J., 1976-85

Williams, R.F., 1944-64

Wilson, L.L., 1944-47

Wilson, W.J., 1971-1974

Chairpersons of the Board of Directors B.C. Central Credit Union

G.M. Holtby, 1944-46

F.B. Dickinson, 1946-48,
  1950-52

L. Morrison, 1948-50

G.W. Ramsell, 1952-55

D.W. Bentley, 1955-57

J.W. Dew, 1957-60

J.H. Lucas, 1960-66

J.W. Darling, 1966-68

I.L. Strang, 1968-70

A.R. Glen, 1970-75

P.P. Podovinikoff, 1975-77

P. Heyming, 1977-1980

T.R. Sankey, 1980-81

W.E. Taylor, 1981-83

H.A. Down, 1983-84

G. Viereck, 1984-86

I. MacPherson, 1986-88

T.T. Manrell, 1988-93

M.J. Tarr, 1993-

Presidents of the B.C. Credit Union League

A.L. Nicholas, 1940-43

J.W. Burns, 1943-45

A.G. Butcher, 1945-47

G.W. Ramsell, 1947-49

J.H. Wallace, 1949-51

G.A. Rasmussen, 1951-52

F.B. Dickinson, 1952-54,
  1955-57

J.H. Corsbie, 1954-55

A.R. Glen, 1957-59

J.P. Lundie, 1959-61

R.F. Williams, 1961-63

A.H.W. Moxon, 1963-65

S. Stonier, 1965-67

G.S. May, 1967-69

P.P. Podovinikoff, 1969-70

General Managers/ Chief Executive Officers of B.C. Central Credit Union

H.H. Brown, 1945-47

J.R. Robinson, 1948-65

G.J. Hook, 1965-70

G.S. May, 1970-77

P.P. Podovinikoff, 1977-84

J.R. Thomson, 1984-85

W.A. Nygren, 1985-

Managers/ Managing Directors of the B.C. Credit Union League

J.W. Burns, 1945-51

R.A. Monrufet, 1951-70

Growth of B.C. Credit Unions, 1940-1994

At Dec. 31	Credit Unions	Members	Assets
1940	43	1,320	$18,790
1945	139	19,027	$1.7 million
1950	182	52,805	$12.8 million
1955	290	125,425	$40.5 million
1960	326	205,308	$107.1 million
1961*	328	209,807	$120.1 million
1965	304	256,424	$174.8 million
1970	223	354,617	$346.0 million
1975	178	595,352	$1.5 billion
1980	153	978,000	$4.8 billion
1985	134	976,000	$6.3 billion
1990	111	1,072,504	$10.4 billion
1994	101	1,270,700	$16.4 billion

* The number of credit unions peaked in 1961.

Source: *Annual Reports,* B.C. Central Credit Union and B.C. Credit Union League.

Co-operation, Conflict and Consensus

Index

Abbotsford Credit Union, 79, 137, 141

Accommodation loans, 138

Adult education, 16, 20, 32, 49, 101, 116, 120

Advertising, 83-84, 166

Agricultural Land Reserve, 224

Alberni Credit Union, 57, 108, 141, 208, 210

Alberta, 57, 59, 76, 84, 95, 127, 145, 198, 203, 207, 214, 220, 228, 238, 246, 254

Alert Bay Credit Union, 241

Allen, Richard, 248

Al-Pine Credit Union, 268

Amalgamated Civil Servants of Canada Credit Union, 26, 31, 39, 41, 49, 63

American credit union and co-operative movement, 15-16, 20, 24-25, 28, 36-37, 40, 44, 48, 51, 55-56, 65, 67-70, 81-82, 89, 91, 93, 98-100, 102-104, 107, 109-110, 113, 116-117, 126, 129, 136, 141, 155-156, 159, 182, 185, 188, 201, 204-205, 208, 224, 227, 229, 241, 248, 263-264, 270

Anderson, Roy, 90

Annual meetings, 33, 39-40, 42, 45, 48-51, 53, 66-67, 70, 74, 77, 79, 82, 85-86, 88, 93, 95, 98-99, 107-108, 110, 112, 115, 117, 119, 129-130, 135, 142, 146, 149, 151-152, 155-156, 162, 172-173, 177, 180, 182, 185, 200-201, 204, 210, 212, 220, 223, 235, 241, 253, 258-259, 261, 272-273

Antigonish Movement, 16, 32, 34-36, 41, 128

Archibald, Jean, *see* Haynes, Jean

Arctic Co-operatives, 260

Army of the Common Good, 18, 23-27, 32, 44, 47, 151

Asian immigrants and B.C. credit unions, 18

Automated teller machines (ATMs), 210, 254, 257-258

Bailey, Ace, 150

Baldonnel Credit Union, 54, 60

Ball, Louis, 58

Bank Act, 132-133, 145, 171

Banks and financial institutions
Alberta Treasury Branch, 76
Bank of British Columbia, 145, 246
Bank of Canada, 145, 216
Bank of Montreal, 58
Bank of Western Canada, 145
Canadian Bank of Commerce, 43, 64
Canadian Commercial Bank, 228
Imperial Bank, 76
Northland Bank, 228
Royal Bank, 77

Baptists and credit unions, 119

Barrett, Dave, 183

Basford, Ron, 179

Bellamy, Edward, 24

Belshaw, Dr. Cyril S., 142

Belshaw Report, 142-143

Bennett, Bill, 210-211

Bentley, Don, 141-142, 148-149, 182

Bergengren, Roy, 67-68, 91, 129

Berner, Bud, 141

Biddlecombe, Harley, 219

Bill C-259, 180

Blackie, Georgie, 141

Blair, Bill, 109

Bleasdale, Walter, 58

Bonner, Robert, 98, 100, 103, 121, 124-125

Bootleg Lending Society, 26

Branching issue, 110, 160-161, 214, 241-243

Briggs, Ron, 198

Bright, Jack, 260

Britannia Credit Union, 120-121

B.C. Central Credit Union
Administration and Finance Division, 173, 216, 247
amalgamation with League, 149-157
annual meetings, 66, 70-72, 84, 99, 152
Belshaw Report, 142
Business Loan Co-ordinating Service, 196

Central Financial Corporation, 175

Central Data Systems (CDS), 149, 162, 175-176, 209-210

Class B Members, 254

Collection Department, 152

control structure, 198-202, 219-221, 223, 253-54

Co-operative Services Office, 178, 215-216

Corporate Affairs, 216, 232

creation, 52-53

Credit Union Services Department, 154

Creekside Drive, move to, 178-179, 186, 189

Development Department, 175-176, 182

"downsizing" in early 1980s, 215-217

Education Department, 50, 74, 116

Finance Division, 173, 216

Financial Advisory Committee, 218

Gill Report, 143

Greentree Developments, 177, 215, 248

investment policy, 249

Legislative Committee, 51, 231-232

Loans Committee, 42, 109

Nanoose Accord, 191, 221, 223, 245-246

Northern Co-op Council, 74

Northline, 59, 107, 110

Pennyfarthing, 212

Planning Committee, 252

problems in the 1980s, 245-248

provincial advertising, 153

Quebec Street and Broadway building, 67, 98, 105

role, 60, 79-80, 82, 85, 142-143, 179-180, 213, 248-252

role of Northline, 59-60

Services Division, 175-176

Small Credit Union Service Centre, 170

Stevenson & Kellogg Report, 143, 149

Supplies Department, 61, 88, 152

System Strategic Planning Committee, 252-253

System Structure Task Force, 253

United Nations Pavilion, 249-250

West Hastings Street offices, 152

Western Management Report, 219

About the Author

*I*an MacPherson is Dean of Humanities and Professor of History at the University of Victoria in Victoria, British Columbia.

A long-time activist in credit unions and co-operatives at the local, provincial, national and international levels, he is the author of numerous books and articles that explore their unique history.

His earlier works include *Each for All – A History of the Co-operative Movement in Canada, 1900-1945*; *Building and Protecting the Co-operative Movement – A Brief History of the Co-operative Union of Canada*; *The Story of CIS (Co-operative Insurance Services) Ltd.*; and *A Very Special Trust Company: A History of the First 25 Years of the Co-operative Trust Company of Canada*.

As well as taking an academic interest in co-operatives, Ian MacPherson knows his subject thoroughly from many years of direct participation as a co-op and credit union leader.

He was chairman of the Co-operative Union of Canada, a forerunner of the Canadian Co-operative Association, and was the first president of the CCA following its formation in 1987. He has served on the Executive Committee of the International Co-operative Alliance, and recently led an ICA Task Force to revise the fundamental co-op principles and develop a worldwide Co-operative Charter for the 21st Century.

MacPherson's involvement in credit unions includes long service as a director of Pacific Coast Savings Credit Union and two of its predecessors. He was a director of B.C. Central Credit Union for nine years, including a two-year stint as its chairman, and also served as a director of the Canadian Co-operative Credit Society, the national credit union organization.